What Happened in the 20th Century?

Peter Sloterdijk

What Happened in the 20th Century?

Translated by Christopher Turner

polity

First published in German as *Was geschah im 20. Jahrhundert?* © Suhrkamp Verlag, Berlin, 2016

This English edition © Polity Press, 2018

The translation of this work was supported by a grant from the Goethe Institut

Polity Press
65 Bridge Street
Cambridge CB2 1UR, UK

Polity Press
101 Station Landing
Suite 300
Medford, MA 02155, USA

ISBN-13: 978–1–5095–1837–1 (hardback)
ISBN-13: 978–1–5095–1838–8 (paperback)

A catalogue record for this book is available from the British Library.

Typeset in 10.5 on 12pt Times by Servis Filmsetting Ltd, Stockport, Cheshire
Printed and bound in Great Britain by Clays Ltd, Elcograf S.p.A.

The publisher has used its best endeavours to ensure that the URLs for external websites referred to in this book are correct and active at the time of going to press. However, the publisher has no responsibility for the websites and can make no guarantee that a site will remain live or that the content is or will remain appropriate.

Every effort has been made to trace all copyright holders, but if any have been inadvertently overlooked the publisher will be pleased to include any necessary credits in any subsequent reprint or edition.

For further information on Polity, visit our website:
politybooks.com

Contents

Contents

1

THE ANTHROPOCENE – A STAGE IN THE PROCESS ON THE MARGINS OF THE EARTH'S HISTORY?

1.1 Weightless Humanity

In the year 2000, when the Dutch atmospheric chemist Paul J. Crutzen suggested that we use the term "Anthropocene" – drawing on an analogous concept of the Italian geologist Stoppani (1824–91) from 1873 – to designate the present age from the perspective of natural history, it was assumed that this term would remain part of a hermetic discourse that is spoken behind the closed doors of institutes for gas analysis or geophysics.

Yet, through a strange series of accidents, the synthetic semantic virus must have succeeded in getting past the quite secure laboratory doors and spreading to the lifeworld in general. We thus get the impression that it easily reproduces itself in the context of the sophisticated feuilleton, the museum, macrosociology, new religious movements, and literature warning of ecological collapse.

The proliferation of this concept can mainly be traced back to the fact that, under the guise of scientific neutrality, it conveys a message of almost unparalleled moral-political urgency, a message that can be explicitly formulated as follows: human beings have become responsible for the habitation and management of the Earth as a whole, since their presence upon it is no longer more or less seamlessly integrated with it.

The concept "Anthropocene," ostensibly a geological term, implies a gesture that in a juridical context would be characterized as the designation of a responsible agency. With the attribution of responsibility, an address is provided to which possible accusations can be sent. This is precisely what we have to do today when we attribute the capacity for geo-historical offenses to "the human being" – without further specification.

When we speak of an "Anthropocene," we only seem to be sitting in a geoscientific seminar. In reality, we are taking part in a court case – in a preliminary hearing before the main trial, to be more precise – in which, as a first step, the accused's culpability is supposed to be settled.

This preliminary hearing is concerned with the question of whether it makes any sense at all to try the offender in question, given that the latter is not of age. This hearing would include the author Stanislaw Lem, among others, who seems to exonerate "the human being" by awarding him,[1] in a tellurian context, the status of a *quantité négligeable*, or as Lem himself puts it:

> . . . were all humanity taken and crowded together in one place, it would occupy three hundred billion liters, or a little less than a third of a cubic kilometer. It sounds like a lot. Yet the world's oceans hold 1,285 million cubic kilometers of water, so if all humanity – those five billion bodies – were cast into the ocean, the water level would rise less than a hundredth of a millimeter. A single splash, and Earth would be forever unpopulated.[2]

In the case of quantitative relations such as these, it does not matter if we introduce present-day humanity, numbering seven billion, into the picture instead of a humanity totaling five billion (as assumed by Lem) or the eight or nine billion that will be reached after the year 2050. In terms of biomass, a randomly and rapidly ever-increasing humanity would remain infinitesimally small, if we could sink humanity *toto genere* into the ocean. But then, what is the point of putting on trial a species that pales in comparison to the material dimensions of the Gaia-system, the hydrosphere? Lem's position, incidentally, is very close to certain classic disparagements of the human being – such as Schopenhauer's contemptuous remark that the human race is like an ephemeral mold on the surface of the planet Earth.[3]

The prosecution will reply to these objections that the whole of humanity at its current stage of evolution simply cannot be defined merely in terms of biomass. If humanity is supposed to be put on trial, this is mainly because it epitomizes a meta-biological agency that is able to exert quite a bit more influence on the environment, by virtue of its capacity for action, than we would assume on the basis of its relative physical weightlessness.

Obviously, in this context, we immediately think of the techno-logical revolutions of the modern age and their side effects, which not without reason are chalked up to collective humanity. In truth, "collective humanity" initially means European civilization and its technocratic elite. It was the latter that introduced a new agency into the game of global powers from the seventeenth and eighteenth centuries onward with the use of coal, and later petroleum, in machines. In addition, the discovery and demonstration of the nature of electricity shortly before the year 1800, and the technical mastery of it in the nineteenth century, gave rise to a new universal in the discourse on energy. Without this new universal, the metabolic interaction of human beings with nature – to recall the Marxist definition of labor – would be inconceivable. The collective that is characterized these days by expressions such as "humanity" mainly consists of agents who within less than a century have acquired technologies developed in Europe. When Crutzen speaks of an "Anthropocene," this is a gesture of Dutch courtesy – or avoidance of conflict. In fact, talk of a "Eurocene" or a technocene initiated by Europeans would be more fitting.

That human actors have an impact on nature in their turn is not really a new observation. Already in antiquity, deforestations were noted in Greece and Italy that were ascribed to the demand for timber in the shipbuilding industry. The emergence of cultivated landscapes, too, is inconceivable without taking the influence of agriculture, viticulture, and animal husbandry into consideration. The latter, in particular, continues to be an unsettling item on the bill that the ecosystem "Earth" will present to human beings. Only in more recent times has the connection between human pastoral power and political expansionism been emphasized.[4] In macro-historical terms, there is quite clearly a relatively recent (that is, spanning about 3,000 years) causal nexus between raising cattle and imperial politics: not a few historical empires – such as those of the Romans, the British, the Habsburgs, and the Americans – were ultimately based on the cultivation of herds of livestock that provided their herdsmen with a significant surplus of labor power, mobility, protein, and leather, not to mention the link between being assured of a certain caloric intake on a daily basis and political expansionism. In more recent times, we have also become aware that herds of cattle have a considerable impact on the environment, because of their metabolic functions.

At present, there are supposedly about 1.5 billion cattle on Earth – if we were to dump them all in the ocean the latter would rise about five times as much as it would if humanity itself were dumped there: even so, we would still be dealing with tenths of a millimeter and yet would have never left the realm of quasi-weightlessness.

Indirect anthropogenic environmental impact due to animal

husbandry is nevertheless striking: every cow maintained by a human being produces a quantity of greenhouse gases in its thirty-year lifespan, owing to digestive flatulence, that would correspond to a trip of 90,000 kilometers with a mid-range engine.

In referring to how widespread the current exercise of human pastoral power has become, we leave the realm of negligible dimensions behind. As the producer of enormous indirect emissions, humanity in the industrial age might actually take on a geologically relevant role, despite its weightlessness, in terms of biomass. This would result in particular from its operation of enormous fleets of automobiles, airplanes, and ships that run on combustion engines, but it would have just as much to do with the heat balance in regions of the world where a pronounced winter gives rise to compensatory pyrotechnic and architectonic attempts at restoring balance. With these preliminary remarks out of the way, the case against the "Anthropocene" can be allowed to proceed to a full hearing.

1.2 Doctrines of Ages of the World

With the concept of the "Anthropocene," contemporary geology once again adopts the nineteenth-century epistemological habit of historicizing anything and everything, and of organizing all historical fields into eons, ages, or epochs. The triumph of historicism is primarily fueled by the idea of evolution, which is taken to refer to all areas of reality, from minerals up to the large composite bodies that are known as human "societies."

Marx and Engels, in harmony with the spirit of their age, could thus claim: "We know only one science, the science of history."[5] In their eyes, human history represented a special case of natural history, insofar as the human being *per se* is the "animal" that has to secure its own existence through production. Consequently, the history of the "relations of production" would be nothing more than the continuation of natural history in another register. Human meta-naturalism would merely be natural history that was technologically alienated. What we call the human being's inner "nature" would be what Spinoza called the impulse (*conatus*) to self-preservation at any price, which marks all life with the form of forward flight.

For a time, the Marxist image of the world popularized the saga of the "relations of production" – along with their great stages of the hunter-and-gatherer era through to slave-holding societies, feudalism, capitalism, and all the way to "communism." This myth had the great merit of replacing ancient doctrines of the ages of the world or eons (which descend from the golden to the iron age), as well as the doctrine of world empire found in the Book of Daniel in the Bible, with a pragmatic theory of epochs. According to this theory, the ages of the world are distinguished from each other by the manner in which human beings organized their "metabolism with nature."

The concept of the "Anthropocene" logically belongs to the group of pragmatic theories of the ages of the world. It posits a state of telluric metabolism in which the emissions caused by human beings have begun to influence the course of the Earth's history. The concept of "emission" helps us to recognize that the kind of influence we are concerned with here has until now taken place in the mode of a "side effect" – otherwise, we would be talking about a "mission" or a "project." The "e" in "emission" reveals the involuntary character of the anthropogenic impact on the exo-human dimension. Thus the concept of the "Anthropocene" includes nothing less than the task of testing out whether the agency of "humanity" is capable of transforming something ejected into a project, or of transforming an emission into a mission.

Anyone who speaks of an "Anthropocene" thus appeals to a still scarcely existent "critique of narrative reason." Since effective histories can only be organized from their end points backwards, the anthropocenic standpoint amounts to a narrative with a stark moral choice. In the narrative culture of the West, this position was formerly reserved exclusively for apocalyptic literature. Apocalypticism is the attempt to evaluate the world from its end – it implies a cosmic-moral procedure of sorting, in which good is separated from evil. To separate good from evil simply means to extract what is worthy of survival from what is not worthy of survival: what one calls eternal life is an intensified metaphysical term for being allowed to carry on, whereas eternal damnation signifies that a specific *modus vivendi* has no future and is to be removed from the series of forms of existence worthy of being passed down.

Everything thus suggests conceiving of the "Anthropocene" as a term that is only meaningful within the framework of an apocalyptic logic. Apocalypticism signifies evidence from the end. Since, as a collective, we cannot be all the way at the end yet, but always have to somehow carry on for a while longer, human intelligence cannot definitively review its own history. It can only try different versions out in diverse forms of anticipation – a fact that is testified to by an illustrious series of simulations, sacred and profane, from the Egyptian *Book of the Dead* to the first report of the Club of Rome.

Current human involvement in natural history shows that Heidegger's original insight of conceiving being as time was fundamentally correct. This intuition was admittedly missing an essential element: namely, that time first becomes noticeable, as time, when its uniform flow is disrupted.

This disruption, which the ancients were the first to perceive, was the delay – it constitutes one of the basic forms of tragedy. Even contemporary humanity is menaced by delays, particularly when it comes to taking measures regarding "environmental policy." Yet time as such generally becomes noticeable for modern humans through accelerations. Accelerating as fast as possible on one's trajectory is what drives apocalypse as a temporo-logical form. Heidegger derived the thought of "running ahead to one's own death" from such acceleration – by accepting an existentialist abbreviation for anticipating the end.[6] In his time, the authentic task of thought already consisted in investigating why modernity, for immanent reasons, is inclined to anticipate a total end. This required an examination of the motif of universal process-acceleration, which imposed the form of absolute progress on modernity's *modus vivendi*.

1.3 Modern Virtuous Circles

Anyone who asks about what drives typical modern accelerations will be mindful of mechanisms of positive feedback, for which the American sociologist Robert K. Merton has suggested the term "Matthew effect," following a well-known passage in the New Testament.[7] The logic of the self-reinforcing sphere of activity that feeds back upon itself is perfectly and intuitively anticipated in the words of Jesus: "For whoever has will be given more, and they will have an abundance. Whoever does not have, even what they have will be taken from them" (MT 25.29).[8] Effects such as these give typical instances of modernization the form of the *circulus virtuosus*, or virtuous circle. Although the modern era is also marked by the emergence of devastating *circuli vitiosi*, its trajectory as a whole to this point has still formed a nexus of virtuous circles, whose cumulative impact amounts to a new perception of time.

At this point, six such self-reinforcing circular processes ought to be mentioned, which are reciprocally interwoven in a variety of ways: the fine arts, banking, engineering, the state, scientific research, and law.

In fact, the fine arts in Europe have exhibited a historic, completely new organization since the fourteenth century. What we call the Renaissance was the result of a self-intensification of artistic skill in the workshops of northern Italy, Flanders, and Germany that lasted for centuries, until finally, thanks to continuous positive feedback – increased by rivalry and mutual observation – a peak of mastery was achieved in the sixteenth and seventeenth centuries that will never be surpassed – one merely has to mention names such as Titian, Caravaggio, or Rembrandt to indicate how artistic ability soared into the stratosphere. The virtuous circle in which art of the modern era, insofar as it was virtuosic, successfully advanced was played out in the studios of humble fourteenth-century masters. However, with the emergence of modern art and the transition to an era of global art, the world market's standard of post-virtuosic productions has prevailed.

Analogous processes can be observed in the realm of positive feedback loops that is commonly referred to as the economy. Even here, a powerful *circulus virtuosus* was set in motion from the fourteenth and fifteenth centuries on. This virtuous circle ensured that great fortunes were made and, from humble amounts of starting capital, developed into worldwide ventures, through the joining together of credit and talent – the latter term understood in its modern sense.

Admittedly, the self-reinforcing dynamic of the economic management of art would have come to a standstill in this part of the world, as it did in classical China, when the latter reached the stage of a developed manufacturing economy, were it not associated with an additional dimension of self-reinforcing processes urging it on, as the seventeenth century ended and the eighteenth century began. We are used to giving roughly approximate names to this sphere, such as engineering, and whoever cannot be bothered to think about such matters can simply say "technology." The close alliance of the second with the third virtuous circle, that is, of an interest-driven economy with innovative engineering, leads to the dynamic monstrosity that is still unfortunately called "capitalism" due to a dullness of mind that has been common since the nineteenth century, although it should have been called "creditism" or "inventionism" all along, if we were concerned with its true name. In 1912, in a statement that sounds harmless but is in fact ominously unfathomable, Schumpeter speaks of this monstrosity that begets itself when he notes that "Every process of development creates the prerequisites for the following [process of development]."[9]

This statement can just as well refer to the following self-reinforcing circle, which has been developed by the modern state. Since its labored beginnings in the age of the Wars of Religion, the modern administrative social-welfare state that is financed with taxes has given rise to a particular kind of Matthew effect, by generating new spheres of activity over which it may exercise authority, additional zones to be regulated, and more in-depth mandates for its interventions. Here one should recall Wagner's law, which is also known as the "law of increasing state spending" or the "law of increasing state activity" – two discoveries, incidentally, that were judged favorably by their author, Adolph Wagner (1835–1917), the doughty development-optimist who held a professorship in Berlin. Wagner, the prototype of the subsequently much-maligned "academic socialists" [*Kathedersozialisten*],[10] possessed the gift of seeing the autogenic expansion of state activities still entirely within the framework of the fulfillment of communal needs, while today we are rather inclined to regard the complex of statism, fiscalism, and interventionism from a skeptical perspective and increasingly suspect it of being the absurd theater of a large, counterproductive institution that serves its own interests.

In addition, the self-reinforcing circle of the contemporary cognition industry deserves special mention. These days, every European schoolchild knows that the modern age is an age of research – this has been the case ever since Bacon wrote his *Novum Organon* and called upon the goddess of experience to increase humanity's stock of "no-nonsense" knowledge and verified information,[11] and ever since Leibniz wanted to found academies so that research would find a home of its own, solely devoted to the search for new truths. For the world in which we live, there is really no characteristic feature more pronounced than the fact that we have become a place to which recently attained knowledge may migrate. This has to be expressed in such unfamiliar terms, strange as it may sound, because research in the modern style does not at all mean the idyllic propagation of bits of knowledge to be stored in separate compartments for the delight of contemplative minds. Research signifies *per se* the generation of new knowledge through knowledge. Furthermore, knowledge typical of the modern era, which revolves around cognitive *circuli virtuosi* in order to continuously proliferate, is for the most part practical knowledge – thus it is truth in search of application. It waits for the next opportunity to insinuate itself into the life of modern populations. We exist in a kind of reality that is characterized by the continual, barely controlled immigration of epistemological and technological aliens, and can only hope that our new neighbors in this cognitive environment will eventually prove to be civilizable ones.

We now come to the last *circulus virtuosus* on this list, though it is not the least in terms of its impact: the legal system in its current systematic form. Only in a modern Europe that was agitated, which was already caught up in all manner of self-reinforcing games, could the apparently trivial but in reality quite daring idea arise that humans have inalienable rights by nature – indeed, that life itself is nothing more than the triumphant validation of rights by their holders. To be sure, from time immemorial human beings have sought protection in local constructions of justice – but only in Europe, in the motherland of the Matthew effect, could a circle develop that emerged from the meta-right as such, the "right to have rights,"[12] to use one of Hannah Arendt's formulations. She succinctly lays bare the expansion of the realm of rights. Only in a civilization in which the right to have rights has become an internalized disposition and an institution sustained by state agencies could the spiral of continually expanded juridification begin to develop, something that has become quite typical of the European social dynamic in recent centuries. This expansion of the space in which rights are claimed admittedly casts an increasingly problematic shadow. A national and supranational regulatory law-monster that is virtually unparalleled in history has been created by the reciprocal interaction of the limitless propagation of rights with gargantuan statist systems of self-reinforcement.

Every mechanism that has been cited to this point has contributed to the temporal dimension's increasing prominence by challenging anticipatory intelligence to go ahead all the way to the end, not only for individual, mortal existence, but for the entire ensemble of relations that we call "modern society."

1.4 Crisis of Severe Externalization

The formulation of the concept "Anthropocene" thus inevitably conforms to apocalyptic logic: it indicates that the cosmic insouciance that was the basis for historical forms of human being-in-the-world has come to an end. In conventional terms, we could describe "the human place in the cosmos" – to recall Scheler's treatise – as a kind of scenery-ontology [Kulissen-Ontologie]: on this view, the human being, as dramatic animal, performs before the massif of a nature that can never be anything other than a placid background for human operations. Such scenic ontological thought remained predominant for quite a while, even after the beginning of the industrial revolution, although nature-as-background is nowadays construed as an integral storehouse of resources and as a universal landfill.

The possibility that resources might be exhausted is only entertained later on: in 1912, the German chemist Wilhelm Ostwald (1853–1932) was the first to explicitly conceptualize the finiteness of terrestrial resources, in his text Der energetische Imperativ [The Energetic Imperative]. In this work, he was already critical of industry and the state: because no infinite superstructure can be erected upon a finite base, humanity is immediately called upon to adopt an alternative ethos in its use of nature. In brief, the energetic imperative is: "Do not waste energy, use it!" Because wars represent the worst form of the waste of energy, they should immediately vanish from humanity's behavioral repertoire – an argument that, two years prior to the outbreak of the First World War, was not entirely beside the point. The "analytic of finitude," which a little later on was translated by Heidegger from the sphere of the natural sciences into an existential dimension, begins with Ostwald's text. Even Max Weber's most famous statement, found at the end of his essay *The Protestant Ethic and the Spirit of Capitalism* from 1920, contains a covert reply to the Ostwaldian ethics of frugality for finite creatures in a finite world: Weber claims that the current economic system holds the human being spellbound within an "iron cage" and "with irresistible force determines the lives of all the individuals who are born into this mechanism . . . Perhaps it will so determine them until the last ton of fossilized coal is burnt."[13] Werner Sombart recalled a more dramatic version of the same thought: in conversation with him, Weber sometimes remarked that capitalism would not come to an end until "the last ton of iron and the last ton of coal had been smelted."[14] The equation of capitalism with old-fashioned heavy industry reveals the extent to which this remark is dated (and not only because of the internal dialogue with Ostwald), although new agents could already be recognized around 1920 as they emerged onto the social-industrial stage, at least in outline: petroleum, chemistry, financial capital, solar power, and telecommunications are not mentioned. Talk of the "last ton" clearly indicates the apocalyptic logic of Weberian reasoning: thanks to his rapid fast-forward to the system's death, the melancholy sociologist attains a synoptic view of "capitalism" as worldwide fatality.

The supplanting of traditional scenery-ontology by an ecological logic reaches far back into the nineteenth century. In their text *The German Ideology* from 1845–7, Marx and Engels had already succinctly postulated a shared history of nature and man, though natural history was subsequently left aside, since they wished to limit themselves to studying the historical formations of "relations of production." This omission characterized an age in which the difference between intended products and unintended side effects had not yet become critical, something that only became typical in the late twentieth century. Furthermore, in their cheerful productivity, Marx and his successors were relying on a basic fundamental assumption of scenery-ontology, according to which nature, reinterpreted as resource, was supposed to perpetually reabsorb industrial production's externalized effects, more or less unnoticeably. The assumption of an infinitely indulgent external nature extended the lifespan of human beings' cosmic recklessness after the industrial revolution, so that it lasted longer than it would have, given the environmental problems that were just emerging. With the end of carelessness, even scenery-ontology and the fundamental age-old distinction of foreground and background reach the limits of their plausibility.

1.5 Ignorance Management

When Buckminster Fuller's famous *Operating Manual for Spaceship Earth* originally appeared in 1968, he boldly assumed, indeed in a utopian manner, that the time had come for social systems to transfer expert control from politicians and financiers to designers, engineers, and artists. This assumption was based on a diagnosis that the members of the first group – like all "specialists" – only ever view reality through a small aperture, which does not allow them to see more than one section. However, due to their professions, members of the latter group develop holistic viewpoints and concern themselves with the entire panorama of reality.

It was as though the Romantic motto "Power to the imagination!"[15] had crossed the Atlantic Ocean and had been decoded on the other side as the slogan "Power to design!" The audacity of Buckminster Fuller's publication, which soon became a "counter-cultural" bible, and later a bible for those seeking "alternatives," was not displayed by his contempt for the seemingly great and powerful of the world, whom he believes are "now only ghostly pre-rogatives."[16] It consisted in the truly prodigious redefinition of our home planet: from this critical moment on, the good old-fashioned Earth may no longer be envisaged in terms of natural dimensions, but is rather to be conceived of as a colossal work of art. It was no longer a foundation but instead a construct; it was no longer a basis but instead a vessel.

It is a testimony to the prodigiousness as well as the irresistibility of Buckminster Fuller's metaphor that in less than half a century it has seeped into our collective consciousness. At the same time, it is indicative of the acute peril on board the spaceship Earth that it brooks no escape into poetic flights of fancy for lack of more precise concepts, as evidenced by the numerous, though admittedly unsuccessful, "summits on climate change." Metaphor here represents the higher form of the concept. Its truth is revealed in the pertinence of its implications for the real situation. If the Earth is a spaceship, then its crew must in fact have a vital interest in the maintenance of livable relations within the interior of the vessel. In this regard, astronautical engineers speak of the life support system (LSS) that controls the biosphere-mimetic constants on board space stations. The first criterion of the new art of piloting that is to be posited for the integral spaceship is thus atmospheric management. We should bear in mind that, in this vehicle, no oxygen masks will fall from the cabin ceiling in the "unlikely event" of the loss of cabin pressurization. It would also be absurd to claim that floor path illumination would guide us to the emergency exits – spaceship Earth does not have any exits, neither for emergencies nor for normal situations. And with regard to floor path illumination, what else is it other than mild hypnosis for passengers suffering from aerophobia? The anxiety of the passengers on board the spaceship Earth must be genuinely alleviated. Treating them requires revolutionary cognitive and technical procedures.

Buckminster Fuller has clearly identified the most important condition for the human stay on board the spaceship Earth: the passengers have not been provided with an operating manual, presumably because they are supposed to get to the bottom of things on their own. In fact, as far as we know, the Earth has been inhabited by human beings and their ancestors for almost two million years, without their "even knowing that they were on board a ship."[17] In other words: in the past, human beings were quite ignorant as they navigated, since the system was designed to bear a high degree of human disorientation. Yet to the extent that the passengers begin to get to the bottom of the situation and seize power over their environment by means of technology, the system's original indulgence of ignorance plummets until it reaches the point where certain kinds of ignorant behavior are no longer acceptable for the passengers' stay on board. Human being-in-the-world, of which twentieth-century philosophy spoke, is thus revealed as being-on-board a cosmic vessel that is susceptible to failure. Some time ago, I suggested the concept of "monogeism" to characterize the human being's appropriate cognitive relation to this vessel – a term that designates the minimum, as it were, of a non-ignorant contemporary relation to the paramount importance of the Earth. It likewise forms the axiom for a political ontology of nature.

Viewed from today's perspective, the history of planetary thought turns out to be a final cognitive and pragmatic experiment, during which the truth of the global situation must be brought to light. Anyone on board the spaceship with the courage to use his or her own mind must sooner or later account for the fact that we must teach ourselves how to travel in space. The true conception of the *conditio humana* is thus: life-and-death autodidacticism. An autodidact is someone who must learn crucial lessons without a teacher. I would like to add that merely falling back on religious traditions in these matters will not help us, because the so-called world religions are without exception bound to a pre-astronautical understanding of the world – even Jesus, with his ascent to heaven, was unable to contribute anything worth mentioning to the operating manual of spaceship Earth.

There is a claim about the relation of being and knowing that is associated with these reflections: traditional knowledge essentially stood at a slight distance behind reality – indeed, we could say that it arrived late, on principle. In light of this and in regard to future problems, the question arises as to whether knowing will always come too late, due to its habitual tardiness. Fortunately, we are in the position to be able to answer this question in the negative. There is a kind of prognostic intelligence that proves itself precisely in the gap between "late" and "too late." I hope to forcefully articulate this intelligence here today. While most human learning to this point has followed the rule according to which we only "learn from our mistakes," prognostic intelligence must wish to learn before the mistake has happened – a novelty in the history of didactics. In order to achieve a deeper understanding of such learning processes, a critique of prophetic reason is necessary. Such a critique must not let itself be daunted by the basal paradox of doomsday prophetism: that, were it successful, it would seem *ex post* like an unnecessary alarm, since what the prophet warned us of will not come to pass, precisely because of his intervention. Outlines of such a critique were presented by Jean-Pierre Dupuy in his 2004 study *Pour un catastrophisme éclairé*. According to Dupuy, only experienced apocalypticists can engage in a sensible politics for the future, because they are brave enough to consider even the worst as a real possibility.

To figure things out today means, above all, to understand that the last century's kinetic expressionism must be radically modified if we remain unable to dispense with it. By kinetic expressionism, I mean modernity's mode of existence, which was primarily made possible by the ready availability of fossil fuel. Since these materials have become virtually ubiquitous around us we have lived life as if Prometheus had stolen fire a second time. The significance of this becomes clear when we acknowledge that this second fire has long powered not merely our engines, but also blazes in our existential motivations, in our vital conceptions of freedom. We can no longer imagine a freedom that does not always also include the freedom to rev our engines and accelerate, the freedom to move to the most distant destinations, the freedom to exaggerate, the freedom to waste, indeed, lastly, even the freedom to detonate explosives and destroy ourselves. We hear the voice of kinetic expressionism when the young Goethe writes in a *Sturm und Drang* letter to Lavater: "I am now entirely embarked upon the wave of the world, completely resolved to discover, to battle, to founder, or to spring into the air with all of my cargo." We hear it when Nietzsche explains in *Ecce Homo*: "I am not a man, I am dynamite."[18] And, in practical terms, we see it at work when, during the final stage of his circumnavigation of the Earth, after running out of coal during the Atlantic passage (from New York back to England), Phileas Fogg, the hero of Jules Verne's *Around the World in 80 Days*, begins to rip the wooden frame of his own ship apart in order to feed the combustion chambers of its steam engines. With the ship of Phileas Fogg burning itself to fuel itself, Jules Verne discovered nothing less than a universal metaphor for the industrial age: it evokes the fatal self-referentiality of a serpent swallowing its own tail – we have to go back to the early Romantic poet Novalis and his insightful vision of the "self-grinding mill" to find a comparably potent image for the description of the current *modus vivendi*. Yet kinetic expressionism already characterizes the gesture with which Queen Elizabeth I of England, in the famous engraving from the sixteenth century, lays her sovereign hand on the globe, as if to show that a new era had now begun in which the rulers of the world were no longer content with their own lands but wanted to extend their power to the ends of the Earth. The principle of growth, essential to modern life, turns out to be nothing but kinetic expressionism in action.

1.6 "We are on a mission"

"We are on a *mission*. Our vocation is the education of the Earth."[19] Novalis

Modern expressionism rests on an assumption that was so self-evident to human beings of earlier times that it almost never had to be explicitly formulated. For our predecessors, nature presented an infinitely superior, and hence an immeasurably resilient, outside realm that absorbed all human discharges and ignored every act of exploitation. This idea of spontaneous nature determined humanity's history until just recently, and even today we have numerous contemporaries who cannot and do not wish to understand that we will need to fundamentally change our thinking on this point. The expressionistic character of lifestyles in today's affluent civilizations has nevertheless made clear that nature's indifference to human activities was an illusion suited to the age of ignorance. There are limits to expression, limits to emission, limits to the indulgence of ignorance – and because there are such limits, even if we do not know exactly where to draw the line, the seemingly immemorial idea of nature as a kind of externality that absorbs everything begins to falter. We suddenly feel it necessary to entertain an idea that appears contrary to nature, namely that the terrestrial sphere as a whole has been transformed by human praxis into a single great interior. Buckminster Fuller wanted designers to take responsibility for this harrowing turning point, and demanded a "comprehensive" and "anticipatory" mode of thought from them. Such thought is supposed to make "world-planning" in the "human being's total communication system" on spaceship Earth possible.

Forty years after the publication of Buckminster Fuller's manifesto, it turns out that it was not so much designers who were concerned with implementing the new idea of the world as a macro-interior, but rather meteorologists. It is evident to us that not design but meteorology has come to power. It has prevailed politically and scientifically, since for the moment it provides the most suggestive model of the global interior: it is concerned with the dynamic continuum of the terrestrial sphere of enclosed gases, which from the time of the ancient Greek natural philosophers has been called the atmosphere – literally, vapor-orb. Conversations about the weather have ceased to be harmless ever since climate scientists established that the atmosphere retains things in its memory-banks, as it were: the atmosphere never entirely forgot the chimney smoke of the early industrial revolution, and it will not ignore anything released into it by the coal-fired power stations of developed countries, the district heating power plants of mega-cities, the airplanes, the ships, the automobiles of the affluent, and the countless open fires of the poor on every continent, although normally half of such emissions is absorbed by the oceans and biosphere. To be sure, other remnants of dubious human behavior are preserved by the Earth: even now we still find horseshoes in the north-German mud that provide evidence of the Roman cavalry's passage. The German soil is neither heated nor cooled by the presence of these Roman horseshoes. In contrast, the Earth's atmosphere is a delicate disposal site: it shows a tendency to respond to past and present emissions by warming up. If meteorologists are speaking the truth, we should expect climate change in many parts of the world to result in situations that are not conducive to human existence as we have known it.

Meteorologists have thus taken on the role of reformers. They call on human beings in industrial nations as well as developing ones to change their lifestyles: they demand nothing less than the decarbonization of civilization in the middle term and a broad renunciation of the enormous conveniences of a fossil-fuel based *modus vivendi*.

These beliefs represent a turning point so fundamental that we are justified in employing grand analogies: the change in thinking that is required of twenty-first-century human beings runs deeper than the sixteenth-century Reformations, in which the rules that governed transactions between Earth and heaven were revised. It immediately brings to mind the voice of John the Baptist, who called for total change. The voice from the desert then called for nothing less than a metanoia, which was intended to replace the trivial egotistical ethos of everyday life with the heart's own moral state of exception – this call was supposed to trigger the permanent revolution that we call Christianity. Finally, the demand to rethink things today even recalls Plato's subtle remark in his dialogue *The Sophist*, according to which the quarrel between the friends of the ideas (commonly known as idealists) and the admirers of perceptible bodies (commonly known as materialists) over the meaning of being amounts to a kind of gigantomachy – a battle that will last as long as there are human beings around to vote for one side or the other, due the contentiousness of the issue itself.

The current battle over the climate no longer aims at the "world domination" that commentators of the imperialist age were fond of talking about. On the contrary, it is concerned with the possibility of keeping the civilizing process open and ensuring its progress. Following the mutual discovery of cultures through long-distance commerce between the sixteenth and twentieth centuries, this process led to a provisional synthesis of global agency through trade and diplomacy. It is expected to soon develop into the positive collaboration of cultures within common institutions capable of action – although we leave aside the question of whether "humanity" is even able to constitute a coherent "we" or a *volonté general*.

Only two things are certain at the moment: first, that the meteorological reformation that has just begun opens up the prospect of an age of major conflicts; second, that the twenty-first century will go down in history as a carnival of redemptive vanities, at the end of which human beings will long for redemption from redemption and salvation from saviors. At the same time, it heralds an era of hypocrisy and the double standard. Nevertheless, beyond vanity, panic, and hypocritical rhetoric, this age will continually confront the question of whether to set up something like a stabilizing regime on board the spaceship Earth. It should be borne in mind that, from the outset, we must have modest expectations regarding the concept of stabilization. Cultural evolution knows no stable equilibrium. At best, it can segue from one livable state of disequilibrium to the next.

The contours of the coming gigantomachy can already be recognized today. The idealistic party is here expressed by the advocates of a new modesty. They confront their materialist adversaries with the demand that all forms of kinetic expressionism have to be reduced to an eco-political minimum. If we have understood that this expressionism is identical to the *modus vivendi* of affluent cultures on the planet, that indeed it permeates the totality of our "metabolism of nature," our production, our consumption, our housing, our business, our arts and communications, and that in each of these domains we still have every indication that there will be no disruption in growth and improvement, then one thing immediately becomes clear: the ethics of the future, hostile to expression and emission, aims precisely at the reversal of civilization's direction to this point. It demands reduction where increase was previously on the agenda, it demands minimization where maximization used to hold sway, it wants restraint where explosions were formerly permitted, it prescribes thrift where profligacy was once considered to be particularly appealing, and it calls for self-circumspection where self-liberation was until now celebrated. If we think these reversals through to their end, then over the course of the meteorological reformation we arrive at a kind of ecological Calvinism. This position is based on the principle that humanity has only one Earth at its disposal. Hence it may not demand from its basis more than the latter has to give – on penalty of self-destruction. Globalization paradoxically works against its own fundamental tendency: by carrying out expansions across the board, it enforces restrictions across the board. In wishing to make affluence a general condition, globalization discovers that ultimately it is only the opposite of affluence – frugality for all – that is practicable on a global scale.

With that said, the giants who will join battle in the impending twenty-first century emerge. We are witnessing the struggle between expansionism and minimalism. We are supposed to choose between an ethics of fireworks and an ethics of asceticism. We will feel the contending alternatives reflected in our attitude toward life and note how we alternate between states of manic profligacy and depressive thrift. Nietzsche sometimes remarked about the Earth that, to an outside intelligence, it must seem like an "ascetic star" on which an elite of depressive spiritualists driven by ressentiment call the shots. The twentieth century has seen the affluent part of the Earth enjoy a hedonistic interlude that might be over before the twenty-first century has ended.

Should the heralded reformation lead to a meteorological socialism, the Earth would soon appear, from an outsider's perspective, to be a frugal star: every single human being on it would be entitled to a small emission-credit, which is due him or her as shareholder in the atmosphere and the other elements.[20] Since Nietzsche was at the same time an expert in questions of gigantomachies and contention between the gods, he knows that neutrality is impossible in conflicts of this magnitude and writes about this in the *Birth of Tragedy from the Spirit of Music*: "It is the enchantment of these struggles that whoever sees them must also struggle with them himself."[21] In wealthy nations, each citizen will not only stage the gigantomachy in their own breast, but will also publicly declare which side they have taken with their own decisions on what to consume.

1.7 "The Power of the Body"

"For no one has thus far determined the power of the body."[22]
Spinoza

At this point in our reflections, it seems as though ecological puritanism might be the only reasonable morality on board the spaceship Earth. We can make of this what we will, but it is clear that during the twentieth century a new form of the absolute imperative has emerged: "You must change your life!" – this principle is authoritative for many contemporary ethical institutions. We realize that we are obligated to cultivate a *modus vivendi* that corresponds to the ecological-cosmopolitan insights of our civilization. This imperative becomes so noticeable that we could liken it to what in earlier times was achieved and is still being achieved by Buddhist, Stoic, Christian, Islamic, and Humanist ethics, respectively, with their significance for both individuals and communities. Because the new imperative, like every great ethical phenomenon, appeals to everyone, we should expect a rampant wave of ethical enthusiasm around the world. In this enthusiasm, the current will to live is combined with the current sense for what is good and proper into a powerful élan that will perhaps shake the world – both within and outside of traditional religions. It is just as realistic to expect a complementary wave of resignation, defeatism, and a cynical "devil-may-care" attitude.

At first sight, it thus seems as if the current imperative could only result in an ethics of global moderation. Perhaps the only question that remains open is whether the turn toward modesty will happen as a result of a voluntary reduction by populations in emission-intensive cultures, or whether the governments of affluent nations – for want of global governance to this point, the only macrosystems capable of action – will find themselves sooner or later compelled to proclaim a kind of ecological martial law in their respective territories, under which what cannot be achieved on a voluntary basis will be imposed instead.

If we reconsider matters, it becomes clear that the demands for a global ethics of moderation or even the hopes for a climactic socialism are illusory. Not only is all of expressionistic civilization's momentum against them, they also contradict our knowledge of what drives higher cultures. In other words, these driving forces are inconceivable if we do not grasp the connection between striving for self-preservation and the will to self-advancement. The link between self-preservation and self-advancement includes the preliminary decision in favor of a culture in which abundance, waste, and luxury have achieved civil rights. In his reflections on the establishment of an ideal polity, Plato soon had to drop the hypothesis of a frugal polis: the wisest of the Greeks had no answer when Glaucon objected to the description of a meal in the frugal city by bluntly asking: "If you were founding a city of pigs, Socrates, isn't that just what you would provide to fatten *them*?"[23] Socrates has to concede this objection and permit the construction of an opulent city. Similarly, in all of our prognoses and projects for the world of tomorrow, we are today compelled to proceed from the fact that human beings in rich nations consider their affluence and its technological premises to be the irrevocable spoils of conquest. They remain convinced that it is evolution's job to make their material affluence and expressive privileges into global phenomena via continuous growth. They will refuse to put up with a future that is founded on negative growth and restraint.

In contrast, the proponents of the new modesty object that sooner or later those who are affluent today will have to accept the ecological facts. To the extent that large numbers of new producers and consumers join the club of profligates, the limits of emission and of expression become increasingly dramatic and become conspicuous even more quickly. The principle that forms the basis of all arguments for limiting growth here comes into play: there is only one unique Earth, and yet the rich nations of the world today live as if one and a half or two more Earths were there to be exploited. If their lifestyle were to be extended to everyone who inhabits the planet, humanity would need no less than four Earths at its disposal. Since, however, the Earth represents a single monad that cannot be multiplied, we must accept the priority of limits over the impulse to transgress those limits.

At first, this argument seems undeniable. As long as the Earth and its biosphere are conceived of as an irreplaceable singularity, the exploitative behavior of modern expressive and comfortable civilization must seem like unpardonable irrationality. The way human beings have treated the planet is then comparable to a disaster film in which rival mafia groups engage in a firefight with high-caliber weaponry on board a plane at 12,000 meters.

At the same time, it is legitimate to ask whether the right consequences have been drawn from the monadological interpretation of
the Earth. Do we understand our situation correctly if we conceive of
the planet and its biosphere as a singularity that cannot be multiplied
and as something that is ultimately fixed? We should remember that it
is no longer merely a matter of the primal cosmological datum, Earth,
and the primal evolutionary phenomenon, life. The technosphere,
which for its part is animated and moderated by a noosphere, has
been added to our basic parameters in the course of social evolution.
In view of both of these parameters for growth, we are justified in
applying Spinoza's statement that no one has thus far determined the
power of the body (that is, the human body) to the Earth: no one has
thus far determined the power of the Earth as terrestrial body. We
do not yet know what developments will be possible if the geosphere
and biosphere are further developed by an intelligent technosphere
and noosphere. It is not impossible *a priori* that such further developments will lead to effects that amount to a multiplication of the Earth.

Technology has not yet spoken its final word. If it has mostly been
considered in terms of environmental degradation and biogenerativ-
ity, this shows that in some respects it is only just beginning. A while
ago, I suggested distinguishing between heterotechnics and homeo-
technics[24] – with the first based on violating and outwitting nature,
and the second based on imitating nature and pursuing natural
principles of production in artificial contexts. A completely different image of the interplay between environment and technology
emerges with the conversion of the technosphere to a homeotechno-
logical and biomimetic standard. We would learn what the Earth, as
terrestrial body, is capable of the moment human beings reorganize
their handling of it from exploitation to coproduction. If we follow
the path of sheer exploitation, the Earth will forever remain a finite
monad. If we follow the path of co-production between nature and
technology, a hybrid planet could result on which more would be
possible than conservative geologists believe.

Around the world, creative thinkers in the environmental movement have put forth similar ideas. They have reckoned that a
doubling of affluence could be achieved by halving our consumption
of resources. Along similar lines, an offhand remark by Buckminster
Fuller suggests a link between the miraculous multiplication of
bread loaves and the metaphysically interpreted history of technology: "By virtue of . . . leverage principles . . . it is literally possible to
do more with less. . . . Possibly it was this intellectual augmentation
. . . that Christ was trying to teach in the obscurely told story of the
loaves and the fishes."[25] The conclusion to his *Operating Manual*
thus includes an appeal to the ethos of creativity:

So, planners, architects, and engineers, take the initiative. Go to work, and above all cooperate and don't hold back on one another or try to gain at the expense of another. Any success in such lopsidedness will be increasingly short-lived. These are the synergetic rules that evolution is employing and trying to make clear to us. They are not man-made laws. They are the infinitely accommodative laws of the intellectual integrity governing universe.[26]

We must guard against reducing these statements to the naivety that they exhibit. If the great autodidact is to succeed in keeping the emissions of ignorance within limits, this will only happen thanks to the intellectual integrity of all those who today assume the responsibility for their positive knowledge and their dark prognoses.

1.8 Politics for the Earth

In the subtitle of this essay, the concept of the "Anthropocene" was called a "stage" [*Zustand*] in the margins of the Earth's history. In this context, it should now be evident just how much the term "stage" is undercut by radical irony: because it is defined by an apocalyptic logic (in which running ahead to the end remains associated with returning to the present moment), the anthropocenic situation is the opposite of everything that in historical times has connected human beings with firm conceptions of what a stage is – whether we call this the state, the status quo [*das Bestehende*], "all that is solid,"[27] the institution, or "enframing" [*Ge-stell*]. Bruno Latour, in an incisive passage from his fifteenth *Gifford Lecture* in February 2013, has noted that Thomas Hobbes' legendary conceptual pairing, that of the "state of nature" and its overcoming by the stage of state formation [*Staats-Zustand*], is currently undergoing an unexpected semantic change: a new state of nature has begun that no leviathan will be able to tame. A new war of all against all has been unleashed in which it is not merely wolves and sheep, or armed nations and homicidal ideologies, which are ranged against each other. The extremely diverse and for the time being stateless ensemble of agents that populate the Earth's field of battle in common with human "societies" now clash on very obscure fronts – CO_2, the sea level, algae, computers, microbes, tuna fish, meteorites, antibiotics, algorithms, methane gas, human rights, wind turbines, genetically modified corn, kidney transplants. The ironically renewed "state of nature" is neither identical to the chaos of creation nor can it provide what used to be offered by the modern conception of a stage.

As a result, the anthropocenic situation requires a new constitutional debate, which in the best-case scenario will result in a process of governing not modeled on that of the leviathan – or, better, in a network of such processes. In such a network, not only are constitutional bodies and those who bear rights defined within the framework of a political relation that is to be newly established – called "Earth-citizenship" – but even the convocation of the collective of Earth-citizens as such is to be conducted anew in diverse formations, both within the terms of the Universal Declaration of Human Rights and beyond it. It is to be expected that these processes will resemble a Titanic clash. The citizens of the Earth shall then assemble themselves, answering the battle cry launched in 1836 by the poet Christian Dietrich Grabbe: "Nothing but desperation can save us now!"

The fact that a few of our most important commentators draw on the memory of religious reform movements, in order to motivate the agents of contemporary civilization to make the necessary change of attitude, reveals how desperate the anthropocenic weather system has become. Since the 1960s and 1970s, authors such as Ivan Illich, Rudolf Bahro, Hans Jonas, Carl Friedrich von Weizsäcker, René Girard, and Carl Amery have argued along these lines. In more recent times, the voices of Robert N. Bellah, Bruno Latour, Pope Francis, and others have been added.

The tone of eschatological despair was nowhere to be heard more clearly than in the left-wing Catholic journalist and novelist Carl Amery, who was one of the intellectual founders of the German Green Party, before he abandoned the party because of its disappointing pragmatic conformism. In light of calamitous contention and resource wars, Amery postulated a mobilization of fundamentalist religious forces on a scale beyond all previous religious practices. On his view – as it is particularly developed in the text *Die Botschaft des Jahrtausend: Von Leben, Tod, und Würde* [Tr. – *The Message of the Millennium: On Life, Death, and Dignity*] – the technologically advanced fraction of humanity must first and foremost learn to rise above its biologically determined, terrestrial, all-too-terrestrial panic over survival.[28] Its task is to create a new *ars moriendi* with a religious foundation, which in the author's sense of the term means with a meta-biological foundation. Such an *ars moriendi* will at the same time facilitate an ethos that is characterized by a more just division of the chances for existence between nations and species.

As desperate as this line of thought might sound, Amery's intervention demonstrates that the political ontology of Earth-citizenship entails the demand for a political anthropology in which human beings would again be understood as they were in the days of Greek epic and Attic tragedy, as fundamentally mortal. Their common point of reference would no longer be an Olympus inhabited by gods who are free from the world's cares. It would be the Earth itself shared in common by mortals throughout its various regions, an Earth that is too real to play the role of traditional transcendence, but also too transcendent to ever become the property of a single imperial power. In this regard, we still consider Hölderlin's vision of the human being poetically inhabiting the Earth to be a compelling one: the concept of the Anthropocene includes a spontaneous *minima moralia* for the present age. It implies care for the cohabitation of Earth-citizens in both human and non-human form. It prompts us to work together on a network of simple and more advanced settings in which the agents of the current world will create their existence in the mode of co-immunity.

2

FROM THE DOMESTICATION
OF THE HUMAN BEING TO THE
CIVILIZING OF CULTURES

Answering the Question of Whether Humanity is Capable of Taming Itself

2.1 Pastoral Metaphysics: The Discovery of the Problem of Domestication

The anthropological discovery that human beings can and must adopt relations to themselves and to those like them that are described by such verbs as taming, breeding, and tending, occurred in the Western evolution of ideas on two occasions in quite singular contexts, each time at a decisive turn in intellectual history. The first manifestation of this complex of ideas is associated with the name of Plato. In a novel manner, the founder of the Athenian Academy attempted to precisely conceive the traditional praxis of educator and statesman, with reference to a kind of anthropological difference that opened up a fissure within the essence of being human. Because human beings in advanced cultures cannot be by nature what they nevertheless are by nature, they must be educated, as individuals, and made to submit to rational governance, as citizens. Education and political stewardship are two fields of praxis in which the incapacity of human beings in advanced cultures to fulfill themselves without guidance from others (putting it in ancient terms: to obey their own nature) is manifested in a particularly noticeable way. In more closely defining pedagogical and state-cybernetic functions, Plato reaches back for images and analogies that are taken from the pastoral sphere. The dialogue *Statesman* is the primary source for Plato's pastoral theory of politics in its fully developed form. Here we encounter a famous and still somewhat scandalous turn of phrase according to which the art of the political steward is an "art of shepherding" the featherless, hornless bipeds of unmixed breeding, along with the telling addition that – since tyrannies are never an option for Greeks in general and philosophers in particular – politics is concerned with a voluntary supervision of a herd of creatures living together of their own volition.[1] A characteristic feature of Greek rationalism is the belief that human beings can only be dissuaded from unreasonable inclinations and induced to enter the house of reason through a specific ascesis – that is, a system of ongoing practices. It is unnecessary to point out how influential Plato's pastoral anthropology was in this regard. Thanks to a series of translations and reformulations, it has left a deep impression on the Western imaginary, particularly the way in which it was blended with the figure of the good shepherd in the New Testament. For almost 2,000 years, Christian communal logic has been based on these Platonic images of herds and their shepherds.

The second discovery that it is necessary to train human beings to be human beings occurs under radically different circumstances in the nineteenth century, after Darwin naturalized the history of the species and placed the human being at the end of an evolutionary line that showed so-called *Homo sapiens* to be a cousin of the hominidae. Ever since, the traditional pedagogical question of how human beings are to be formed into human beings has been overshadowed by evolutionary biology. Instead of the tension between unreason and reason, we now have the antagonism of wilderness and civilization or, to put it in mythological terms, of Dionysian and Apollonian powers. Only in such a situation can the talk of domestication assume a serious tone. Now, the formation of human beings is no longer merely to be conceived metaphorically, as entry into the house of reason, but is supposed to literally be conceived as leaving behind the animal wilderness for civilized domesticity. This occasions Nietzsche's unsettling intervention: he was one of the first to recognize that the process of generation, in the literal sense, always also implies instances of self-breeding and, on his view, usually as a kind of a progressive self-abnegation in thrall to the ideal of priestly and anti-aristocratic prejudice. Hence the provocative verse from the song *On Virtue That Makes Small* in the Third Part of *Thus Spoke Zarathustra*:

At bottom these simple ones want one simple thing: that no one harm them. . . . To them virtue is whatever makes modest and tame; this is how they made the wolf into a dog and mankind himself into mankind's favorite pet.[2]

It is enough for us to note here that though Nietzsche's observations continue to be well-understood, his concerns are no longer ours at present. While the author of *Thus Spoke Zarathustra* toiled away on the problem of how the suppressed sheen of the wilderness could be saved from castrative civilization's total triumph, the question for us is rather how to succeed in putting a halt to the running wild of civilization at its height.

2.2 Beyond Taming: From Pedagogy to the Discovery of Neoteny and Back Again

The twentieth century's specific contribution to a new definition of the *conditio humana* begins with the realization that domestications cannot be sufficiently defined with the categories of evolutionary theory – neither for household pets in general nor for the king of household pets, the human being. Successive generations that follow a trend toward domestication are not governed by the normal evolutionary pressure of a purely natural environment. They benefit from a special climate that has been created half naturally and half culturally, in which it is not necessarily those who are optimally adapted for external nature who survive but rather the specimens that do well in internal conditions: these are the living beings who distinguish themselves by their exceptional agility, their increased capacity to learn, their engaging sociability, and, finally, by their bio-aesthetic advantages. Nest-building creatures, particularly birds, provide a natural-historical prelude to this, but even individual reptiles, such as the well-known Mexican salamander, retain their larval form for the duration of their lives, as do those particular mammals that are able to offer a high standard of nest-security and parental care to their young. In the case of such living organisms, biologists have observed a complex of characteristics that since the late nineteenth century were described by the term "neoteny," that is, the retention of juvenile features (or were described with the concept "paedomorphism"). This includes the trend toward accelerated births, which leads to the emergence of quite immature young, a feature that is inconceivable without the luxury of a secure nest. These tendencies all come together in *Homo sapiens*, whose young are characterized by extreme immaturity at their time of birth. "Premature birth" [*Frühgeburtlichkeit*] among humans, to use the *terminus technicus* coined by Adolf Portmann in the middle of the twentieth century, not only implies that the human life cycle has an unusually prolonged juvenile phase, but also paradoxically entails that specimens that are "mature" in the biological sense die off, while premature, larval, or fetal forms acquire a monopoly on sexual reproduction. According to the Dutch paleoanthropologist Louis Bolk, whom we have to thank for having already formulated these dramatic insights in the 1920s, the evolutionary-theoretical truth of *Homo sapiens* is to be found in the provocative thesis that we represent a species of culturally and biologically successful fetal primates, who despite their juvenilization form a species capable of sexual reproduction.

A third discovery of human domestication is associated with these references to the neotenic condition of the human species, and gives a new meaning to the previous two. Disclosing the mystery of neoteny confirms the insight of cultural anthropologists that human beings, even in their early stages, must be conceived as cultural creatures. From this point on, the fundamental enculturation of human beings appears under a twofold light: First, culture signifies the resumption of a biological nest-privilege with the resources of civilization – in this context, domestication means neither entry into the house of reason nor into the house of civilization, but rather the gradual transformation of nest-security measures into architectonic protections and socio-technological privileges. It has since been very clearly recognized how culture as a whole functions like an immersive incubator that envelops its members. Second, through these reflections it becomes clear that *Homo sapiens* is dependent on cultural guidance for even its motivational disposition. After the breakdown of a purely biological programming of orientation, due to its extreme neoteny, the instinctive framework of *Homo sapiens* no longer guides it from within and it loses the firm linking of brain and environment, losses that require compensation. This compensation is provided by systems of symbolic guidance, which replace the instincts with authorities – a motif that was developed in the mid twentieth century by Arnold Gehlen. Symbolic ordering systems disburden all human young of the insoluble problem (at least on the individual level) of having to create the experiences and discoveries of their ancestors over again all by themselves.

The introduction of the concept of neoteny into the science of the human being clearly represents the most subversive innovation on record in the field of anthropological knowledge after Darwin. Its consequences should not be overlooked now, especially since most disciplines in the human sciences have yet to understand them at all yet or else have done so inadequately. The discovery of neoteny is also significant because it allows phenomena such as the passing down of traditions and education, which were supposedly already exhaustively researched, to appear in a different light. On the one hand, thanks to neotenology it is evident that pedagogy always comes too late, because the newborn human being, due to its premature birth, does not initially need education but rather demands the resumption of gestation by extra-uterine means (a motivation that Kant had already grasped in his anthropological writings, when he emphasized that deficient education can always be compensated for, while deficient discipline means that something is missing that can never be redeemed again). On the other hand, this theory reveals that human beings can never be educated enough, because their entry into the house of symbolic orderings forever remains a labile operation susceptible to disruption. Psychologists today are especially aware of this, and increasingly warn us of the dangers associated with the weakening of symbolic authority in postmodern ("fatherless") society.

2.3 Naive Pacifism as the Refusal of Cooperation in Cultural Limit Situations

With what has been discussed to this point, I hope to have explained in broad outline why the members of the species *Homo sapiens* as such always already represent products of domestication: biologically through neotenization, and culturally through their integration into self-generated symbolic orders. Owing to the synergy of these two aspects, historically developed cultures first and foremost amount to (relatively) closed survival units, in which individual cultures are kept as though in artificial enclosures, or incubators. This was the issue that was occasionally described metaphorically as the "human park."

In light of these reflections, it should be clear that self-domestication is a concept that encapsulates humankind's past. The mystery of *Homo sapiens* – that it exists despite its biological impossibility – is only to be interpreted in terms of an anthropology of domestication. At the same time, we must acknowledge that prior methods for domesticating and taming the human being were obviously inadequate. When we see what an advanced pedagogy for our species involves, we immediately realize that the work of civilization is only half done. Even if human domestication appears to be a *fait accompli* in some respects (inasmuch as human beings only exist in the incubators of their respective cultures), it remains incomplete. The reason for this is easy to see. Cultures may respect domestic orders in their own internal solidary systems, yet domesticity in their relations with what is outside remains unfinished, because single cultures do not gather together under one roof very often, instead forming environments that are strange to each other, and not seldom hostile. The historical trace of the enduring lack of domesticity in external human relations is war, which has occasionally plagued the evolution of the species, but that first developed into a stable, somewhat professionalized institution approximately 7,000 years ago in Eurasia.

If we define more recent cultures as unified entities capable of war, we have a concept that allows us to see how the lack of domesticity has cast its shadow over internal cultural relations. Insofar as successful cultures prepare for war, their members never really feel secure in the shelter of their own homes. Anyone who wishes to overcome the poisoning of domestic life by preparing for war abroad must therefore reflect on the extension of domestication beyond older ethnic solidary unities. We find attempts at this, particularly in early Buddhism, in Stoicism, and in early Christianity. All three wisdom teachings (that are often misunderstood to be religions) are essentially movements for de-domestication: their founders demand that followers break with traditional domesticating systems. Buddhism refers to those who turn away from their old communities to enter the path of the Dharma, the house-abandoners *expressis verbis*. Jesus' shocking demand that one must leave behind father and mother for the sake of the heavenly kingdom is well known. The ethical demand that the wise human being should prove himself to be a citizen of the universe (*kosmopolitēs*) and not merely a member of his own primary ethnic community goes back to Stoicism. Of course, these programs of radical de-domestication never aim at a return to the wilderness (although there are eremitic phenomena in all three movements), and even less at a regressive break with national symbolic orders. Uprooting from former dwelling places is part of a relocation effort to a higher domesticity, which for now can only be articulated in spiritual or cosmic symbols. In essence, Buddhist, Christian, and Stoic de-domestications are to be interpreted as acts of conscientious objection, indeed as respective metaphysics of desertion. They put an end to membership in cultural communities whose existence is based on war against foreign cultures. War is the limit situation of unified domesticated entities that simultaneously forms the fundamentally non-domesticated situation between unified foreign entities. Given these premises, only someone who rejects cooperation with their own collective in order to devote themselves to a domestication of humanity beyond polemical, individual cultures can conscientiously object to military service.

At this stage of moral evolution, we can ask how the naive pacifism of the great wisdom teachings and philosophies can be developed into a scientifically grounded pacifism. The answer to this question is provided by a second-order theory of domestication. Such a theory at the same time offers the foundations of a general theory of extended solidarity.

2.4 Maximal Stress Cooperation in Cultural Groups

We now understand that individual cultures function as primary domesticating agents by safeguarding their members in a symbolic and material order. At the same time, it is evident why domesticating agents cannot themselves be domesticated: they are still oriented to the emergency of non-domesticity, to a life-and-death battle with foreign cultures – however muted this battle may have become in many places over the course of the modern era, reduced to merely economic competition. In view of these conditions, the phenomenon of culture – that in everyday consciousness is not entirely incorrectly equated with the concept of a "nation" [*Volk*] – can be redefined as a symbolically integrated population whose members cooperate with each other not only in domestic situations, but also in situations of life-and-death struggle. Cultures thus represent real operative survival units – in Heiner Mühlmann's terminology, they are maximal stress cooperation units (MSC units).[3] This definition has the advantage of clarifying why the most successful cultures are simultaneously the most domesticated and the most warlike, as a rule. The classic example of this in the cultural milieu of the West is offered by the Romans, whose civilization formed an enormous parallelogram of familialism and militarism. The secret of Roman culture's success – as with every other distinctive military culture – consisted in the creation of a military technique whose principle could be characterized as the moral control of high-stress reactions in the face of present life-threating dangers. The fact that human beings are able to cooperate in relaxed [*entlasteten*] situations does not require much explanation. Conversely, the fact that men cooperate under maximal stress or pursue common goals even in battle and close proximity to death represents a phenomenon that is very much in need of explanation. Cultural theory shows us that the creation of extremely improbable patterns of conduct such as "maximal stress cooperation" requires a great deal of moral injunction (categorical prohibition of cowardice), cultural idealization (heroism), and technical preparation (weapons training, drill formations).

All of this suggests that maximal stress cooperation be viewed as key to the successful survival of cultures in the historical era, or the age of advanced cultures. At the same time, we should add that such acts of cooperation represent a paradoxical form of domestication. This is evident in the training of animals, which renders the most difficult biological processes – high-stress reactions – subservient to strategic goal-planning. Anyone who reflects on the continuation of humanity's self-domestication and its integration into overlapping solidary communities must consequently turn to the question of whether traditional, culturally formative kinds of maximal stress cooperation can be overcome.

2.5 The Culture of Taming the Wild Animal

With this, a fourth sense of self-domestication emerges. After the talk of taming and domesticating human beings through neotenic juvenilization, and then additionally through political pedagogy, and finally through the internalization of symbolic orders, a rather technical version of the problem of domestication comes into view when we consider the military training of stress reactions. A pacifism elaborated in terms of anthropology cannot be content with the fact that rational individuals move out of their family's or nation's house into the house of God or the Dharma – or join the invisible nation of the wise. At moments of crisis, these morally fastidious movements lead to martyrdom, insofar as the latter provides justification for the belief that it is better to be killed than to remain in solidarity with a murderous cultural group. From the perspective of cultural theory, we would need to examine whether this exceptional form of non-cooperation with maximal-stress cooperators can be revised into a practicable general rule. This can be verified, although the difficulties associated with it remain great indeed. If cultures are to be understood as systems of domestication that are not themselves domesticated, the concern with higher-order domestications can only be assuaged by a revision of how cultures have been designed to this point, as polemical survival units. In this context, the concept of "solidarity" attains its specific transcultural resonance.

By its very nature, the work of the culture of taming the wild animal is carried out over three stages. The first stage is reached when a number of survival units, through mimetic assimilation, reach the point of being able to hold each other in check. In so doing, they do not aim at any internal domestication or demilitarization, yet are able to provide the deterrence needed for a containment that is prerequisite for progressive civilizations.[4] At this stage of interethnic relations and relations between states, diplomacy arises – as an art of well-tempered hostility. This civilizing effort experienced its juridical fallout in modern Europe's *ius publicum*. In this regime, it is obvious that regressive tendencies are not to be eliminated. The reason for this lies in the still unchanged equation of culture and survival unit.

Hence the second stage, that of the containment of polemogenic cultures, consists in reforming such cultures into interdependent systems. In doing this, cultures make their vital interests so dependent on association with their partners from other cultures that we may here speak of the emergence of a higher-order survival unit. This can be observed at present in the economically interdependent states of the West, whose likelihood of regressing to war with each other has become minimal. The effect of domestication here proceeds from the reformatting of a perceived survival unit. Such a survival unit transgresses its previous external borders so as to render the former enemy or rival into a cooperator, making them advantageous for its own survival. This process is readily apparent in the historically unique construction of the European community, which, in a fascinating process of self-containment, has transformed itself – against a backdrop of war that is not so far in the past – into an advanced political domestication unit. That even such self-containment units have to contend with the endogenous forces of disintegration is shown by the results of the referenda on the European constitution, in France and in the Netherlands, in May and June of 2005, respectively. Clear popular majorities made it known that they still consider their own nation, and not the European Union, to be their survival unit. The voting results in both countries are *de facto* profoundly illusory, since the respective survival interests of both can only still be satisfied in the European format, and this has been the case for some time already. (At the core of the will to illusion lies the fear of losing economic privileges, which we might prefer to believe have been earned by nations as such and not by the system of interactions between nations.)

The third stage of the culture of domestication of the wild animal would be achieved the moment the great, internally domesticated survival units, which one may call civilizations,[5] using Samuel Huntington's terminology (namely "the West," "Islam," India, China, Africa, Latin America), would have again developed among each other such a high degree of affirmed independence that they progress beyond the stage of non-domestication in their external relations. Present tendencies point in this direction. Nevertheless, they do not yet lead out of the stage of reciprocal containment. We should just as little ignore the fact that immense conflicts arise on the front lines, between large units – particularly between the Chinese and the Americans, and between the West and Islam. The contending cultural blocks are a long way from effectively gathering under the roof of a common civilization. In the external relations of large units, there can be no talk of the law of the excluded emergency, which was formulated by Bazon Brock and that governs internal civilizations. Indeed, containment as such is itself always put into question again, not least by the tragic double role of the monopolar world power, the United States of America. This country has dedicated itself to a global civilizing mission, on the one hand, and follows a crude regional pressure-group politics, on the other. It presents the spectacle of a civilization that simultaneously seems to be domesticator and wild animal. Thus the USA has quite rashly discredited the ideas whose creditability must be maintained at any price, if the progressive civilization of individual cultures is supposed to advance beyond the level of polemical containment.

2.6 The Disarming of the Population Bomb

In conclusion, I would like to point out a fifth sense of the concept of domestication. Aside from the still insufficiently tamed external relations of cultures, the sore point of their internal relations (biological reproduction) is also very much in need of regulation. Even in this regard, the culture of the wild animal proves to be an entity that requires domestication. This clearly entails lowering the birthrate in all cultures, to a degree compatible with their socioeconomically prevalent living standards. It rules out any kind of population increase for the poor, as well as fierce reproductive conflicts – as have been observed for a long time in Arab lands. The population there, from 1900 to 2000, grew from 150 million to 1.2 billion humans, which amounts to an eightfold increase. Immense violent discharges will be the almost unavoidable consequence of such an increase. Recent demographic research has made clear that there is a positive correlation between excessively high birth rates and war or occurrences of genocide. Through polemically motivated overproduction of human beings, whether latent or manifest, young men in particular between the ages of fifteen and thirty become a risk group that overstrains their own cultures' potential for domestication. Information provided by institutes for strategic research reveals that in the Arab and African world over the next twenty years several hundred million young men will be ready for all manner of polemical activities. There is fear that not a few of them will make good recruiting material for religiously coded programs of self-destruction.

In view of these circumstances, we must split the question of whether humanity can domesticate itself into two halves. The first would be whether such self-taming should be expected in the near future. The answer to this question is clearly no. In all likelihood, the first half of the twenty-first century will remind us of the excesses of the twentieth century. The loss of life will probably be immeasurable, the damage to morality and culture incalculable. The second half of the question is related to longer-term perspectives. Despite everything, they are to be assessed with cautious optimism. If the attempt to bring the two biological *explosiva* of human cultures, polemophilic stress-programs and excessive reproductive tendencies, under control is successful in the long term, the process of global self-domestication (in other words: "the civilizing process") may then receive a favorable prognosis.

3

THE OCEAN EXPERIMENT

From Nautical Globalization to a General Ecology

3.1 Globalization as a Maritime Experiment

If there were a copyright for single words, then the heirs of the Harvard economist and marketing theorist Theodore Levitt (1925–2006) would have to be included among the richest families in the world. Since 1983, when Levitt, in an article for the *Harvard Business Review*, spoke for the first time about the "globalization of markets" (or, to put it better, when he unleashed a wave of imitators by employing this term, which had already been used on occasion), the word "globalization" has risen to become one of the most widely used terms in the modern lexicon. It is undoubtedly the most infectiously energetic word in the vocabulary of the past quarter of a century. This is really saying something in an age in which many terms have spread like epidemics throughout the world of discourse – especially ones such as terrorism, sustainability, greenhouse effect, precariat, celebrity, structured products, and the like. Furthermore, this term has a quasi-magical character. It has the power to produce what it names all by itself: it globalizes itself by creating a name for the most important occurrence of our time – the transformation of the world into a dynamic context in which almost everything interacts with almost everything else almost everywhere.

The market's transformation into a world [*Weltwerdung*], or the world's transformation into a market, as envisaged by Levitt, could not have taken place were it not sustained by a technological innovation that since the 1970s and 1980s has fundamentally transformed most of humanity's mode of existence: I am referring to the introduction of digital procedures into the communicative activities of civilizations. Thus, to begin with, we are completely justified in describing globalization as the digital revolution. Its hallmark is the incredible acceleration of communications that results from the alliance of digitalization and computerization. The world had previously always been characterized by relatively slow movement, significant distance, and cultural asynchronicity. It was only able to be transformed into a synchronous world, whose agents mutually reach across great distances in real time, because computerized world communication made maximum speed into the standard of symbolic transactions. Spatial distances seem to lose their meaning in a synchronous world. It is hard to avoid the impression that high-speed movements have made slow voyages a thing of the past.

We do not really understand the essence of globalization if we allow ourselves to be dazzled by digital revolution's glittering surface. As dramatic as the changes to our *modus vivendi* may be, and as profoundly as the volatile financial markets of the last decade have shaped our understanding of the reality and unreality of monetary transactions, they still form but the surface layer of a multilevel transportation system, which is based on the interconnection of relatively slow, flowing masses and quick signal transmissions. In the current phase of globalization, both poles are already inseparably intertwined – the massive and the subtle, heavy traffic and flying sparks, slow navigation on the surfaces of the Earth and the transmission of messages via distance-negating transmission channels.

From a systemic perspective, slow movements are still primary, since ultimately it is they alone that fill rapid transmissions of information with their substantive contents. From a historical perspective, this is especially true: globalization is not only the effect of the most recent interaction between markets and digital technology – it is the result of a long history that began the moment when the sailors of the Iberian peninsula, in the middle of the fifteenth century, were seized by the audacious idea that the Atlantic Ocean must have another shore – and that this shore could be reached. Viewed in terms of its origins, real and genuine globalization was thus initially a nautical fact. Globalization originally means nothing but the Atlanticization of seafaring: it implies the transition from coastal navigation in the Portuguese manner to navigation of the high seas, based on the model of Columbus' voyages. Globalization therefore presupposes belief in the spherical shape of the Earth.

For this reason, it is not advisable to derive the word "globalization" from the adjective "global," as is typical, but rather from the noun "globe," the central cartographic medium of the modern world, which discloses to terrestrial inhabitants the truth about the shape of their planet and reveals the preponderance of the oceans.

Globalization is based on the belief in the accessibility of other shores. Indeed, even more than this, it is nourished by the conviction that great fortunes are to be found on the other shore. The extreme risks of seafaring are only to be accepted because distant worlds are imagined as immense treasure troves, from which the successful entrepreneur returns to sea, laden with riches. In short, the adventure of nautical globalization is only conceivable if we recall the beginnings of the modern world, when European sailors transitioned from cartographic theory to nautical praxis and dared to demonstrate the unity of the Earth as a round, navigable space for transportation.

It would not be appropriate here to discuss the psychosocial premises of the oceanic turn. All we know for sure is that there must have been something like a primitive accumulation of daring among human beings of the fifteenth, sixteenth, and seventeenth centuries. The demographic policy of early European nation-states undoubtedly contributed to such an accumulation. In fact, Europe – today a region of the planet in demographic decline – was engulfed by a deliberate political population-tsunami between the sixteenth and nineteenth centuries whose consequences included a massive export of human beings. Research has shown how fifty million human beings then left behind what we now call the old world, some voluntarily and some involuntarily, as merchant adventurers and as desperados. They did so to escape from misfortune, to seek a new fortune, most without the prospect of a return voyage, not a few filled with the above-mentioned faith in the primacy of another shore. The world now belongs to the ambition of the second son (the Spanish called them the *secundones*), who leaves home to either find his fortune abroad or die trying.

These brief remarks should be enough to illustrate the thesis that, from its nautical, mercantile, and colonial beginnings, globalization has represented the inclusion of the entire Earth in the psychodynamics of the pursuit of happiness – or in the escape from local misery. It thus becomes evident that globalization is not merely a technological or political phenomenon, that it does not merely indicate the extension of international relations and the consolidation of economic networks. Nor is it merely the addition of an informational and computerized superstructure to a nautical base. We can only really understand it if we recognize in it the expansionism of the pursuit of happiness. Turned unflinchingly outwards, this pursuit considers the entire globe to be its area of operations. Modernity as a whole is therefore based on a psycho-political fact: the pursuit of happiness become planetary. Because becoming planetary in an operative sense means seafaring (as well as aviation, since the second

half of the twentieth century), we today find nautical industries at
the center of events, as in the previous five centuries. One should
not be confused by the media-savvy clamor of the information
industry: the reality of reality is not found in a cyber-café, nor is
it defined in search engines. Its momentum is still in relatively slow
transportation systems that make the spatial world accessible via
roads, rail, and above all via maritime routes, on which activities
devoted to seeking one's fortune motivate enterprising humans. Up
to the present day, globalization remains bound to routines that
were developed by early sailors to conduct the oceanic experiment.

3.2 The Experimental Spirit and the Externalization of Side Effects

After a half-millennium of such practices, the time has come to
review the established routines and to reconsider the experimental
conditions as a whole. I have indicated why globalization is inseparable from oceanization, and at the same time have suggested that
the adventure of modernity, which results in the integration of the
Earth into progressively consolidated transportation networks, can
only be rendered conceivable by the dynamism of the globalized
pursuit of happiness. However, if globalization is oceanization, and
if oceanization signifies the pursuit of happiness by nautical means,
then it is evident that the reality of the global oceanic era of the
pursuit of happiness must *per se* take on the form of an experiment,
and the reasons why this had to happen are likewise clear. The term
"experiment" is obviously not only associated with procedures in
laboratories and research institutes, where scientists and engineers
have more or less well-defined objects "react" to each other under
controlled conditions to compel previously "mute nature" to speak.
Nor can it be reduced to empirical modes of thought that are largely
responsible for the material growth of knowledge in the modern
world. First and foremost, the *modus vivendi* of human beings
also now becomes experimental. Such human beings devote their
whole existence, by land and by sea, to spotting new realities, new
opportunities for profit, and new procedures for controlling nature.
From this perspective, sailors, long-distance traders, ethnographers,
naturalists, but also utopians, schemers, and perhaps charlatans
and soldiers of fortune, as well, should be included in the extended
family of experimenters. Without the actions of such experimenters
the modern world would be unthinkable – beginning with the great
figure of Francis Bacon, whom we remember as the author of the
Novum Organon and as the founder of inductive logic, and whose

death typified the risks of the experimental life: he died, at the age of sixty-five, following a cold that he had caught when, in the winter of 1626, he attempted to preserve meat by freezing it instead of the more traditional method of salting it (in particular, he wanted to discover whether one could better preserve gutted chickens by filling them with snow). Ultimately, the constitution of modern "societies" as a whole is experimental or, to put it better, the constitution of active populations who are surrounded by ever-more numerous technological objects and engaged in ever-closer interactions as they pursue ever-more ambitious goals in ever-more artificial environments is experimental.

The conversion of the modern *modus vivendi* into experimental forms not only involved a dizzying acceleration of technological and cognitive progress. It also set off great cultural shockwaves, accompanied by enormous moral and political crises. These crises are partially discharged into conservative reactions, culminating in present-day fundamentalisms, and partly translated into totalitarian concepts of progress, climaxing in the idea of the "permanent revolution" (Trotsky). Yet the most important result of the generalized experiment has only first dawned on current generations. It has become increasingly apparent that every experiment *per se* is continually accompanied by a systematic neglect of constraining conditions. This holds true for controlled scientific experiments, and it holds all the more true for the wild experiments that remain characteristic of modernity's *modus vivendi* on all fronts.

One of the virtues of a well-constructed experiment and one of the conditions for its success is that it limits itself to a few precise isolated factors and studies their behavior in a narrowly delimited test site. Hence the art of ignoring is inseparable from successful experimentation – we could even say that the ability to disregard [*Vernachlässigung*] what can be disregarded distinguishes the good experimenter *lege artis*. However, if virtually all domains of life become experiments, in the world of work and in that of leisure, in communities as well as in private life, the consequences can easily be gauged: every experimental zone engenders its own surroundings from disregarded variables. As a result, with the increasing consolidation of experiments, we always find that neglected zones [*die Zonen der Vernachlassigung*] increasingly overlap – with more or less severe consequences.[1]

In other words, precisely because the globalization of the pursuit of happiness leads to a widespread proliferation of experimental behavior, it must also involve an inflation of negligence. Environmental awareness, as it has been articulated in the last third of the twentieth century in the industrialized world, arises from the unbearable effects of this inflation. What we call the *environment* is initially nothing more than the disregarded variables in an experiment, which are only noticed after the fact.[2] The obligation to take note of such things proceeds from the fact that negligence (in technical terms: the externalization of apparently irrelevant factors) is everywhere reaching its limits. Side effects become ever more apparent and begin to overshadow the main effects. For this reason, disregarded variables must be combined with conscious and deliberate products – these latter not infrequently form the majority of the equation. Where externalization was, internalization shall be. The age of side effects at the same time represents an age of integral balances.

We now understand that the globalization of happiness-experiments cannot occur without the globalization of side effects. This is a morally demanding and economically costly realization, which has tragic implications in some instances. On the one hand, we are increasingly better able to recognize why and on what grounds modern agents devote themselves to enterprises that are supposed to convey them to their other shore. We see how each individual experimenter moves ahead in his or her own tunnel of chances [*Chancen-Tunnel*] by focusing on a few elements, namely costs and profits, and ignoring countless external factors. At the same time, it is more evident by the day that this *modus operandi* is no longer compatible with the fact that we coexist with billions of other experimenters pursuing their happiness on an interconnected globe.

This was the great insight of the engineer Buckminster Fuller, who in his visionary text *Operating Manual for Spaceship Earth* (1968) called on us to finally compose a general codex for navigating the ship of all ships.[3] His argument is as relevant today as it was when he first authored it. The vast majority of human beings have populated spaceship Earth in both prehistoric and historic times without ever noticing that they were on board a cosmic vehicle. Human beings started to form an idea of their actual situation when they began to voyage across oceans. Only today have conditions become such as to make the demand for a general policy of on-board management imperative. As long as human beings thought exclusively in local categories and acted in small and medium-sized radii, their existence was similar to that of ants on a Persian carpet: for all their eagerness to scurry around on it just as they wished they remained unable to appreciate the carpet's pattern.

From Buckminster Fuller's perspective, globalization primarily signifies an event in the history of thought – or better, a reversal in the ethics of knowledge: globalization is the rapid repeal of the right to ignorance. The evolutionary reserves of ignorance-indulgence, which seemed to place the Earth forever at the disposal of its inhabitants, will run out within a few centuries. Ever since enterprising humans began acting on a global scale, they ventured into an era in which the only thing that will be of any help to them is to deal perceptively with circumstances on board the great ship – that includes in particular the recognition that in all too many ways they do not know enough to be able to act reasonably and without causing further harm.

3.3 Limits of Externalization, or a New Labor of the Argonauts

Interiorization must take the place of exteriorization: this is the axiom for any future realism in the globalized world. This has quite astonishing, even alarming consequences as regards the ocean, that primordial element. In every image of the world hitherto, the high seas, insofar as they already played a role for land-based cultures, epitomized an insurmountable externality. Even the fact that oceans have been navigable for centuries has hardly changed this view. Indeed, universal seafaring initially only seemed to prove what little consequence human activities have in the face of the supremacy of the elements. So it is no wonder if, in the modern world, all negligence flows into the sea, as used to be said of rivers.

Over the last few decades, the observations of sailors and scientists at institutes of oceanography and marine biology from around the world have combined to form an alarming picture. I will mention only the most well-known phenomena: the great garbage patches of the North Atlantic and Pacific Oceans, a few of which have already become as large as Central Europe and whose impact on the maritime environment has yet to be reliably gauged; the increasing acidity in the oceans, which, assuming ongoing business-as-usual by humans until the end of the twenty-first century,[4] will no longer be compatible with numerous maritime lifeforms;[5] the dramatic reduction of marine fauna, threatened by decades of industrialized overfishing;[6] the growing risks of submarine oil spills due to increasing off-shore drilling;[7] the polluting of the atmosphere above the oceans by the emissions of marine engines powered by heavy fuel oil; the contamination of enormous bodies of water through extensive aquafarming; the chronic polluting of oceans from the runoff of countless coastal cities and the refuse dumped from on board more than a hundred thousand ships that continually navigate the oceans, only a small number of which (namely, cruise ships) have self-contained waste-management systems.

The list could be extended. The gravity of globalization is palpable at every single point: the sea can no longer fulfill its supposed role as absorber of the disregarded factors of human experiments. The absolute imperative of the future requires that transactions on the seas and coasts become civilized. Civilization means the integration of an external world into an internal world, the subsumption of disorderly praxis into a regulated sphere, and the subordination of a field in which irresponsible actions have prevailed to the jurisdiction of an authority capable of acting responsibly. It would be delusional to expect the imperative of civilization to be realized solely on a voluntary basis. For its implementation, two mechanisms, or objective trends, are necessary, in the absence of which goodwill alone remains powerless: First, in view of existing calamities and those to come, the agents in question will have to mutually compel each other to finally submit to a universally binding set of rules whose introduction and oversight is the vital business of an organ of global governance.[8] Second, technological developments will have to occur that ensure that the civilization of maritime practices happens at a reasonable price. The synergy of law, science, and technology will be necessary for the civilization of globalization to succeed.

In the final analysis, all legal and technological contributions to the civilization of globalization will remain merely superficial modifications if they are not properly embedded in a comprehensive transformation of the moral and spiritual forces that drive globalization. Such a transformation would have to assume the proportions of a cultural revolution: it would involve civilizing the pursuit of happiness itself. I have indicated how the mundane pursuit of happiness, symptomatically embodied by Columbus' legendary obsession with gold, has provided the motive of motives, the motor of motors, the energy of energies that we see at work from the beginning of seafaring, globalization, and modernity in the fifteenth century. The dream of finding good fortune on another shore has driven the world-experiment of modern enterprising cultures.[9] For some time now, there have been indications that this dream is transitioning into another mode, if it is not already exhausted – I would like to mention two such indications.

We find the first in outer space just above Earth, that is, in a region that in more naive times used to be called the heavens: since 1998, the International Space Station has been under development as a joint effort of America's NASA and Russia's Roscosmos, as well as the space-travel agencies of Europe, Canada, and Japan. Since the year 2000, 220 people have stayed on board the station for various lengths of time. This group can be considered an elite of present-day humanity, insofar as they presently comprise the only members of our species who, owing to their eccentric observational position, have seen spaceship Earth *in situ* with their own eyes: during one of the station's orbital periods of 92 minutes, astronauts experience no less than sixteen Earthrises and Earthsets every day. This small group's privilege of observing such a spectacle immediately leads to a radical transformation of our image of the world. Whereas modern humans believe in the possibility of finding a fortune on another shore and plunge headlong into the tunnel on their search, disregarding all other aspects, observers in the space station have taken up a standpoint that immediately allows them to see that there can be no other shore for the Earth as a whole.[10] One could say that they travel into space as modern humans and return as postmodern humans – insofar as postmodernism is defined as a mode of thought that fundamentally requires giving up the illusion of the other shore. For the time being, conventional inhabitants of the Earth's surface remain modern – which means that they revert to the position of ants on the carpet that fail to appreciate the pattern, even though attempts to explain it to them are not lacking.

Reference to the astronautical change of perspective can be complemented by a second observation. One of the most fascinating phenomena on today's oceans is the emergence of a cruise industry over the last thirty years. Some experts declare it to be the surprising rebirth of aristocratic travel in the age of mass tourism. According to insiders, there are currently about a million human beings on board cruise ships at any given time. There is reason to believe that even these travelers should be considered to be a group of postmoderns, since, in their own way, they have dispelled the illusion of another shore – at least for the duration of their cruise. They intuitively understand why being underway is the goal itself and why their happiness is to be found on board or nowhere at all. Incidentally, environmental awareness is unusually more developed in this group of passengers and in those who operate ships. Indeed, if one may believe this industry's self-image, the facilities that are characteristic of this class of ships form a technological avant-garde of maritime environmentalism. The spokespersons for the industry to some extent speak as realists, and to some extent still as prophets, when they assure us that sea voyages are no longer the problem but are instead the solution, due to the legal and technological standards that the industry has voluntarily adopted.

I would like to conclude by recalling the voyage of the Argonauts, the most ancient seafaring adventure in the European tradition, which was already sung of in pre-Homeric times and that again became the subject of a great epic poem by Apollonius of Rhodes, a librarian and writer of the Hellenistic era. Having stolen the Golden

Fleece in far-off Colchis (in present-day Georgia) with the help of the king's daughter Medea, the daring sailors find themselves in a difficult situation as they return home, which almost results in the end of their enterprise. Zeus is angered and sends an unfavorable wind, which causes the Argo to run aground on a shoal of Syrtis Major on the Libyan coast, without any hope of returning to open sea. For days, the heroes are stuck on the shoal and see their end fast approaching. There the local tutelary deity appears to the desperate Jason with a mysterious command: ". . . do ye pay to your mother a recompense for all her travail when she bare you so long in her womb!"[11] Jason seeks out the counsel of his companions, and finally the hero Peleus solves the riddle: the Argonauts have been ordered to lift their ship into the air and carry it across land! In fact, we would expect the sons of kings to think themselves too exalted to perform a labor that one would not ask of slaves. Full of admiration, the poet turns to the men of days gone by: ". . . by your might and your valor ye have raised high aloft on your shoulders the ship and all that ye have brought therein, and bare her twelve days and nights alike over the desert sands of Libya."[12]

In this tale, we for the first time encounter the figure of reversal between passenger and vessel, between bearer and what is borne, between environment and inhabitant.[13] One can glean from this a first indication that ships – and environments in general – can no longer be regarded merely as maternal containers that protect and care for us under all conditions. As soon as human beings run aground on the shoals of false social or technological evolution, they must learn to repair their ships, their systems, their institutions for use outside, even if they cannot take them on their shoulders and carry them through the desert. We are not going to carry a ship for twelve days over the dunes. Argonauts today will have to struggle through the entire twenty-first century so that the ocean experiment will once more run its course successfully through all dangers.

4

THE SYNCHRONIZED WORLD

Philosophical Aspects of Globalization

Ladies and Gentlemen,
Before such an eminent audience, I would like to contribute a few
thoughts to serve as a basis for reflection – reflection that is here
concerned with the autonomy of a branch or sector of the economy.
I will try to speak with the necessary and unavoidable indirectness
that a philosophical contribution must assume when treating a topic
such as this.

In essence, I would like to call upon us all to think more deeply
about the process of globalization, in both cultural and historical
terms, than we usually do in the hustle and bustle of the contemporary business world and its representation in the media. In fact,
whoever claims that globalization is nothing new is absolutely
right. We only obtain a proper view of the present situation when
we realize that Europeans have been continuously involved in the
adventure of globalization for the last five hundred years. But this
also requires noting that terrestrial globalization and the flight from
its consequences are of the same age – namely, half a millennium
old, insofar as we interpret Columbus' first voyage in 1492 as the
beginning of the age of genuine globalization. The fear of older
Europeans confronted with the newly discovered extent of the world
was expressed as the fear of agrarian and physiocratic mentalities
confronted by emerging industries and the global maritime economy.
The leading anti-globalists of past centuries were oceanophobic in
character. In contrast, today we are more phobic about globalized
stock exchanges, which to some degree represents the continuation
of the oceanic game on another level.

I begin my inquiry by taking the etymology of the term "globalization" more seriously than has been typical in public discussions.

Germans, along with Americans, prefer in this situation to use the correct term – that is, "globalization," as distinguished from the French, who speak of *mondialisation*, which is misleading. As a matter of fact, the globe as such is at issue here. But what is a globe? To begin with, a globe is nothing more than a mathematical construction, and is thus initially the province of geometers and philosophers, and only afterwards that of globographers, cosmographers, and, last of all, that of economists and tourists. The globe is certainly not a German patent, even if the first extant example of a globe was made in Germany, as you may perhaps know. It is located in the German National Museum in Nuremberg – a globe made according to Portuguese models by the Nuremberg merchant Martin Behaim in the fateful year 1492. It features a pre-Columbian outline of the continents and thus still presents us with the old Ptolemaic image of the world with three continents, and yet already has the proper form, namely that of a spherical planet. Hence one can say that Behaim got it just as right as Columbus did. To discover America and depict the globe are, analogously, the same action in two distinct media.

In short, I would like to point out that globalization was initially a concern of ancient mathematics. In this regard, the meaning of globalization is entirely different from our perception of it today. The fundamental thesis of all ancient discussions of globalization, familiar to us under the title of metaphysics, can be encapsulated in the following statement: "The form of the circle and the sphere is of the utmost importance." The sphere is the most serious thing that human beings can ponder. Why? Because the shape of the sphere allows us to discover a way of ascertaining the world's form. In addition, the sphere is the only shape that successfully provides us with a convincing rational representation of the cosmos. The classical treatment of this view is to be found in Plato's later dialogue *Timaeus*, a work of natural philosophy, which was concerned with the creation of the world by a perfect and wise creator. This creator of all things, because he was the best, could do nothing but give the best of all forms to his first work – which is why the cosmos inevitably ended up spherical.

The cosmos is a sphere containing everything: the real beginning of globalization is to be found in this insight of natural philosophy. Hence philosophers are ultimately to blame for globalization. Ladies and gentlemen, if you are ever at a loss for where to find culprits, and should Mr. Martin and Mr. Schumann, and Frau Forrester, who have been most effective in indicting economic globalization for its horrors, one day wish to turn to the real culprits, then you should send them this philosophical address and explain to them that national economies were only partly responsible for the situation. Complete responsibility is to be attributed to ancient metaphysics and its modern heirs, if anywhere at all.

Broadly speaking, the significance of this philosophico-geometrical construction clearly consisted in the fact that it provided human beings with a representation of where they are when they are in the world, and it did so in a novel and engaging manner. The advantages of such a representation are obvious: we feel lost in the world, and would like to know our location. The answer of ancient metaphysicians was the first convincing, indeed perhaps even the most convincing, system of orientation that was ever offered to human beings in the Western world. It provided details to those in search of answers: "Wherever you may be, you are in a sphere out of which you cannot fall. You are in an ordered structure that simply cannot be left behind, because the sphere is precisely what encompasses everything. You are in the right place, wherever you are." This information amounts to a morphological gospel that was heralded by early philosophers in order to reassure human beings in troubled times, as were antiquity and late antiquity. Cosmic-philosophical consolation conveyed a kind of good news from that world of order that we half share in, insofar as we ascend to the intelligible sphere with the enlightened part of our intellect, while we are otherwise engulfed by empirical turbulence.

Globalization starts out as a geometrical revolution of thought or, more precisely, as an uranometric revolution. This requires careful elaboration: "geometry" here does not refer to what our mathematics teachers have done with the term. As a rule, we are told the edifying story of how the Egyptians, attempting to survey fields of arable land flooded by the Nile, discovered the art of working with angles and radii. This is not entirely false and yet only a small part of the truth. More significant is the fact that Greek philosophers made a discovery in the sky above, whose feedback still influences our lives today. They discovered something in the sky that we do not find on Earth: namely, the pure point, the pure point of light on a dark background. There are no points on Earth, but looking up to the sky lends empirical plausibility to the quasi-mathematical idea that there are points whose only use, in practical terms, is to serve to construct geometrical figures. The Greek approach to geometry begins with the insight that we can mentally visualize drawing a line between two points – which is completely different from what motivated Egyptians toiling in the mud. The Greeks are not geometers in the strict sense of the word (that is, earth-surveyors), but actually uranometers, surveyors of the sky, who with their passion for the sky's structure set us Europeans on the path to a science of the whole, under the auspices of the sphere, or circular cosmos. Incidentally, the Greeks would not have spoken of globalization, but of spherization, which in fact amounts to the same thing, since what the Greeks consider a sphere is a globe to the Romans.

How do we get from this starting point to our current questions in the present context? I have already shown us one way, when I indicated that the ancient metaphysical knowledge of globalization was intended as a response to human questions about our location: wherever you may be, you are in the right place when you exist in a massive sphere. Whoever is truly wise has understood that he or she can only function anywhere as a local function of the cosmos. Wherever you are, you are a worker of the whole. You are a relay, a switch point for the totality. You cannot extricate yourself from the whole. Incidentally, for the precursors of globalized everyday culture in antiquity, for intellectuals, for itinerant philosophers, for business people, for officers in the field, for far-flung officials of the empire, this entails having to learn how to function outside of their homeland, too – an ability that is not self-evident, as is well known. Whoever has been abroad knows that the capacity for exile is something quite valuable, which must be instilled through training. In the modern age, the Jesuits, in my view, were the first group of Europeans who systematically cultivated human beings to be sent abroad – and indeed with a quite harsh psychological training. Graduates of such training would not be much impressed by the altogether soft and spoiled ways of contemporary human beings. These days, when we are abroad, we demand that the same Hilton we find in Munich or Vienna should be waiting for us in Sydney and Singapore. The Jesuit of former times could not expect this on his trip abroad, which required him to adapt to outside circumstances under the harshest of conditions.

The problematic of globalization in the modern age begins the moment it becomes clear that it's not just the sky that has a spherical shape; the Earth does too. The Christian Middle Ages, as you know, led to a relative slowdown of the cosmological enlightenment and professed the remarkable worldview that, whether round or flat, the Earth is surrounded by a system of spherical layers.

The historical caesura at the dawn of the modern era, associated with the name of Columbus, is an essential part of the history of our present-day concerns. When Columbus found the way to America, to the Indies, strictly speaking, which to his surprise turned out to be an unexpected double continent named America (something only realized after his death), he showed Europeans the way west and opened up the Atlantic as their new Mediterranean sea, as a modern *mare nostrum*. His surge westward across the sea had world-historical consequences, fifteen years after his death – I am referring to Magellan's voyage to the Maluku Islands, which supposedly resulted in the first complete circumnavigation of the globe. The story whose sequel we are still writing begins in the year 1519: the Spanish crown outfitted a small fleet of five ships, with a crew of between 240 and 280 men on board, under the command of a renegade Portuguese captain.

The trip that set out from Seville in August 1519 still presents us with a problem today. What happened? Magellan, in accordance with the designs of the Spanish crown, wanted to be the first to find a way to the fabled Spice Islands by traveling westward. Spanish rulers were just as capable at that time as are the rulers of Bavaria, Saxony, and Schleswig-Holstein today. They sought to corner the market in spices, the most lucrative market at that time. Europeans, as you know, traveled the wide world over primarily because they were hooked on spices. They were addicted to the luxury drugs of their age and were trying to find a way out of this dependence – admittedly not by quitting such tasty drugs, but rather a way out of their dependence on the Venetian monopoly in this most lucrative of all markets. We may even go so far as to claim that, at the end of the Middle Ages, the spice trade was the drug trade – and it is no wonder that not only spices themselves but the legendary profit margins at stake in trading them particularly aroused the appetites of people at that time. Thus the Iberian rulers began to dream of fleets whose outfitting, despite all the risks and costs, made for ideal business if they could just reach the mysterious Spice Islands on which the most coveted goods were to be found at this time: pepper, clove, ginger – the aphrodisiacs of the era's business class.

Spice merchants stand out among the pioneers of early terrestrial globalization. These long-distance traders believed in the European palate's potential for development and set up shop confident that the modernization of the palate had just begun. In this regard, the spirit of utopia and entrepreneurship are one and the same: because both are oral functions, both cater to the same appetite, which clearly reveals its insatiability. Magellan himself died in a needless skirmish in the Philippines. Most of the ships in his small fleet were lost to storm and mutiny, and only a single damaged frigate, the small *Victoria*, returned to Spain in September 1522 with eighteen of the previously mentioned sailors on board, who had almost starved to death. They landed in the seaport of Sanlúcar de Barrameda and, simply by physically returning, bore witness to the facts that form the basis of the entire modern era: first, that the Earth can be circumnavigated in a single direction, and thus that the so-called Seven Seas are connected and globally navigable, and ultimately that the entire planet is enveloped by an atmosphere that can be breathed by European sailors – which, before it was proved through experience was by no means as self-evident as it seems in hindsight. The sailors returning from the Magellan voyage brought back evidence with them, no longer possible to ignore, of the atmospheric unity of the Earth's surface and of global wind patterns and the climate system, which within certain limits operate in a predictable manner. We now know that not only can we venture to make outbound voyages, but that the return home is just as possible. In fact, globalization precisely means that we increasingly come to see Europe through the eyes of those returning.

This is the exact moment when the question of location becomes world-historically significant for the first time. A location [*Standort*] – as anyone who uses the word knows, without needing it to be philosophically clarified – is a familiar place [*Ort*], which in a typically modern, indeed revolutionary way has been drawn into the comparison and competition between places. What is special about a location is not the fact that we live in it because we were born there – location signifies the opposite of an original homeland. Rather, it is a way of viewing a place that we have claimed after having been uprooted from it – a place that we have left behind to go around the world and that we reach again after looping around the whole.

The key word that lurks behind the question of location is reachability [*Erreichbarkeit*]. This term allows one to explain why so many people in Europe, the Germans in particular, debate location so intensely and with such concern: reachability is in fact the latent and manifest underlying theme of the present epoch. Its hallmark is the fact that those who reach outwards are no longer merely others, but we ourselves. It is thus evident that we have entered the second phase in the history of reachability: for 450 years we have only discussed the theme of reachability from the perspective of the outbound journey and thus acted as though globalization were a European privilege. In the process of globalization, Europeans have been outbound voyagers *par excellence*, they have held the capacity for preemptive strikes in matters pertaining to globalization and have very much relished the primacy of the outbound voyage, often to the bitter end, for others who were adversely affected. They have reaped profits and felt themselves to be the legitimate masters of the globe. But they have now entered a phase where others have learned how to travel there and back again just as well as they do. From this point on, Europeans are no longer only discoverers, but also the discovered, no longer those who reach distant shores, but also those who are reached across distances.

We have thus entered the age of counter-discoveries and must come to terms with the fact that perspectives have become reversible. To be sure, we discovered others first, but in the meantime they have discovered us, and not only as individual tourists, but as massive waves of refugees seeking asylum. It becomes clearer every day that the others have nothing more for us than we do for them – and this is true for persons, goods, and information. Our experiences involving two-way traffic with others results in a new, particularly bewildering wariness about globalization. We sense that epochal privileges are a thing of the past and that a new reality principle is issuing its demands. All things considered, Europeans have gained very valuable experience through their outbound voyages, with globalization in its active phase, and they are now asking themselves whether they will be able to keep their customary globalizing privileges in the future. A period of self-critical reflection has dawned upon Europeans, ever since they had to recognize the injustice of their imperialist and colonialist one-sidedness. They have to put up with two-way traffic now more than ever, something that they unleashed and incited.

A bird's-eye view of the process of globalization reveals a situation that we must face more resolutely now than ever before, not merely for economic reasons, but even in terms of our overall moral responsibility for the world's course. A reflection on much more than the usual five-hundred-year history of globalization has now become unavoidable for Europeans. It is time for them to recall their own project, precisely in the age of two-way traffic and counter-reachability – and thus of migration into their traditional spaces. And this is best facilitated by admitting to a problem that began in Seville in the year 1522.

At that time, when the Earth had just been circumnavigated and the homecoming sailors entered their town, the hometown was for the first time transformed into a location. The basic kinetic pattern of the age of globalization is capital departing from its location on a voyage around the Earth and returning with a surplus on its ledgers. Karl Marx described the movement of capital perhaps a little too one-sidedly, in depicting it as a classical metamorphosis of commodities in which capital shifts from having the form of gold to that of commodities and then back to the form of gold. On his account, the touristic portion of the transmigration of value, so to speak, receives short shrift. Today we see more clearly that capital's long-distance travel constitutes the secret internal connection between the realization of capital and globalization. The spice trade of the early modern era is a paradigmatic instance of this. In fact, in order to realize commercial capital in the spice trade, in order for gold to metamorphosize into commodities on the Maluku Islands (that is, in the land where pepper grows), the entire globe must be circumnavigated.

Globalized capital is money that needs to circumnavigate the Earth completely to be realized. This is a striking observation, and it already reflects a truth of the early sixteenth century. The significance of this fact can hardly be overstated. In light of this, I would like to share an anecdote with you that not only expresses the chaotic character of early globalization, but even helps refute the oft-heard thesis that the global economy has only begun to engage in speculative cash flows in the last twenty years. The following story makes clear that this is a half-truth, at best. In 1529, King John III of Portugal and Charles V, the Holy Roman Emperor, came to a remarkable agreement with each other that has entered the history books as the Treaty of Saragossa. An important part of this treaty was an agreement on the already mentioned Spice Islands. With the help of his legal counselors, Charles applied such pressure on his Portuguese rival that the latter bought the claims to the Spice Islands in perpetuity from the Spanish for the sum of 350,000 gold ducats – which were brought over in a long mule caravan from Lisbon to Madrid. What were the conditions for this payment? Naturally, they were made on condition that neither party knew to whom the islands belonged, because neither had a very clear idea where the islands were. Yet what does "belong" mean in the case of islands that are merely known to be somewhere in the antipodes and that are inhabited by people who cultivate and harvest pepper, the very same pepper that Europeans simply cannot live without? The Treaty of Saragossa is proof positive that even early state capitalism already exhibited a fundamentally speculative character. Two kings spent a long time trying to force each other to fold, like poker players, until one of them lost his nerve and became a businessman. This led to the great speculative coup of the sixteenth century – a coup that becomes even more interesting when one considers that, due to the Treaty of Tordesillas of 1494 (that is, the division of the world between the Spaniards and the Portuguese), the Maluku Islands would turn out to be found in the Portuguese half of the world, something that could not yet be known with certainty absent precise enough longitudinal measurements on the other side of the globe. Ten years later, the geographical facts were clearly established by improved methods for determining longitude, and Charles V is supposed to have been quite amused by the fits of rage that this provoked in his royal colleague.

Having considered this anecdotal evidence, I return to my main thesis: Europeans cannot argue their way out of responsibility in the questions concerning globalization. Having been so vigorously occupied for the last five hundred years, they might now begin to feel sorry for themselves. Such a defensive and evasive attitude would not only be undignified but also wrong, not merely in historical terms, but also politically and economically.

If I may, I would like to conclude these reflections with a couple of general remarks on the social-psychological consequences of globalization, as they are exhibited, for instance, in migration flows. It would be misguided to not take European nervousness regarding this process very seriously. In fact, we are facing a crisis – a social-psychological crisis and a fairly profound crisis over ways of life. It is not easy to transform national human beings into post-national human beings. By national human beings, I mean a social character that arose in Europe over the last two hundred years and has become second nature for how we live our lives in a nation-state. These are human beings who experience their land and their nation as a fortified container – mostly monolingual, rooted in their native soil, vernacular, as Ivan Illich used to say: at home in their own nook and pledged to the dialect of life that flourishes there and nowhere else. If people with such character types are now suddenly called on to realize overnight that asylum seekers who break through the container are part and parcel of globalization, a certain initial hesitancy is understandable.

Allow me to conclude these reflections and suggestions, ladies and gentlemen, with the thesis that we are today living through a dramatic crisis of reformatting. On a fundamental level, so-called globalization calls upon human beings in nation-states to reorient ourselves from a society fortified by strong walls (one could even say from a society that is tightly contained) to a way of life that may be characterized as "particularly thin-walled." In other words, we are entering an age in which weak borders and porous shells become the distinguishing feature of social systems. Above all, this means that we have to develop a deeper understanding of the human needs for immunity and identity – needs of individuals who to this point have found their immunological optimum (in terms of their social definitions) in regionalism and nationalism, that is, in relatively tightly sealed container-societies whose members have generally believed that the borders of their own nation-state were part of their own personal immune system. In such social formations, it seems obvious to react to what is foreign with a corresponding selectivity *a priori*. In the case of immigration into European countries, we are today confronted by situations in which social and political immune systems are thrown into a tumult in unpredictable ways – with the result that the search for identity and immunity must increasingly shift from collective to individual strategies.

We see how population groups respond to this controversial issue in a way that can best be viewed from an allergological or immunological perspective. Such reactions are to be taken seriously, because, broadly speaking, we are today faced with reprogramming the human being's immune response from its orientation to a state that envelops and protects it to one of self-protection and self-care. While human beings in traditional, well-functioning protective states have tended to expect the latter to provide them with immunity via order and provisioning, it will be more realistic in future to increasingly rely on self-immunization. Human beings are now beginning to understand that no one will do for them what they will not do for themselves. In all likelihood, immunological problems (in the broadest sense of the term, including the biological, social, and spiritual condition of individuals) will in future have to be dealt with more at the individual level than at the collective level. This is what fills present-day society with such anxiety about its future. The more the political sphere succeeds in distancing itself from excessive demands projected onto it from a society tantalized by desires, the better it will function under the changed conditions of the thin-walled world.

5

WHAT HAPPENED IN THE 20TH CENTURY?

Toward a Critique of Extremist Reason

Human civilizations have occasionally been characterized as the outcomes of a permanent struggle between remembering and forgetting. If one takes such an image as a basis, positive cultural content and features would be like reefs rising out of the sea of forgetting, due to the sedimenting labor of repetition, tradition, and archiving. Should the sea currents change, these emergent reefs can become increasingly inundated, and traditional subjects, which only a short while ago were still considered to be up to date and contemporary, sink beneath the waterline.

In the following reflections, I proceed on the assumption, or better, from the observation, that, as far as the Western hemisphere is concerned, something like a reversal of the currents has taken place in contemporary culture. As a result, the balance of memory with regard to the recent past has dramatically shifted in the last few years. Hence, in the first place, I would like to refer to the synergies of triumphant consumerism with its imagery of the beautiful life and how this is further developed by neoliberal doctrines – which leads to the jettisoning of the greater part of our dark and disturbing memories. Secondly, we have more than one reason to assess the collapse of leftist traditions, a collapse that has given rise to the fear that they could sink forever into the capitalist Lethe before we even have the opportunity to map the sinking reef systems, which are to a large extent already submerged. Such "fear" is a symptom of conservative anxiety, not the commitment to a political standpoint.

You can glean the extent to which these reflections are justified from a remark by Alain Badiou, one of the last guardians of a now defunct radicalism at the beginning of the twenty-first century. In the introduction to his remarkable book *The Century*, which appeared in 2005 and obviously speaks not of the century to come, but rather of the one that has just ended, he felt impelled to cite an aphorism by Natacha Michel, which runs: "The twentieth century has taken place."[1] This statement would be foolish or trivial if it did not represent the antithesis of another statement that is not explicitly referenced but is easy enough to figure out, the statement that, at bottom, the twentieth century never took place.[2] With all of its battles and atrocities, it has faded into a mere phantom that can no longer be reconstructed from the present generation's attitude toward life – and, it would seem that no other future looms than that of a stock of myths and a desolate disposal site for scenes of violence. Should something of its great motifs remain of significance for later ages, this is only because they will still serve, for some time, as a repository of materials for popular films with tragic settings. The twentieth century's phantomization was carried out behind the backs of today's generation, without our being able to point to a single event through which the gravity and passion of the past age was extinguished in us – neither the disaster of Chernobyl nor the fall of the Berlin Wall, neither the space station *Mir*'s controlled plunge back into the Earth's atmosphere nor the sequencing of the human genome, neither the introduction of the euro nor the attack on the World Trade Center. No other event from recent times can be identified as the culprit either.

The infinitely banal statement "The twentieth century has taken place" can best be appreciated by relating it to Hegel's dictum that the life of spirit is not "the life that shrinks from death and keeps itself untouched by devastation, but rather the life that endures it and maintains itself in it."[3] Elevated to this level, Badiou's thesis imme- diately leads to an overwhelming logical and human challenge: it requires thinkers to pause beneath the petrifying gaze of the Medusa and contemplate it as an icon of present-day being – a demand that corresponds to the spirit of a century in which philosophy's basic emotion changed from wonder to horror. To be sure, even ancient wonder was never entirely free of dark emotions, and it must have already cost the ancients a certain amount of effort to adhere to the ontological dogma according to which all that exists is good. Only as tragic excess could a remark like that of Philoctetes – "How can I praise the gods when their ways are so evil?"[4] – break through the universal imperative of positivity. However, only in recent moder- nity, more precisely in the philosophical witches' Sabbath from the time between the world wars, and then more fully after 1945, could the thesis that being is anything but good, indeed that the good must be wrested from being, be explicitly stated by making a case for something that is fundamentally constituted *"otherwise than being,"* to recall Emmanuel Levinas' post-ontological or meta-ontological figure of thought,[5] whose claims reach further than we can explain at the moment, and whose implications may well exceed the discursive capability of contemporary philosophy. At the beginning of the nineteenth century, Hegel's sublime sangfroid had been necessary to conceptualize a spirit that had the virtue of looking steadfastly at the sun and at death while engaged in its learning processes. Thinking at the beginning of the twenty-first century has lost the strength of this elevated indifference. We find ourselves compelled to return to La Rochefoucauld, in making the observation: *We cannot look squarely at either death or the sun, or the twentieth century.*[6]

With this in mind, let us take a closer look at the question that forms the title of this lecture. If the question is: "*What happened in the twentieth century?*," then surely a historical account is not expected as an answer. We know from the start that no enumeration of the changes for good or for evil would tell us enough about what constituted the twentieth century in its dramatic and evolutionary substance. The difficulties in accounting for the era are rooted in more than just the fact that, in hindsight, this century manifests itself as a Medusean and extremist one, particularly in the violence unleashed during its first half. The key complications that hinder a reconstruction of the twentieth century are connected to the fact that this era, which is dubiously referred to as an "age of extremes," was in truth even more an age of complexities. Looked at from our present situation, this way of characterizing the era seems to be self-evident. It would remain the most vacuous of all possible statements on the subject, if it did not derive a specific historical significance from the fact that the dominant discourses and actions of the epoch were engaged in a furious struggle against the emergence of complexity.

The formulation "reduction of complexity," which has characterized a general aspect of the functioning of social systems since Luhmann, has a quite specific meaning for the twentieth century. It must be emphasized that the Medusean extremisms of that era all possessed the character of fundamentalisms of simplification – including even the fundamentalism of militancy and the myth of a "new beginning" through revolution, that bitter and proud attitude of a radical break with the given world. In the meantime, among Europeans, this attitude has lost its radiance, yet it continues to have a sporadic influence, particularly in the *Maquis* of latter-day leftist radicalism, down to the present day. Wherever manifestations of the extreme were encountered in the course of the twentieth century, there was always an uprising against complexity, that is, against the formal law of the real as conceived in contemporary terms. To be sure, this uprising was carried out entirely in the name of the real itself, of which all camps had formed extremely reductionist concepts.

Because a quasi-formal gigantomachy was embedded in the heart of the twentieth century as a duel between the logics of complexity and their polemical simplification, we must not be surprised when this age strikes us in retrospect as a century of confusion, as a time devoid of an overview and an era in which contingent standpoints were exaggerated. In this case, the main form of exaggeration consisted in the reduction of all things to an all-powerful ground or underlying factor (an observation already noted by the critic Carl Christian Bry in 1924, in his forgotten masterpiece *Verkappte Religionen* [Tr. – Religions in Disguise], without causing the followers of reductionist, extremist religions to question their beliefs).

The "age of extremes" suggested by Eric Hobsbawm has never remained silent about itself.[7] As an age of total chatter, it has already said everything there is to say about itself, and the opposite of that, too, and even this observation was made long ago, as one can gather from Karl Jaspers' text on *Man in the Modern Age*, for instance, where analogous statements can be found *passim*. What the author describes in this book as the phenomenon of "the struggle with no fighting front"[8] was able to recur a half century later in the case of leftists suffering from disappointed or delayed complexity, under the heading of a "new obscurity,"[9] the only difference being that the source is no longer recognized. It would hence be a difficult if not futile undertaking, and would furthermore condemn us to a methodologically false approach, if we wanted to appeal to what was said and written about the epoch in order to learn what kind of a century we are dealing with. We would come face to face with the darkest of all hyperboles, as formulated from the standpoint of the murdered Jews, the exemplary victims of the century-long madness, viz. the definition of the twentieth century as the era of the great breakdown of civilization symbolized by names such as Auschwitz and Treblinka. Even if the whole truth about the Shoah were empirically brought to light and the sources of the extermination were fully grasped, one would have presumably understood only a small segment of the twentieth century's global drama. Even less would be achieved if one wished to add that the supposedly "short twentieth century" reached from 1917 to 1991 and thus ran parallel with the history of the Soviet experiment. Its core process would have consisted in nothing other than the Titanic clash between liberalism and egalitarianism, in which the latter manifested itself as a two-headed monster, with a fascist and communist one. Hobsbawm's theses can be read as an echo of another interpretation of the twentieth century (proposed by Ernst Nolte and modified by Dan Diner), according to which the century was shaped by its main conflict, the so-called *Weltbürgerkrieg*.[10] The same author gives the lie to the title of his all-too-successful book when he explains in its crucial chapter why it was not so much the clamorous drama of the struggle between ideologies that decided the epoch's outcome, but rather the quiet upheaval of all traditions that was triggered by the decline of an agrarian culture and the triumph of urbanization. However that may be, this suggestion sheds light on the situation at present, where in a highly industrialized country such as the Federal Republic of Germany only two percent of the population lives on and from farms, while even in a supposedly agro-centric nation such as France the corresponding numbers no longer exceed three to four percent.

If one looks back at the remaining overarching interpretations that were proposed either during the course of the twentieth century or in retrospect, it remains puzzling that in every case particular events, motifs, or features have been elevated into epochal images. No contemporary of the early twenty-first century can imagine themselves circa 1950 without feeling strange, a time when the term "atomic age" was uttered with a pronounced tremolo informed by the history of philosophy, convinced as they were that the essence of the epoch was finally in sight. One spoke in those days about the atom and fission with the same uneasy piety, indeed with the same ontological lasciviousness, with which one began to speak about the genome and its manipulation around the year 2000. Likewise, Arnold Gehlen's suggestion around the middle of the century, that the present age was to be understood as the era of "crystallization," is today remembered by only a few experts – although it was a brilliant insight that articulated a transformation of present social circumstances into the forms they would have in a pacified, post-revolutionary condition. Even such an eye-catching title as "sexual revolution" has largely faded from sight today (more precisely, it has fallen victim to anniversary-culture, as one can see from the journalistic campaigns for the fiftieth anniversary of the appearance of the Kinsey Report) – and the current slogan of the senior-citizen revolution is likely to suffer a similar fate. Only a few experts on the Third World still remember what the "age of decolonization" involved. For historically minded political theorists, the twentieth century may signify the era of the *translatio imperii* from the British to the Americans (in which the British retreat from their engagement in the Balkans and the Middle East in February 1947 can be considered a key date), while Europeans tend to have their twentieth century limited to the span from August 1914 to May 1, 2004 – in other words, to the complete cycle of Europe's fracturing and the restoration of its integrity. This view, based on historical events, might have a dramaturgical plausibility going for it. In any case, it results in Europeans looking back on the lost century *summa summarum*, without knowing for sure whether, having experienced their own self-destruction, they have now found a more adequate conception of themselves and their role in the world.

To say a word in conclusion about so-called globalization, which monopolized all discourse about the present age at the close of the twentieth century: this term, insofar as it is used sensibly, is a synonym for the consolidation of the world into a great artificial system, which distances itself with increasing speed from twentieth-century problems that now already seem to be mere phantoms. We will have occasion to consider whether the current forgetting of the twentieth century does not lead to the fulfillment of the innermost intentions of that century itself.

5.1 The Apocalypse of the Real: Toward a Logic of Extremism

The preceding reflections suggest that we shall not discover the core process of the twentieth century by referring to historical events, nor by drawing on intellectual history or the history of discourse. The essence of the epoch cannot become completely manifest in a single event, or in a sequence of events constituting a trend. Nor is it to be found in concentrated form in some absolutely privileged text, however eminent the philosophical and poetical writings of the century may have been. In retrospect, one cannot help but feel as though pretty much every historical expression of that age about itself evinces a certain bias. Everywhere one looks one has the impression that the actors were hypnotized by the programs and the witnesses were dazzled by the dramas. Hence Alain Badiou is right when he argues, in his aforementioned book *The Century*, that the passion of the twentieth century is sought in vain as long as one presumes to find it in ideologies, messianic programs, or phantasms: the predominant motif of the twentieth century is rather that terrifying *passion du réel*, which manifests itself in the action of the protagonists as the will to *actualize the truth directly in the here and now*.[11]

I am convinced that this view actually provides us with a fruitful approach to the complex of the twentieth century. Not only is the dignity of philosophy vindicated by it, with its insistence that the truth of concepts is always also at stake in the tumult of battle. In addition, with such a view, we claim to know that the real is always only given to us through the filter of variable formulations and that the way we grasp reality is blended with the latter into an amalgam. Basically, we are concerned here with a contemporary revival of the Platonic doctrine that the eternal gigantomachy over being is fought out in thought itself and nowhere else, and that only in this struggle can the grounding of reality come to light. This thesis is reflected in Nietzsche's dictum on Greek tragedy, that the enchantment of these struggles consists in the fact that whoever sees them must also struggle with them himself.[12] As in Badiou's thesis, we find in the classics the insight that there is a convergence between understanding and struggle that is not easily avoided and may indeed be inescapable. According to Plato, to think means to take part in logical civil war, in which truth takes to the field against opinion. According to Nietzsche, to think even means to realize that the thinker himself is the battlefield on which the parties of the primal conflict between energies and forms collide. Even in Badiou's effort to save radicalism, the ideal of a detached theory is rejected, by drawing on contemporary resources to show how a thoroughly polemical praxis is at work behind the façade of liberal pacifism that is dominant today.

In what follows, I would like to translate the thesis that the twentieth century was characterized by a "passion for the real" into a context that is informed by my own studies of the emergence of imponderous elements, atmospheric facts and immunitary systems – studies that have materialized primarily in the trilogy *Spheres* (Volume I, *Bubbles*, 2011; Volume II, *Globes*, 2014; Volume III, *Foams*, 2016), and in *In the World Interior of Capitalism: Towards a Philosophical Theory of Globalization*, 2014. The central theme of the spherological project is articulated in the observation that modernity can only be understood as the epoch of a struggle for a new definition of the meaning of reality. In contrast to the polemical ontologies that dominated twentieth-century discourse, I attempt to show that the main event of this age consisted in Western civilization's breaking free from the dogmatism of gravity. That the twentieth century was primarily a matter of the *passion du réel* may well be a statement that turns out to be quite correct. However, that the actualization of the real primarily manifests itself in a passion for antigravity – only this additional observation will put us in position to understand the meaning and the progression of the clashes over the real on their own terms. The drama of the century only properly comes to light if we understand the obvious battles, both physical and discursive, as ways of expressing a widespread agony. I am speaking of the agony of the faith in gravity, which since the nineteenth century has manifested itself in ever-new convulsions, reactions, and fundamentalisms.

The spherological approach is based on a hermeneutics of an antigravity or unburdened existence, which includes both destructive and constructive parts. While from the constructive perspective there is talk of the discovery of atmospheric facts and of concealed immuno-systemic realities, the general theory of antigravity and exoneration, with its destructive élan, is devoted to ideological fabrications, which since the days of the French Revolution shackled the human being to the galleys of modernity: the galleys of scarcity, need, lack of resources, violence, and transgression. At the core of all of these theories, which for the most part emerge as anthropologies, as economies, and as theories of a parsimonious nature, statements about the real, aka "nature" or "history," can be found that limit the realm of human freedom to the reluctant gesture of submission to the law of the real. Wherever new realisms find their voice, human beings are declared to be vassals and media of superior realities – regardless of whether the latter are invoked in naturalistic, voluntaristic, economistic, vitalistic, drive-theoretical, or genetic idioms.

The following reflections aim to shed more light on precisely this condition of being a vassal and a medium in relation to a dominant real. They should put to the test Hegel's dictum according to which philosophy is its own age conceived in thought.[13]

Allow me to include a warning with this allusion to Hegel. I have never made a secret of my view that Hegel's dictum could indeed be valid from a perspective informed by ideal types. However, it is completely off the mark in empirical terms, since philosophy, as we have been familiar with it for nearly the last two hundred years both publicly and academically, has almost exclusively consisted of a most carefully organized flight from time. But the fact that each and every time flees from itself in a different way offers an involuntary contribution by philosophy to the characterization of its own respective age. The honor of philosophy as the current voice of truth has always only been preserved by the marginalized, who have been called, not without reason, "the dark writers of the bourgeoisie."[14]

I intend to show that the breakthrough into the aforementioned *passion du réel* cannot be restricted to the twentieth century. To be sure, this passion reaches its peak in that age of contending realisms, but the dispositions that made such clashes possible and unavoidable date back to the French Revolution. Not only did the latter create the archetype of modern aggressive fundamentalism in the form of Jacobinism; not only did it introduce the schema of the unfinished revolution into the world, which since that time has remained influential as a matrix of radicalism; it has also fostered activist and materialist ontologies that have to be read as the true textbooks of a modern society oriented around labor and struggle. In another passage (and yet in the same place), I have suggested the somewhat dramatic term "apocalypse of the real" for this comprehensive caesura in the history of mentalities,[15] in order to point out that more was involved in the radical transition to modernity than merely a generational shift in the flow of the old European metaphysical tradition. The real shift in the balance of the European conditions of thought was lucidly articulated by Nietzsche, who succeeded in condensing intellectual history, to say nothing of Europe's onto-history, into the format of a telegram: "How the True World Finally Became a Fable."[16] By registering the implosion of the world hereafter, this dire text sums up the main logical event of its epoch. Whoever is interested in the long version of this dispatch can still find a magisterial and comprehensive reference point in Karl Löwith's work *From Hegel to Nietzsche: The Revolution in Nineteenth-Century Thought*, from 1941.[17]

The point of this event becomes apparent in the fact that the traditional relations between the esoteric and the exoteric were reversed in the course of the nineteenth century. As long as old Europe's theologically tinged idealist metaphysics maintained its dominance, the main emphasis of all esotericism lay in the realization, to be kept secret at all costs, that there is no God and that there are no gods, and thus that all ideas of a higher world hereafter are pure fictions, castles built in the clouds, which are constructed out of anxiety, weakness, and longing. Until well into the nineteenth century, atheism, that life-threatening wisdom, disguised itself as the true occultism, while metaphysical theology was allowed to play the role of public opinion for more than a millennium and a half. But then the tide turns: what was a secret doctrine becomes common knowledge and public opinion, while, conversely, an alternative esotericism is constituted, emerging as empirical theology or as an ethnology of the world hereafter, in order to meet the requirements of a new realist, pragmatic zeitgeist – the concept of the unconscious could only begin its career in this neo-esoteric context. This concept, which became topical around 1800, signals that the world hereafter is nearby and that nature's dark side begins right on the threshold of consciousness.

The young-realist break in nineteenth-century thought manifested itself in a torrent of literature that aimed to expose and that was devoted to the task of providing hitherto suppressed or concealed dimensions of reality with their rightful seats in the parliaments of knowledge.[18] Such literature aspires to be actually scientific, but due to its performative features is simultaneously composed in a prophetic manner, insofar as it does not merely describe newly thematized realities in their exposed state (the will as foundation of the world, human labor, class struggle, flows of capital, natural selection, and the sexual libido). Rather, the realm of the real to come is also continually proclaimed, and the public is called upon to prepare itself for what is coming. This modern-realist speech act has both prophetic and apostolic features, combining the epistemological apocalypse of the real with a moral adventism that describes the realm of the real as nearly imminent, indeed as a regime that is already present in the depths. To indicate at this point the Medusean dynamic of the young-realist practice of exposure that only later became manifest, we should observe that where prophets and apostles take hold of the Word, martyrs of the real cannot be far behind, too – and we might as well also include the persecution of enemies of the real.

Such young-realist discourses are polemical – and indeed not only in the trivial sense that the best is always the enemy of the good. All of the new realisms understand themselves as figures in an evolutionary or revolutionary tableau in which they play an unavoidable exterministic role. To a certain degree, nineteenth-century evolutionism offered historicized versions of an ancient Eastern ontology of contending principles, which had not entirely faded away under the predominance of monotheism and lived on in the cryptic, dualistic undercurrents of Western metaphysics.[19]

In contrast to classical dualism, nineteenth-century young-realist ontologies of struggle do not conceive the conflicting or antagonistic factors as eternally symmetrical opponents facing off, but rather believe them to be their historical predecessors. An asymmetrical conception of the adversarial object as obstacle arises as a result, regardless of whether this is defined as the overarching term for relations, as a complex of ideas, or as social groups. No one understood this more clearly than the young Marx, who in a significant note on the essence of new activist critique declared that such critique did not want to contradict its object, but rather annihilate it.[20] Exterminism, essential to the *modus operandi* of contentious twentieth-century radicalisms, is rooted in evolutionarily inclined conflictual ontologies, according to which the truth of the real must be effectively implemented against the status quo, which despite being current has already been superseded and is only a temporary semblance of the real. The predominance of the unreal, which still clings to power thanks to an illusory covering over and distortion of the real, is to be broken, so that the realm of the real may arrive.

With these remarks, we have mainly been outlining the situation of Young Hegelian thought, which was the broadest manifestation of the invasion of the real. It heralded the triumph of realisms as a

public and political fact, despite every attempt at neo-idealist restoration. This triumph led to the flowering of "critical theory," which
flourished from 1831 to 1969 (if we choose the dates of Hegel's and
Adorno's deaths, respectively, as parameters). A deeper analysis of
the older sources of this movement would be well-advised to start
with Lenin's reference to the "Three Sources and Three Component
Parts" of the Marxist worldview, where explicit reference is made to
eighteenth-century French materialism.[21]

What Lenin did not mention, or did not know, is that the paradigmatic thinker embodying this tendency was the Marquis de Sade,
who portrays the advent of the real as a criminal realm-to-come. De
Sade is the occult genius of modern radicalism, because he was the
first to demonstrate how nineteenth- and twentieth-century activists
would envision their union with the operative principle of reality.
For de Sade – as for Spinoza – nature takes on the function of an
omnipresent active substance. If the task of modern thought is to
develop substance as subject; if, consequently, nature must become
human in order to completely come into its own and to realize
its ultimate possibilities, then, conversely, the human being must
completely become nature, too. Or, to put it better, the human
being, as an agent of nature, must settle into a mediumistic relation
with nature. In modernity, nature summons its own apostolate. This
turn to a mediumistic or apostolic naturalism would perhaps not
be cause for further concern had de Sade not defined the essence
of nature as that of an absolute criminal. (In contrast, German
Romantics developed a completely different version of mediumistic
naturalism, according to which nature is a healer that communi-
cates through salutogenic media – a motif that led to scandal in
the case of Franz Anton Mesmer but was popularized by Wolfart
and Carus.) Yet because, for him, nature as such is the embodiment of a principle of criminal indifference and pure arbitrariness
in the pursuit of desire, which can be actualized as soon as one
sheds the inhibiting effect of religion, human beings will only be
able to naturalize themselves successfully, or develop into media of
absolute criminality, if they transforms themselves into sovereign
criminals – and even more, if they take up the criminal apostolate,
so as to simultaneously proclaim with each act of their life the gospel
of primal criminality. It is not enough to commit crimes, we must
also actively become teachers of crime – and indeed, as Dolmancé,
the hero of *Philosophy in the Bedroom* (1795),[22] explains, this must
initially happen within secret societies, but then also in a constitutional republic. Criminal prophetism is articulated in modernity's
first naturalist manifesto: *Frenchmen, Some More Effort If You Wish
To Become Republicans*.[23] This singular pamphlet, which must be

read alongside the great texts of the French Revolution as excessive libertinism's declaration of human rights, heralds not only the emancipation of criminal initiative, but for the first time also defines the essence of specifically modern reaction: reaction is now seen to be at work everywhere the powers of the religious *ancien régime* establish contrived impediments to the free operation of the natural principle in individuals. This entails nothing less than the claim that the natural subject in need of real emancipation can only come into its own against an obsolete moral background, and thus can be freed for the consummation of its current desire. The essence of subjectivity is here interpreted as something only to be actualized by a specific disinhibition, in other words, by removing the inner *ancien régime* and its repressive authority.

It could be argued that de Sade, two generations before Bakunin, was the true discoverer of the superego, insofar as he successfully revealed the true identity of prohibition, namely as the rule of priests over authentic nature. At the same time, he was the father of radicalism, because he formulated the categorical imperative of every revolt, the psycho-political sublation of the *ancien régime*. Every radical has since been able to affirm the maxim: you may do what you want, provided that what you want actualizes a drive of nature, the great criminal. Realism now means nothing more than the submissive correspondence of the intellect to an order of things outside of us; it implies the activation of the real as an ongoing intensification of causes that aim to produce new effects. Uncommitted crimes wait for their perpetrators – just as still incomplete revolutions wait for their activists. What the twentieth century recognized as "grand politics" [*großen Politik*] – the term goes back to Nietzsche – thus continually assumes the form of the "good crime" on a grand scale, with Lenin and Stalin no less than Hitler and Mao Zedong. The realist is the agent, medium, and apostle of a power that only achieves what is called "free expression" after its disinhibition. The revolutionary is the good criminal.

Is it still necessary to say that with de Sade, modern expressivism also begins in an aesthetic regard, with the real itself defined as the continual transition of powers into their expression? The schema of power and expression, incidentally, is also easily transferred to so-called "history," which refers to its media as though they were nature at work. Political activists, however, believe that history is not so much a criminal as it is a surgeon, who amputates the diseased tissue of the past.

The key point in this brief philosophical portrait of the divine Marquis is to see that the structure of modern radicalism is only understandable if we begin with him. Young-realist authors since

Marx have assured us that to be radical means to understand things from their roots – but the roots are sought in a fundamentally dynamic realm that is constructed from the bottom up, which is indicative of the Sadean paradigm. Because roots are to be thought of as basal powers, to be radical means to join with the powers at the base of relations in order to move them toward newer, freer, more uninhibited forms of expression, regardless of whether they manifest themselves as crimes, revolts, revolutions, works of art, or acts of free love.

The vegetative metaphor of the root, incidentally, is obviously connected to the architectonic metaphor of the fundament or basis. Just as true radicalism sets new expressive action to work from the roots, so true fundamentalism wants to revolutionize or restore the basis, in order to move things in the superstructure around. Radicalism and fundamentalism are synonyms, insofar as both seek to form an alliance with the lower depths, regardless of whether these are thought to be powers or values. Both rest on the assumption that what is below has more reality than what is above. Both are derived from the same ontology, insofar as they are bound to a metaphysics of gravitation, according to which substantial, weighty, and serious things strive downwards to form the soil from which everything else must be yielded.

I will show that this ontological fundamentalism, which is inherent in all forms of modern realism and their radical crescendos, rests on a mistaken conception of the real that is certainly understandable, but nonetheless objectionable, and I will also show why this is the case. In the nineteenth century, when Marx taught that all critique begins with the critique of religion, his thesis implied that it was enough to identify religion as a superstructural phenomenon, so that critique could focus on the base of the relations of production. The work of critique entails eradicating things by reducing them to a deeper ground and really resolving them. Only in rare moments does Marx deviate from this reductive praxis and suggest the possibility of a redemptive critique, when he characterizes religion as the heart of a heartless world. This line of thought is in fact not critical but dogmatic, since its arguments rest on an inadequate ontology of the basal.

Critique can only really begin at all as a critique of gravitation – but this presupposes that thinking renounce its dogmatic opportunism vis-à-vis the real as basal power from below and freely shift to the midpoint between weighty tendencies and antigravity ones.

There is good reason to believe that the issue of antigravity in modernity is not built on sand – if a metaphor referring to the ground is not out of place here. The following considerations will show that uplifting forces have seen dramatic gains in enthusiasm and become more wide-ranging over the course of recent social evolution, far beyond the illusory religious ascension to heaven. I believe this can be demonstrated by inquiring into the dynamic of antigravity that belongs to the real, as it manifested itself in the course of the technological modification of the world. I thus take up Nietzsche's formulation of the transvaluation of all values (leaving aside the conflict over values) in order to deploy it in an event that I consider to be the real *novum* of the twentieth century: I mean the construction of the Western system for easing life [*Lebensentlastung*] on the basis of an extensive tax regime and a civilization of mass comfort founded on fossil fuels. We only gain a clear view of these phenomena when we obtain enough distance from the rachitic dogmas of leftist radicalism. We must brace ourselves for an inversion of radicalism – for a change of direction toward the airy, the rootless, and the atmospheric. Whoever would like to get to the bottom of things today must fly into the air. It remains to be shown that light, quasi-immaterial objects, although opposed to all "soils," are more elementary than the fictions of gravity that enthralled the twentieth century's *passions du réel*. Since I still have to gather my thoughts here into a general theory of antigravity, I will present the outlines of an interpretation of technology as an agency of relief. I will then supplement the anthropological theory of relief with a post-Marxist theory of enrichment.

5.2 Revaluation of all Values: The Principle of Abundance

Anyone inquiring into the general premises of relief in the age of its technological intensification would do well to consult the early French socialists, specifically Saint-Simon and his school, whose publications – their journal was not named *Le Globe* for nothing – are the starting point for an explicit politics of pampering from a genre-theoretical perspective. The formula of the era of relief, still valid to this day in theory and practice, originates with Saint-Simonism; it states that with the rise of major industries in the eighteenth century, the time has come to end the "exploitation of man by man" and to replace it with man's methodical exploitation of the Earth. In the present context, we can acknowledge this statement's epochal significance: the human race, represented by its avant-garde (the *industriel* class), is thereby identified as the beneficiary of a comprehensive relief movement – or, in the terminology of the time, as the subject of an emancipation. Its goal was expressed in the secular-evangelical gospel of the resurrection of the flesh during one's lifetime.

Such a thing was only conceivable provided that the typical distribution of weight in agro-imperial class societies, namely the relief and release of the ruling few through the exploitation of the serving many, could be revised thanks to the relief of all classes through a new universal servant: the Earth of resources, taken over using large-scale technology. What the Saint-Simonian keyword "exploitation" means, in processological terms, could only be articulated once the philosophical anthropology of the twentieth century had developed a sufficiently abstract concept of relief, particularly in the wake of Arnold Gehlen's efforts.[24] When the cultural sciences were able to employ this concept, it became possible to formulate general statements about the evolutionary direction of advanced technological social complexes that are substantially more practical, in systemic and psychological terms, than the palpably naive nineteenth-century theses on emancipation and progress. If we trace both the phenomenon and the concept of relief back to Saint-Simonian *exploitation*, it becomes evident that the effect in question, relief via technology, cannot be achieved for the majority without a shift of exploitation to a new bottom.

Against this background, it can be argued that all narratives about changes in the human condition are narratives about the changing exploitation of energy sources – or descriptions of metabolic regimes.[25] This claim is not only an entire dimension more universal than Marx and Engels' dogma that all history is the history of class struggles; it also reflects the empirical results far more accurately. Its generality extends further because it encompasses both natural and human energies ("labor power"); it is closer to the facts because it rejects the bad historicism of the doctrine that all states of human culture are connected in a single evolutionary sequence of conflicts. Futhermore, it does not distort the existing data despite its high level of abstraction. Such a distortion can be found in the polemogenic didacticism of *The Communist Manifesto*, which passed over the comparably rare phenomenon of open class struggles – at the risk of ascribing a significance to the slave and peasant revolts of earlier history (along with their desperate, undirected, and often vandalistic tendencies) that was supposed to be exemplary for the struggles of wage earners to achieve redistribution.

The story of the exploitation of energy sources reaches its current hot spot as soon as it approaches the complex event known in both older and newer social history as the "Industrial Revolution"[26] – a misnomer, we now know, as this too was by no means a "radical change" in which above and below switch positions; rather, it heralded the manufacture of products using mechanical substitutes for human movements. The key to the transition from human labor to machine labor (and to new human–machine cooperations) lies in the coupling of power systems with executive systems. Such couplings had usually remained latent in the age of physical labor, insofar as the worker him- or herself, as a biological energy converter, embodied the unity of the power system and the executive system. However, once crucial innovations were implemented in mechanical power systems, these couplings were able to be explicitly elaborated.

Thus begins the epic of motors: with their construction, a new generation of heroic agents stepped onto the stage of civilization, a generation whose appearance radically changed the energetic rules of the game for conventional cultures. Since the advent of motors, even physical and philosophical principles such as force, energy, expression, action, and freedom have taken on radically new meanings. Although these forces are normally tamed ones, bourgeois mythology has never completely lost sight of their unbound, potentially disastrous side, describing it in terms of the pre-Olympian race of violent Titanic deities. Hence the profound fascination with exploding machines, and indeed with explosions in general.

Ever since neo-Titans appeared in the midst of modern life, nations have changed into immigration countries for machinery. In a sense, a motor is a headless energy subject that was created because we are interested in using its power. However, it only possesses the impulsive attributes of the agent [*Täter*], and is not burdened by reflection. As a beheaded subject, the motor does not move from theory to practice, but from standstill to operation. In motors, that which disinhibits human subjects who are about to take action is triggered by the starting mechanism. Motors are perfect slaves, since we need not worry about complications, such as a concern with human rights, if we make them work around the clock. They do not listen to abolitionist preachers who have a dream: the dream of a not-too-distant day when motors and their owners have the same rights, and the children of humans and machines play with one another.

To integrate motors systematically as cultural agents requires fuels of a very different nature than the food that sustained human manual laborers and beasts of burden in the agro-imperial world. This is why the most dramatic sections in the epic of motors are the cantos on energy. We could even ask whether the formulation of the abstract, homogenous energy principle – energy *sans phrase* – by modern physics is not merely the scientific reflex of the principle of motorization, whereby the vague coupling of nutrition and organism was replaced by the precise relation between fuel and machinery. In the grand narrative of the procedures and stages of energy source exploitation, the transfer of power from the organism opens what could very well turn out to be a permanent final chapter.

As we know, modernity's grand narrative of relief begins with an account of the massive invasion by the first generation of mechanical slaves, which from the eighteenth century onwards came into use as "steam engines" in the burgeoning industrial landscapes of northwestern Europe. Mythological associations were readily apparent in regard to these new agents, as their operating principle – the expansion pressure of trapped steam – immediately recalls the Titans of Greek theogony, who were condemned to subterranean bondage. Since steam is initially caused by the combustion of coal (it was only with twentieth-century thermonuclear power plants that a completely new agent was introduced), this fossil fuel had to become the nascent Industrial Age's heroic bearer of energy. It is one of the numerous "dialectics" of modernity that coal, a powerful pampering agent, usually had to be extracted through the inferno-like labors of underground mining. Thus the miners of the coal-hungry nineteenth and early twentieth centuries could be presented as living proof of the Marxist thesis that the wage–labor contract was merely the legal mask of a new slavery. From the later nineteenth century on, petroleum and natural gases (also relieving and pampering agents of the highest order) joined Promethean coal as additional fossil carriers of energy. Their extraction required overcoming obstacles to development that were different than those encountered in underground mining. Occasionally, the process of acquiring them exhibited what could be called a natural accommodation, as if nature itself wished to make a contribution of its own to ending the agriculturally defined age of scarcity and its reflection in ontologies of lack and varieties of misery.

The primal scene for this accommodation of human demand by natural resources took place in 1859 in Pennsylvania, when the first oil well was uncovered near Titusville, and with it the New World's first great oil field, in a very shallow layer hardly more than twenty meters below ground. The image of the eruptive oil well, known among experts as a "gusher," has since become an archetype of not merely the American Dream, but the modern way of life as such,[27] which was made possible by easily accessible energies. The petroleum bath is baptism for contemporary human beings – and Hollywood would not be the central issuing facility of our popular myths had it not shown one of the great heroes of the twentieth century, James Dean, bathing in his own oil well as the star of *Giant* (1955). The steadily growing influx of energy from fossil stores, which for the moment remain unexhausted, not only enabled constant "growth" – positive feedbacks between work, science, technology, and consumption over more than a quarter of a century – together with implications that we have described as the psychosemantic modification of populations due to prolonged relieving and pampering effects; it also involved an abrupt change of meaning for such venerable categories of Old European ontology as being, reality, and freedom.

The concept of the real has now come to include the constructivist connotation that things could always be different (something of which only artists, as guardians of the sense of possibility, were previously aware). This stands in contrast to the traditional conception of the real, in which references to reality were always infused with the pathos of not possibly being any other way. As a result, the concept demanded submission to the power of finitude, harshness, and lack. In the past, a phrase like "crop failure," for instance, was loaded with the admonitory severity of the classical doctrine of the real. In its own way, such a phrase reminds us that the ruler of this world can only be death – supported by the Four Horsemen of the Apocalypse, his tried-and-true entourage.

In today's world, which is characterized by the basic experience of surplus energy, the ancient and medieval dogma of resignation is no longer valid; there are now new degrees of freedom whose effects extend to the level of existential moods [*Stimmungen*]. Small wonder, then, that Catholic theology, which essentially thinks in premodern and miserabilist terms, has completely forfeited its connection to present-day facts – even more than Calvinist and Lutheran doctrines, which at least take a semi-modern approach. Accordingly, the concept of freedom also had to shed its conventional connotations over the last hundred years. It sounds new dimensions of meaning on its harmonic series, especially the definition of freedom as the right to unlimited mobility and festive squandering of energy.[28] The two former prerogatives of lords, namely gratuitous freedom of movement and whimsical spending, are thus democratically generalized at the expense of a subservient nature – this is only true, of course, where the climactic conditions of the great greenhouse are already in force. Because modernity as a whole only takes shape against a background whose primary hue is abundance, its denizens are struck by the constant dissolutions of boundaries. They can and must acknowledge that their lives now occur in a time without normality. They pay for their thrownness into the world of excess by feeling that the horizon is drifting.

The sore point in the reprogramming of existential moods in modernity thus concerns the experience of de-scarcification, encountered early on by the inhabitants of the crystal palace – something that they have hardly ever acknowledged sufficiently. The sense of reality among people in the agro-imperial age was attuned to the scarcity of goods and resources, because it was based on the experience that their labor, embodied in onerous farming, was just enough to establish precarious islands of human artificiality in nature. This was already addressed in the ancient theories of ages, which bear resigned witness to the fact that even great empires crumble, and the most arrogant towers are leveled by inexorable nature within a few generations. Agrarian conservatism expressed its ecological-moral conclusions with a categorical ban on wastefulness. Because the product of labor could not usually be increased, only augmented by looting, at best people in the ancient world were always clearly aware that what they value, that which they generated, was a limited, relatively constant factor that had to be protected at all costs. Under these conditions, the squanderer must have been considered insane. Hence the narcissistic profligacies of noble lords could only be considered acts of hubris – and their later reinterpretation as "culture" could not yet be foreseen.

These views ceased to be relevant when, with the breakthrough into the fossil-fueled style of culture a little more than two centuries ago, a sinister liberalism appeared on the scene and resolutely began to overturn previous standards. While wastefulness had traditionally been the ultimate sin against subsistence, as it jeopardized the always scarce supply of the resources necessary for survival, the age of fossil energy saw a thoroughgoing change in the meaning of wastefulness: we can now calmly term it our first civic duty. It is not that supplies of goods and energies have become infinite overnight, but the fact that the limits of the possible are constantly deferred further and further, which gives the "meaning of being" a fundamentally altered complexion. Now only Stoics still carefully take inventory. Ordinary Epicureans in the great comfortable greenhouse assume that the "inventory" is something that can be infinitely increased. Within a few generations, the collective willingness to consume more was able to ascend to the level of a systemic premise: mass frivolity is the psychosemantic agent of consumerism. Its blossoming indicates that recklessness has assumed fundamental importance. The ban on wastefulness has been replaced by a ban on frugality, expressed in perpetual appeals to encourage domestic demand. Modern civilization is based less on "humanity's emergence from its self-incurred unproductiveness"[29] than on the constant influx of an unearned profusion of energy into the space of entrepreneurship and experience.

In a genealogy of the motif of wastefulness, we would have to note how the verdict of tradition on the luxurious, leisurely, and superfluous was rooted in theological values. On the conventional monotheistic view, everything superfluous could only be displeasing to God and nature – as if they were also taking inventory.[30] It is remarkable that even the proto-liberal Adam Smith, as willing as he is to sing the praises of luxury-stimulated markets, clings to a markedly negative conception of wastefulness – which is why his treatise on *The Wealth of Nations* is pervaded by the refrain that wastefulness is a submission to the "passion for present enjoyment."[31] It is a habit of "unproductive hands" – priests, aristocrats, and soldiers – who, due to a long-entrenched arrogance, subscribe to the belief that they are called upon to waste the riches generated by the productive majority.

Marx likewise remains bound to the agro-imperial age's conception of wastefulness when, following in Smith's footsteps, he adheres to the distinction between the working and wasting classes, albeit with the nuance that it is capitalists, much more than feudal "parasites," who now occupy the role of malign squanderers. At least he agrees with Smith in conceding that new economic methods have brought a surplus product into the world that surpasses the narrow surplus ranges of agrarian times. The author of *Capital* stylizes his bourgeois as a vulgarized aristocrat whose greed and baseness know no bounds. This portrait of the capitalist as a pensioner ignores the fact that the capitalist system also introduced the new phenomenon of the "working rich," who balance out "present enjoyment" with the creation of value. Nor does it take into account that in the modern welfare and redistribution state, unproductiveness switches from the tip of society to the base – leading to the virtually unprecedented phenomenon of the parasitic poor. While in the agro-imperial world, it could normally be assumed that the impoverished were an exploited productive class, the paupers of the crystal palace – bearing the title of the unemployed – live more or less outside the sphere of value creation (and supporting them is less a matter of demanding "justice" than of national and human solidarity).[32] Their functionaries, however, cannot refrain from claiming that they are exploited individuals who are lawfully entitled to compensation because of their hardships.

So, even if liberals and Marxists alike undertook far-reaching attempts in the nineteenth century to interpret the phenomenon of industrial society, the event of fossil energetics was not perceived in either system, let alone conceptually thought through. By making dogmatically inflated labor value the most important of all explanations for wealth, the dominant ideologies of the nineteenth and early twentieth centuries remained chronically incapable of understanding that industrially extracted and utilized coal was not a "raw material" like any other, but rather the first great agent of relief. It was thanks to this universal "worker of nature" [*Naturarbeiters*] (for which alchemists searched in vain for centuries) that the principle of abundance found its way into the greenhouse of civilization.

Yet even if the pressure of new evidence compels us to understand fossil energy carriers and the three generations of motors spawned by them – steam engines, combustion engines, and electric motors – as the primary agents of relief in modernity, even if we go so far as to welcome, in them, the *genius benignus* of a civilization beyond lack and muscular slavery, we cannot ignore the signs that the inevitable shift of exploitation in the fossil energy age has created a new proletariat whose suffering enables the relaxed conditions in the palace of affluence. The main emphasis of current exploitation has shifted to livestock, which is produced and used in massive quantities by industrialized farming. On this subject, statistics are more informative than sentimental arguments: according to the German government's 2003 Animal Welfare Report, almost 400 million chickens were slaughtered in 2002, along with 31 million turkeys and nearly 14 million ducks; of large mammals, 44.3 million pigs, 4.3 million cows and 2.1 million sheep and goats. Analogous figures can be assumed in most market societies, not forgetting that the national statistics must be augmented by vast quantities of imports. Animal proteins constitute the largest legal drug market. The monstrous scale of the figures exceeds any affective judgment – nor do analogies to the martial holocausts of the National Socialists, the Bolshevists, and the Maoists fully reflect the unfathomable routines in the production and use of animal carcasses (I shall refrain from addressing the moral and metaphysical implications of comparing large-scale cases of human and animal exterminism). If we consider that intensive livestock farming rests on the agrochemically enabled, explosive growth of animal feed production, it becomes evident that the flooding of markets with the meat of these animal bio-converters is a consequence of the oil floods unleashed in the twentieth century. "Ultimately we live on coal and petroleum – now that these have been transformed into edible products through industrial farming."[33] Under these conditions, one can predict that, in the coming century, an internationalized animal rights movement, already almost fully developed, will emphasize the unbreakable connection between human rights and animal suffering, which will lead to a growing unease among the populations of the great greenhouse.[34] This movement could end up being vanguard of a progressive development that redefines non-urban ways of life.

Thus, if we are to name the axis around which the revaluation of all values in our developed comfortable civilization revolves, the only possible answer is the principle of abundance. Current abundance, which always wants to be experienced within the horizon of reinforcements and dissolutions of boundaries, will undoubtedly remain the decisive hallmark of future conditions, even if the fossil-energy cycle comes to an end a hundred years from now, or slightly thereafter. In broad terms, it is already clear which energy sources will enable a post-fossil era: primarily a spectrum of solar technologies and regenerative fuels. At the start of the twenty-first century, however, the details of the shape this will take are still undecided. We can only be sure that the new system – some simply call it the coming "global solar economy" – will have to move beyond the compulsions and pathologies of current fossil-resource policy.[35]

The solar system inevitably poses a revaluation of the revaluation of all values – and, as the turn toward current solar energy is putting an end to the frenzied consumption of past solar energy, we could speak of a partial return to the "old values"; for all old values were derived from the imperative of managing energy that could be renewed over the yearly cycle. Hence their deep connection to the categories of stability, necessity, and lack. At the dawn of the second revaluation, a civilizing weather condition on a worldwide scale will emerge that will quite likely display post-liberal qualities – inaugurating a hybrid synthesis of technological avant-gardism and eco-conservative moderation. (In terms of political color symbolism: black-green, which it would be a grave mistake to only interpret as a "restoration.")[36] The conditions for the ebullient expressionism of wastefulness in current mass culture will increasingly disappear.

Insofar as the expectations created by the principle of abundance in the industrial era remain in force, technological research will have to devote itself first and foremost to finding sources for an alternative wastefulness. Future experiences of abundance will inevitably see a shift of emphasis toward immaterial streams, as ecosystemic factors preclude a constant "growth" in the material domain. There will presumably be a dramatic reduction of material flow – and thus a revitalization of regional economies. Under such conditions, the time will come for the as yet premature talk of a "global information or knowledge society" to prove its validity. The decisive abundances will then be perceived primarily in the almost immaterial realm of data streams. They alone will authentically possess the quality of globality.

At this point we can only vaguely predict how post-fossility will remold the present concepts of entrepreneurship and freedom of expression. It seems probable that from the vantage point of future "soft" solar technologies, the romanticism of explosion – or, more generally speaking, the psychological, aesthetic, and political derivatives of the sudden release of energy – will be judged in retrospect as the expressive world of a mass-culturally globalized energy fascism. This is a reflex of the helpless vitalism that springs from the poverty of perspectives in the fossil energy-based world system. Against this background, we understand why the cultural scene in the crystal palace betrays a profound disorientation – beyond the aforementioned convergence of boredom and entertainment. The cheerful mass-cultural nihilism of the consumer scene is no less clueless and without future than the high-cultural nihilism of affluent private persons who assemble art collections to attain personal significance. For the time being, "high" and "low" will follow the maxim *"Après nous le solaire."*

After the end of the fossil-energetic regime, there may *de facto* be what geopoliticians of the present have referred to as a shift from the Atlantic to the Pacific space. This turn would primarily bring about a change from the rhythm of explosions to that of regenerations. The Pacific style would have to develop the cultural derivatives of transition to the techno-solar energy regime. Whether this will simultaneously fulfill expectations regarding worldwide peace processes, the even distribution of planetary wealth, and the end of global apartheid remains to be seen.

5.3 Beyond Expensive and Free: In Favor of a New Alliance with the Worker of Nature

Looking back on the question of what happened in the twentieth century from our present vantage point, it is apparent that in a number of ways this era represents a time of fulfillment. Badiou has rightly emphasized the extent to which this century broke with the prophetic habits of the previous one. It is the century of triumphant impatience, which is capable of anything but waiting a while longer for things to mature gradually in their own time. It is the century of immediate implementation, in which the martial law of taking action replaces patience, delay, and hope. Contra Ernst Bloch, we should now recognize that the twentieth century never knew a principle of hope, but only ever a principle of immediacy [*Sofort*], which consisted of two cooperating factors, the principle of impatience and the principle of getting something for free [*das Prinzip Gratis*].

The unleashing of impatience is one of the social-psychological mysteries of the twentieth century. Without it, neither the realist excesses of the first half nor the second half's mass-cultural forms of recreation can be understood. Epochal impatience dates back to the diffusion of new motorized powers into the propulsive tendencies of human action. Power can become an omnipresent theme in the twentieth century because this was when its technological organs formed their new alliance with available energies.

Thus in order to do justice to yesterday's aspirations for the twentieth century as an age of seriousness, we must recognize its resolute actualism and review the reasons why the age of anticipation transitioned to an age of deeds. This cannot be accomplished, as we have already indicated, if we limit our analysis to the span from 1914 to the present. Even to extend our inquiry to motifs dating back to the age of the French Revolution, as we have already done, remains inadequate. The real dynamic of the twentieth century cannot be explained merely by the emergence of radicalism, in which new subjects or agents wanted to make themselves into the media of nature or of history to come. Instead, we must return to the era of Renaissance arts and Baroque universal magic, in order to trace there the crucial lines of power whose triumphant manifestation becomes evident in the twentieth century.

The reference to magic of the early modern era is no accident, since anyone who would like to track present-day culture's dynamic actualism, with its explosiveness, impatience, instant gratification, and smug dissatisfaction, must focus their attention on the crystallization phase of a new mental structure that extends from the sixteenth into the twenty-first century. I am referring here to a reversal in which the formulation and formatting of human desire shifts from a religious to a secular object. From the sixteenth century on (including a few preludes in the fourteenth and fifteenth centuries), the *summum bonum*, which generally shows desire the way, is translated from the striving for resolution into the search for ease [*Erleichterung*]. With this change of emphasis, immanent conditions assume the function of the highest good. This leads to immense interest in so-called natural magic, which initially seems to mean nothing more than providing the human being with a way to escape from the prisons of old necessity. (On a deeper level, we should here note that it also leads to the discovery of the first depth psychology and to a symbolic technique of self-birth.[37]) Consequently, human life in the modern age can take on the form of a treasure hunt. Treasure is imagined to be the means for the universal easing of life, and only needs to be found for this to immediately happen.

We must once again visualize the paradoxical course of this search. It is hard not to notice an effect that could be called irony: scarcely had the modern era's *magia naturalis* taken shape as the epistemological matrix of research into means for the easing of life before it devolved into an endless task whose enormous difficulties belied the imagined result of the search. This is obvious from the vast resources that Baroque thought and experimentation invested in so-called alchemy, particularly the art of making gold, today forgotten and considered to be absurd. This branch of alchemy, undoubtedly its most fascinating offshoot, is based on the grandiose pre-capitalist dream in which the quintessence of value or the substance of treasure could be directly produced. If this were true, whoever mastered the production of gold would be able to conduct the treasure hunt as though it were a scientifically controlled manufacturing process. Such an alchemist would be freed from external fortune and would have found the source of wealth. The dominant motif of fairy tales in the modern world here emerges in crystalline purity: from now on, it will always be a matter of working in order to never have to work again. In the new regime, all effort has merely a preliminary character; the meaning of all exertion is to be found in striving for effortless homeostasis. We are patient one more time, so that after the great discovery we will never have to be patient again. Europe's deepest dream is the unemployment that results from affluence.

I am suggesting that we recognize the realization [*Wahrmachung*] of the alchemical dream as the main event of the twentieth century. We have seen that it is characteristic of this age's style that realizations cannot occur without bringing the dream's latent horrors to the light of day. The irony of realization [*Verwirklichung*] is connected to the irony of the search. From the beginning, the search for wealth was unmistakably inherent in the conflation of working and searching. As soon as the search itself took on the form of organized work it also transformed the concept of wealth as such, and from the figure of treasure there gradually emerged that of capital, which tested the acuity of economists, as well as critics of political economy, from the late eighteenth century onwards. The treasure hunt became less meaningful as economists increasingly took over the topic. The concept of treasure was only then able to eke out a dreary existence on the fringes of both the capitalist and socialist imaginary, under the amazing and envy-arousing heading of the capitalist's or oligarch's private fortune. The last character-mask of treasure was the deplorable Count of Monte Cristo, who as treasure-finder was a figure from the past, but as avenger was entirely a man of the future.

I will conclude these reflections by observing that a general economy, still longed for by contemporary thought, even after Bataille and after the work of ecologists and deep ecologists, will not avoid returning to the much-maligned concept of treasure. Of course, the right lessons must be drawn from alchemy's fate. It is no longer a matter of searching for the treasure-function, the sudden and magical easing of life, by fetishizing gold. Under present-day conditions, this would amount to the suggestion that we operate as counterfeiters or try our luck in the casino and on the stock market. In light of historical experience, we must remain resolute in understanding that there would be no capitalism, no widespread affluence, no welfare state, and no trace of anything that constitutes

the *modus vivendi* of the current Western system of comforts without
the intervention of the most immense of all treasures (as we have
already discussed). Yet the treasure assimilated by capitalism was
neither found in pirates' chests nor in alchemists' cabinets, but was
found in terrestrial real estate. This treasure, even if it is occasionally
called "black gold," is not part of the monetary aspect of the economic process, but belongs to labor (I am referring to the Marxist
dual opposition of capital and labor). However, it also does not
play any role in the ordinary concept of the laborer, since the latter
is not a person but the pure carrier of energy. The new concept
of treasure to be incorporated into post-Marxist terminology thus
requires an explicit concept that would allow us to express the fact
that it belongs to the sphere of labor in an essentially different way
than the former so-called proletariat or some other form of wage-
dependency. Active treasure, which is what we are here referring
to, coal and petroleum (other forms of biosynthesis, too, later),
embodies the principle of getting something for free in a typically
modern way. This is because such a principle is suited for rapid combustion and for producing immediate effects, in stark contrast to its
predecessor – the Earth as bearer of slow growth. Active treasure is
the actual agent of the principle of immediacy.

The agent in question here, which can neither be capital nor labor,
signifies nothing less than nature understood in post-conventional
and post-metaphysical terms – and indeed in its twofold differentiation as a source of fossil fuels and as laboratory for organic syntheses.
Hence, the name we are looking for can only be *worker of nature*.
The anticipated general economy will only be able to be elaborated
in the form of a tripolar theory that is applied to the juncture of
labor, capital, and worker of nature. Since Nietzsche, and once
again since Bataille, we know that the sun has always played the
role of the first profligate. For now, it is the greatest embodiment of
the virtue of generosity, which forms the absolute counter-principle
to capitalism's principle of acquisition. A post-capitalist form of
the world and a corresponding ethics can only proceed from a new
interpretation of the sun. Of course, current capitalist intellectuals
are clueless when it comes to an agent like the sun, because – even
after the ecological caesura – they are still completely in the habit
of absolutizing the interaction of capital and labor and continue
to ignore the contribution of the third side, that of the worker of
nature. For the moment, let us content ourselves by concluding that
the golden age of such ignorance is coming to an end.

If the twentieth century aimed to realize the dreams of the modern
age, without having interpreted these dreams correctly, then we can
say that the twenty-first century must begin with a new interpre-

tation of dreams. Such interpretation will require examining how humanity pursues the treasure hunt that is the *sine qua non* for expressing what being-in-the-world means for us.

6

THE THINKER IN THE HAUNTED CASTLE

On Derrida's Interpretation of Dreams

Until the beginning of modernity, the classical philosopher's image included practicing his profession as a kind of *ars moriendi*. The conception of philosophy as an art of dying was quite influential in the older European tradition and acknowledged to be self-evident by such contrasting figures as Plato, the founder of philosophy *more academico*, and Montaigne, the father of the anti-philosophical essay. The early Heidegger still unmistakably belongs to this line when he links resolutely reflective *Dasein* to an act that he called "running ahead to one's own death." Yet "being-toward-death,"[1] as he described it under the shadow of two world wars, ended up amounting to nothing more than the bleak acceptance of an ultimate fate. In this regard, classical philosophy can be called an unarmed heroism. The hero, whether heading onto the military battlefield or that of finitude in general, is always someone who has affirmed his end in advance and without reservations.

In contrast, Derrida, whose "sur-vival" [*Fortleben*], "survival" [*Überleben*], and "spectral" projections are to be examined here, spoke out at the end of his life against the archetype of a death we have "mastered" or "learned" how to do. He did this quite emphatically in his quasi-testamentary conversation with Jean Birnbaum (in March 2004), which was published later that August in the newspaper *Le Monde* – two months prior to the philosopher's death.[2] In this interview, the author confessed that, on a personal note, "I have not learned to accept death. . . . I remain impervious when it comes to knowing how-to-die. I have yet to learn anything about this particular subject." This is a very striking remark, indeed it is almost terrifying in its implications, precisely because its authenticity cannot be called into question. It could be read as a sign of the fact that, *in extremis*, Derrida rejected philosophy as such, whether classical or modern, and denied its most existential dimension (excuse my clumsy use of the superlative) – he of all people, who in numerous other contexts never tired of pointing out how much he understood himself, faithfully or unfaithfully, to be an heir of the tradition and how deeply the traces of the philosophical past, from Plato to Hegel and Heidegger, had informed his own existence.

In doubting that death is something we can learn to live with – or that we can accept our own finitude – Derrida is not alone among moderns. For example, we should recall Gilles Deleuze, who, before he jumped from a window to his death on November 4, 1995, emphasized that his gesture did not belong to the tradition of the philosophical death, nor did he think it should be compared to Empedocles' leap into Mount Etna. Rather, it confirmed that a depleted potential for life actively acknowledge its exhaustion. And we should recall Elias Canetti's entire body of work, which is permeated by an almost unparalleled protest against the absurdity of death and against the obscenity of the "wisdom" advising us to resign ourselves to finitude.

Derrida's rejection of wisdom had long been observable in his theoretical activity – particularly in his meta-psychological meditations on the difference between mourning and melancholy. These meditations culminated in the claim that the "work of mourning" – to straightforwardly take up the Freudian term adopted by Derrida – is never finished after the death of someone close to us, because to mourn – if it is supposed to be carried out successfully as psychoanalytical "work" – amounts to a betrayal of the unfathomable otherness of the other. If mourning were carried through to the end, it would reveal the moral scandal of its fungibility in the survivor's "psychic economy." With his demand that all mourning become melancholy, Derrida already set the guidelines for how posterity would deal with him – and at the same time provided a theoretical basis for his personal aversion to the idea of one day bidding farewell to himself.

In what follows, I will attempt to do justice to Derrida's line of thinking here, to the best of my abilities. To this end, I am encouraged not least by his observation (while speaking in the mode of philosophical anthropology) that life [*Leben*] always structurally signifies survival [*Überleben*]. Hence it must continually face the dilemma of melancholy. Melancholy today proceeds from the fact that Derrida has already been gone for five years. It retains a special character, since it becomes increasingly clear as the years go by that he was irreplaceable. The only time things lighten up or there is at least some relief is to be found in Derrida's own emphatic thought that insofar as we are still alive, we can never avoid being survivors who always feel some guilt toward those who went before us.

From the beginning, we have proceeded in a quite somber way, so that we could approach the domain of a philosophical thanatology from a distance, and so an apparently humorous digression would not be out of place here. To this end, I refer to the great ironist Richard Rorty, whose theoretical and existential trajectory crossed with Derrida's at more than one point. One could even go so far as to say that Rorty (who lived from 1931 to 2007) and Derrida (who lived from 1930 to 2004) led something like philosophical *bioi paralleloi*, insofar as both were trying to achieve a post-metaphysical position for both contemporary and future thought. Both thinkers developed a personal strategy for acting as curator and guide of the haunted castle of ancient Western logos. Rorty's life was only a bit longer than that of his French counterpart or rival. In the summer of 2006, the American thinker wrote a letter to a German colleague,[3] who later reported that after a few paragraphs of conventional political content – talk of the damage that the Bush administration had wrought in the US and in the world – he suddenly came across an alarming private message: "Alas," Rorty notified him, "I have come down with the same disease that killed Derrida."[4] Rorty is here alluding to the fact that, like Derrida, he had been diagnosed with incurable pancreatic cancer. He sarcastically added that his daughter had formed the hypothesis that this kind of cancer was caused by reading too much Heidegger.

I can safely assume that Rorty had an idiosyncratic knack for making cryptic jokes about Derrida and himself. This was true in two respects: first, he could exhibit a macabre humor, because, having received the same terminal diagnosis, he found himself subject to a dire twist of fate that was similar to his renowned French colleague's; second, because, as a reader of Derrida, he had already for some time suggested not taking the latter's dramatic grappling with the spirits of the metaphysical tradition quite so seriously. With the clear gaze of a diagnostician schooled in Nietzsche, Rorty saw the weak point, or blind spot, in Derrida's oeuvre: namely, that Derrida had made a heroic choice and deliberately resolved to suffer from the problems for which deconstruction was supposed to be the solution or, better, the perpetual form of non-solution. From Rorty's perspective, Derrida can be compared to a lodger who chooses a suspicious old house for his residence, one that is rumored to be haunted by ghosts, when he could have easily found a building that was unburdened by a problematic past.

"Alas, I have come down with the same disease that killed Derrida." Allow me for a moment to yield to the temptation to speculate on how Derrida would have commented on this fateful statement, were he able to make posthumous notes in the margins. In the first place, he certainly would have expressed doubts about the phrase "the same disease,"[5] since it is well known that the "same disease" only exists in medical textbooks, while the spectacle of really existing morbidity has as many diseases as there are patients. Second, he doubtless would have contested the legitimacy of the phrase "that killed Derrida,"[6] not merely because he would have pointed out the terrible imposition of the syntagm "to kill Derrida,"[7] but also because he probably would have emphasized that his proper name designates a singularity that in essence cannot be killed – which is why one should beware of hastily concluding that a philosopher named "Derrida" can be killed.

Yet, the crucial difference between the two thinkers was expressed by Rorty's daughter's sarcastic diagnosis about the dangers of excessive Heidegger reading: at the very point when Rorty resorts to black humor (which already settles the matter for him), it is quite safe to say that Derrida would have displayed a more thoughtful reaction and having begun somewhat playfully would have shown with increasing gravity how a bitter seriousness is to be extracted from the pain. From his perspective, it would be entirely possible that Rorty's daughter and even Rorty himself, indirectly, were alluding in a satirical manner to a hitherto rarely explored dimension of "intellectual metabolism" (if we are willing to provisionally accept such an unusual term). Indeed, they might even be suggesting in a laconic way that they were engaged in developing a mental toxicology. If this assumption seems at all plausible, we then enter a realm that in pre-psychoanalytic times would have been referred to as magic, while today one speaks of psychosomatics or psychoneuroimmunology. From an ethnological perspective, we here find a modern articulation of the archaic belief that there is no such thing as a natural death. Rather, the end of any life is to be attributed to an evil spirit who arbitrarily cuts a human being's thread of life. Every death would be the work of something malicious, of a curse, or a poison that is administered – in this case, of a philosophical poison from a suspect German apothecary, from a true devil's workshop that obtains its lethal ingredients from afar and is associated with the ancient Platonic pharmacy.

There is something to this interpretation, even if it might seem at first sight to be more of a surrealist response than an intellectual one. To its credit, it takes seriously the idea that reading is a kind of metabolism. Philosophical reading, indeed reading in general, would thus be interpreted as an act of assimilation – and we all know that assimilation of what is indigestible can sometimes have dramatic consequences. The risks and side effects of such mental processes are hence emphasized with an unprecedented explicitness. Indeed, the entire organismic and psychosomatic apparatus that since Schelling, Schopenhauer, Eduard von Hartmann, and Freud has been called the unconscious would accordingly be depicted as a nervous stomach or a baroque digestive system, in which dangerous transformations occur unbeknown to their subjects. This digestive system forms a crypt full of engrams or neural deposits that are associated with only a small part of the discursive dimension of a person's memory, but which for the most part remain unable to be represented and yet at the same time have quite an influence on the manifest behavior of human beings. In light of such quasi-psychoanalytical or, better, psychotoxicological considerations, intellectual life as a whole turns out to be a subtle metabolic drama. There would thus no longer be any thought process that was not involved in a permanent and relentless struggle between the administration of poisons and antidotes.

I probably do not need to emphasize here that such conjectures are much closer to Derrida's line of thinking than to Rortyian irony. Before Derrida, no one so consistently advocated the thesis that assimilation is not innocent – and thus also that the reproduction and proliferation of earlier impressions is never innocent. Wherever traces remain embedded in material bearers, whether the latter are alive or dead, made out of stone or nervous systems, written on paper or carved into skin, the unity of poison and its administration is unmistakable. According to Derrida, deconstruction is unavoidably and continually also a praxis of antidotes and counter-administrations, which are reactions to previous poisons and the acts of administering them. Derrida referred to the site where the interaction of poisons and antidotes (as well as the interaction of the administration of poison and antidotes) is documented as the archive, while hinting that he was running for the office of archivist. The significance of this office could justifiably be interpreted as a democratic analogue to the Platonic fantasy of the rule of philosopher-kings.

In what follows, I would like to pursue this psychoanalytic or psychotoxicological line of thought a little further and discuss the question of how Derrida discovered an approach to the psychodynamics (or to the semiodynamics or the somatodynamics, respectively) of the philosophical tradition. For connoisseurs of such things, incidentally, it may be obvious that I am once again taking up, from a contemporary perspective, a question that about twenty years ago was the occasion for a conference in Paris concerning the state of the Freudian project after Lacan's death: is there such a thing as Derridean psychoanalysis? René Major was then responsible for formulating this question, and as we know, it led to a fierce dispute, because it was suspected of being a rhetorical question that aimed to enthrone Derrida as a guru of the post-Lacanian scene.

My response to this question is no secret, both in the earlier context and today, a few years after the thinker's death: it is emphatically affirmative. I would go so far as to claim that Viennese psychoanalysis was but a particular instance of something universal, which Derrida thematized as a mostly neglected sphere of psychosemiotic processes where the mechanical and the organic merge into each other. He thus offered a few prescient suggestions for a response to the question of how psychological iteration is to be thought over the course of successive ages and generations. In so doing, he indirectly contributed to the solution of the greatest of all problems of cultural theory: how are we to understand the phenomenon of a civilization that is able to regenerate itself by learning? This problem seems even more difficult when we recognize that the tradition inherited from all dead generations really and quite literally weighs like a nightmare on the brains of the living, as Marx put it in 1852 in his great essay on the situation in France after the coup d'état of Napoleon III.[8] This famous statement, by the way, shows that we can recognize Marx as an expert in historical nightmares, an early spectrologist, a secularized ghost-seer [*Geisterseher*] in the Derridean sense.

If that faded myth of the twentieth century that we call Freudianism, is to be successfully passed down to future generations despite its current decline (and indeed not merely in the ossified form of therapeutic organizations, but as a medium of living, inquiring thought that has a role to play in a prospective theory of civilization), then this will be accomplished not least because Derrida opened doors to future psychological knowledge of human beings and cultures with his reflections on a general theory of the trace, i.e. of materialized "spirit" [*Geist*] and of ghosts [*Geister*]. These are the same doors or at least ones adjacent to those through which, over the past century, thinkers such as Ernst Bloch, Gotthard Günther, Jean Baudrillard, and Niklas Luhmann, as well as contemporary pioneering intellects including Bruno Latour, Peter Galison, Heiner Mühlmann, and Roberto Esposito – to name only a few of many colleagues – have passed and continue to pass. Despite their different approaches, these thinkers are all searching for a complex concept of culture that would overcome the conventional binaries of metaphysical, political, and scientific vocabularies – whether we are dealing with the ancient dichotomy of spirit and matter, or with that of human beings and things, or with that of nature and society, or with other similarly venerable dichotomies.

To proceed a bit further in this direction, I would like to return to some thoughts that I presented in the spring of 2005 at a conference held on the first anniversary of Derrida's death at the Centre Georges Pompidou in Paris. At that time, I resolved not to speak directly about Derrida's work and specific passages in his texts, but to employ a method of indirect reflection [*Spiegelung*] – a way of proceeding that has elsewhere been called "constellation research."[9] In the short essay titled *Derrida, an Egyptian*, I was concerned with illustrating a few basic figures of deconstructive thought by redeploying them in closer or more distant proximity to analogous intellectual projects – Niklas Luhmann's systems theory, Freudian psychoanalysis, the humanist mythology of Thomas Mann, Franz Borkenau's cultural theory, the mediology of Régis Debray, Hegel's theory of signs, and Boris Groys' theory of the archive and museum. Because circumstances dictated that everything that I said on that occasion would have to be more cursory than rigorous and more suggestive than probing (serving to deepen our understanding), I am glad that in today's lecture I will be able to go into more detail on at least one matter. I acknowledge, a little apprehensively, that we will now be considering my most speculative remarks in Paris, which wander the furthest from Derrida's own text.

I am referring to the section of my presentation titled "Thomas Mann and Derrida." I there suggested that while composing his four-part work "Joseph and his Brothers," the great novelist had to a certain degree poetically anticipated the phenomenon of Derrida, by portraying the character type of the highly talented outsider in the enchanting figure of the young Joseph. This outsider, owing to his unusual talents, succeeds in advancing from an empire's periphery to the inner circles of the center of power, so as to make himself indispensable there as a dream interpreter, as an adviser, indeed as the Pharaoh's own better self. I called this structure, or position, "Josephism" and wanted to thus indicate a volatile and dynamic cultural configuration that has been quite significant in modernity. I argued that we could not possibly understand the dramatic struggles over authoritative interpretation in Western civilization since the late nineteenth century if we ignored this configuration.

The Josephistic position is so compelling because it allows its agents to advance to the "center of the center" and thus to create a novel and eccentric interpretation of centrality. Yet even though such interpretation can be very appealing to the holders of central positions, it often turns out to be subversively dangerous. The procedure that leads to the problematic site that I called the center of the center can only be that of dream interpretation – as is evident from the Biblical story that Thomas Mann expanded upon in a fantastical manner. In other words, dreams in the middle make it clear that the middle can never actually be its own middle. Let me clarify from the outset that we are not here concerned with the interpretation of just anybody's dreams, but are directly concerned with interpreting the noble lord's dreams, and even more with the lord of lords, with the exalted Pharaoh's dreams, which are about the fate of the empire and of the throne, though in a way that is initially obscure.

Thomas Mann presented this situation in a grandiose narrative sequence: the Pharaoh had dreamed the famous dream in which the lean cows devoured the fatted ones, and asked his court oneiro-mancers what these visions could mean. Unsatisfied with their answers, the Pharaoh eagerly heeded the rumors of a young Jew, who was imprisoned in a jail in the southern part of the empire. This young Jew had been imprisoned because, though a slave, he was suspected of an affair with the wife of a senior official. He was also said to possess the gift of interpreting dreams to a wonderful degree. Pharaoh had a boat sent down the Nile to bring the young man to his court so that he could put his art of dream interpretation to the test – you are probably familiar with the rest of the story. What might be less well known is the fact that many hermeneuticians who interpret great texts have since been haunted by their own dream, one that also requires interpretation. They are constantly dreaming that one day a ship will come from the middle of the empire, or a vehicle with a chauffeur from the capital, from which a messenger will emerge to invite them very politely to the palace where the powerful have unsettling dreams. However, since this second-order dream has yet to be adequately understood, let alone ever fulfilled, later dream-interpreters felt compelled, in the absence of a formal invitation, to head at their own expense from the periphery into big cities, so as to wait for an opportunity there.

I argued in my Paris lecture that the twentieth century was a golden age of Josephism. Dream-interpretation as a career (the structure of which I just outlined) was expressly realized at least three times in this century, as far as I can tell. It happened for the first time before the First World War, when Sigmund Freud, who, although born in a province, had spent his youth in Vienna, set himself the task of interpreting the dreams of his contemporaries. Even if these were not directly the dreams of the Emperor Franz Joseph, under whose rule the bold new hermeneutician lived for several decades, they were still the dreams of your typical late-monotheistic neurotic, all the way to the highest levels of society. It happened for a second time when the young Ernst Bloch, after the First World War and in scandalous synchronicity with the young, still hopeful Russian Revolution, attempted to interpret humanity's widespread dreams of a better world in terms of their real content, or, better, in terms of their utopian relevance and their anticipatory significance. And it happened for a third time after the Second World War, when Jacques Derrida built up the arsenals of deconstruction, in order to thereby subject the dreams of old European metaphysics to a treatment that was both meticulous and subversive – the word "arsenal" here suggests the image of a shipyard whose dock workers never really know whether the ship they are working on is supposed to be scrapped or made into a new, seaworthy vessel.

Today I would like to slightly amplify the all-too-laconic reference to this threefold twentieth-century dream-hermeneutics and thus to indicate, at least in outline, how the third instance, which I have characterized as Derridean dream interpretation, is distinct from the two preceding models and yet closely linked to them on a few points.

It is immediately evident that the three versions of Josephism that I have just mentioned do not simply converge. On the contrary, each of the three approaches involves a subtle and radical shift of subject matter. With Freud, as with Bloch and Derrida, the concept of the dream itself is always defined in a very idiosyncratic manner, and indeed each author even provides us with a new definition of the oneiric function as such. In summary: Freudian dream interpretation primarily discusses dreams at night, tapping into the deactivation of the sleeper's consciousness in order to project the traces of a forbidden and impossible infantile desire onto the dream-theater's screen. In contrast, Blochian dream interpretation foregrounds daydreams, which provide fantasy material for the technological and political improvement of the world. Derridean dream interpretation is ultimately concerned with fragile fabrications through which metaphysical speculation rises above the difference of life and death. To put it much more concisely: Freudian dreams are regressive, Blochian dreams are progressive, and Derridean dreams are spectral. The first are dreamed in beds and written down in journals, or recounted in therapy sessions. The second present themselves in folk tales and utopian novels, as well as in rapturous string quartets and heavenly symphonies, or are translated into party programs and five-year plans. The third are dreamed in the place where writing goes to die, the library, and transformed into contributions to a universal archive.

At this point, I do not wish to speak about the mechanisms of "dream-work" investigated by Freud in his early publication *The Interpretation of Dreams* (from 1899–1900) – they have been trivialized in twentieth-century culture, mostly indirectly via film. Instead, I would like to point out that there is an attempt at a kind of second dream interpretation in Freud's late work. Here it is not so much a matter of the psyche's nocturnal fabrications, but of those dream-analogous figments of the imagination that Freud called illusions, or to put it more clearly, religious ideas. In fact, with the expansion of psychoanalysis into a multinational therapeutic movement, its founder inevitably turned his attention to manifestations of collective consciousness, or cultural phantasms. Freud was aware of which approach he should avoid at all costs, thanks to the work of his dissident colleague Jung, and was thus inclined to adopt another approach to the sources of the religious dream. He could not escape into the psycho-ontological mode of thought that characterized Jung's problematic doctrine of archetypes, but had to remain faithful to the discrete genetic methods that were distinctive of psychoanalytic procedures in the Viennese School.

It is testimony to the sublime impartiality of the later Freud that, in his attempt at a second interpretation of dreams (I will use this term for the time being), he did not adhere rigidly to the parameters of his earlier theorizing, but made a fresh start so that he could do justice to the phenomena before his eyes. While most theoreticians are hypnotized by their own ideas and thus satisfy the preconditions for self-repetition, which the contemporary world construes as their "system" or trademark, Freud was wide awake, enough to occasionally see through the veil of his own conceptual terminology. This allowed him to approach and reformulate phenomena that had not been treated adequately with his earlier concepts. In terms of the dynamic of the religious formation of illusions, we might say that he put his own libido-dogma to one side for the moment and developed a proposal for the interpretation of religious matters with a completely different orientation that was to some degree extra-psychoanalytic. In *The Future of an Illusion* from 1927, we find his hypothesis that "religious ideas have arisen from the same need as have all the other achievements of civilization: from the necessity of defending oneself against the crushingly superior force of nature."[10] Just after this we read of "the urge to rectify the shortcomings of civilization that made themselves painfully felt."[11] We thus see how effortlessly Freud transitions from a theory of desire to a theory of compensation – the famous transformation of the human being into a kind of prosthetic god is to be found here, something more reminiscent of Herder, Adler, and Gehlen than of his earlier writings. In my view, this maneuver indicates that Freud was on his way to an early form of general immunology. As I tried to show in my *Spheres* project (and in a few other works), immunology allows us to reformulate the entire field of metaphysics, religious studies, cultural theory, and therapeutics in a compellingly intercultural and progressively civilizing way.

If it is indeed true that all achievements of civilization including religions stem from motivations to protect and resist, as Freud puts it in the passage cited above (or, in my terminology: that they primarily arise from the immunitary imperative), then a new page has been turned in the book of psychoanalytic cultural theory. To be sure, Freud stuck with his approach in interpreting phenomena genetically, from out of infantilism, yet we are no longer dealing with the precedence of the child's libido, which formed the indelible seal of classical psychoanalysis. Rather, the pressing demand for a power that can protect against unbearable risks to existence now becomes prominent. Accordingly, Freud here finally attempts to establish the validity of his system's core by emphasizing that the libido prefers to attach itself – in the "mode of anaclisis" [*Anlehnungsmodus*] – to objects that provide us with "narcissistic" gratification, thus initially to the mother, and later to the father, so as then to remain forever attached to the latter. Yet, in the final analysis, it is evident that this "choice of an object" [*Objektwahl*] is not primarily based on a libidinal cathexis, but rather expresses the frightened individual's attempts to form an immunitary alliance with a power that is able to protect it. Nevertheless, the link between the need for protection and love is not to be taken lightly – this is confirmed whenever we regard the genesis of the dependence between children and parents. At the same time, libidinal desire and the striving for immunitary alliances and envelopments are two psychodynamical categories that should be strictly distinguished from each other.

What we have here called Freud's second dream interpretation, that is, his later theory of illusion, thus begins with the bold thesis that every adolescent sooner or later recognizes that in a certain sense he or she is condemned to remain a child forever. The adolescent somehow becomes aware that he or she will never be able to do without protection against superior extrinsic forces. The psyche then creates its gods, especially male divinities, from this "recognition" – Freud also calls it an "impulse." This creation of gods from the need for protection reaches all the way back to the God of monotheism, the father of fathers. Freud may have devoted particular attention to this form of divinity because he knew he could rely on the household god of Western and ancient Near Eastern civilization as the main evidence for his thesis. In the midst of his reflections, reaching ahead into uncharted territory, he could not resist returning to his earlier theoretical accounts. Thus in a later passage he claimed, rather abruptly and without arguing for it sufficiently, that religious infantilism is a "universal obsessional neurosis of humanity" that arises from the Oedipal complex.[12] It benefits individuals by allowing them to find shelter in the system of collective delusion, so that they do not need to form a "personal neurosis." Freud hereby touches on a fruitful distinction between neurotic constructs and symbolic immune systems, yet is unable to explain this distinction clearly enough without a developed immunological logic.

The second Freudian interpretation of dreams would remain incomplete, inconsequential, and speculative in the bad sense of the term, had it not exhibited an at least rudimentarily practical and therapeutic perspective. In this regard, the older Freud to some extent broke new ground by discreetly intimating that when we are faced with perpetual infantilism, becoming an adult is ultimately all that can help us – yet, at bottom, the will to become an adult is more a matter of individual morality than of following medical directions. Hence one can probably understand why he called the religious illusion a "sweet poison"[13] – we suddenly find ourselves in the realm of drug phenomena and their corresponding processes of withdrawal. Yet we are faced with a "bitter-sweet poison" – this is not too different from the Marxist dictum regarding the "opium of the masses": its agreeable side includes the promise of suggestive infantile indulgences, but its bitter flip side entails the subject's fixation in a system of psychical servitude. The cost of religious symbolic immunity has never been expressed so harshly and clearly, in my view. Freud explicitly makes it clear that this price is unacceptably high – regardless of whether we are concerned with the price of monotheism in particular or with the price of illusion in general. At another point, the psychoanalyst is unable to adequately explain, with his conceptual apparatus, why human beings should ever develop the wish to become adults. By focusing his attention on *Homo libidinosus*, the human being as a desiring creature, or in any case a creature motivated by fear, he remains unable to explain why that same human being sometimes straightens up, develops a firm sense of pride, and opposes its fate, regardless of whether this manifests itself in everyday acts of courage or in great moments of *amor fati*.

In brief, classical psychoanalysis lacks the conceptual resources to grasp the thymotic dimension of psychical life, owing to its systematic tendencies. At the same time, Freud had always recognized this, having made no secret of his affinity to Stoicism, which in its diminished bourgeois form amounts to a heroic conception of life. He thus paid indirect tribute to the equality of thymos and eros. The consequences of this hardly need to be explicitly spelled out: psychoanalysis is only apparently a medical procedure or one

of the healing arts – in reality, it offers a way to develop adults
[*Erwachsenenbildung*]. Yet a belated development of adults, in the
stricter sense of the term, can only make headway where the striving
to one day belong among the "greats" is reinforced. Adulthood *per
se* is a thymotic dimension. The way this tendency functions is not
very well understood by the members of contemporary, excessively
eroticized, and thus appetite-driven Western civilization, if they do
not simply ignore or dismiss it. For this reason, we should not be
surprised to observe a progressive infantilization in the present-day
world that is accompanied by pervasive eroticization, a one-sided
thought that thinks merely in terms of the libido, an invasive thera-
peutism, a widespread cult of consumption, and an ever-increasing
incapacity to understand thymotic phenomena.

The second Josephistic phenomenon on a grand scale was to
be observed in the early twentieth century, when the young Ernst
Bloch, born in 1885 as the son of petit-bourgeois Jewish parents
in the southwestern province of Germany, conceived the outlines
of his sprawling philosophical oeuvre while in exile in Switzerland
during the First World War. The author later remarked that his
early work *The Spirit of Utopia* (from 1918, revised in 1923) had
been a test, a mere probing of its content – it represented a work of
anticipation and a piece of "revolutionary gnosis," that is, a sign
that the most radical knowledge of the soul goes hand in hand with
the most radical dissatisfaction with the world hitherto. Bloch's
interpretation of dreams goes far beyond that of psychoanalysis,
because it is not content to interpret the nocturnal psychological
fabrications of bourgeois wives and senior civil servants. Bloch's
Josephistic operation begins by immediately marching to the political, indeed to the cosmic center. His ambition is nothing less than to
interpret humanity's (this means Jewish–Christian civilization first
of all) millennia-long dream from the vantage point of an authentic we-experience in a non-alienated collective. As a Schellingian
Marxist, Bloch believed the human spirit to be a cosmic site in which
fettered and bound nature is freed from its bonds, and opens its
eyes to behold itself and the universe. For this reason, a humanist
interpretation of dreams is of no interest to him: dream-functioning
does not merely involve the addition of the human nervous system
to lifeless matter, but is rather living, fermenting matter itself, full
of tendencies and teleologies, which dreams in and through us and
is propelled *per homines*. In a passage from *The Spirit of Utopia* that
is as famous as it is obscure, we read: "But we walk in the forest
and we feel we are or could be what the forest dreams."[14] With an
enthusiasm that would be worthy of one of the prophets, Bloch –
proceeding from such intuitions – cleared a path from Jakob Böhme

to Karl Marx. Driven by a ruthless apostolic energy, he drew a line from Christ to Lenin – hence his famous expression *ubi Lenin ibi patria*,[15] for which Jacob Taubes never forgave the author of *The Principle of Hope*. Bloch was uninterested in the regressive dynamic of the imagination and in the psyche's fixations in childhood. Rather, he understood childhood to be a manifestation of the capacity for anticipation that runs through all of nature, but which comes into its own with the human being and culminates in the *Homo sapiens* child. Orbiting the logic of the not-yet his whole life long, Bloch was in this sense the metaphysician of youth – and it is no accident that, after leaving the DDR following the construction of the Berlin Wall in 1961, he became one of the figureheads of the last youth movement in West Germany and a sympathetic mentor for the student protests in the 1960s.

The innumerable day-dream images that Bloch compiled with encyclopedic thoroughness in his magnum opus *The Principle of Hope* have one stark feature in common, which concerns their temporo-logical status. They are all "ahead of their time." They signify neither the haunting memories of older, better conditions nor deferred reproductions of inhibited infantile wishes, but are supposed to be deciphered as harbingers of a better world in the future – and where there is a harbinger, the thing-to-come itself seems intent on demonstrating the possibility of its own realization. If a marked attention to various kinds of haunting phenomena can be observed in Bloch, it is obvious that he is less interested in what haunts us afterwards than he is in what haunts us in advance. Bloch encapsulates such phenomena with the term *Vor-Schein* [Tr. – "pre-appearance"]. This term brings to light an unusual, even paradoxical concept of the trace: things in the future have the ability to symbolically manifest themselves in advance – as though that which has not yet existed could already leave behind footprints in the present. The better world is already here right now, as advent and friendly ghost. Bloch had to devote great energy to create a novel futuristic philosophy of nature so that he could lend plausibility to such seemingly outlandish claims. The author's posthumous papers on the *Logos der Materie* [*Logos of Matter*], which are devoted to the question of "bringing out" [*Herausbringen*], provide compelling evidence of this devotion.[16] In these papers, Bloch demonstrates the manner in which the not-yet can latently be at work in the already-now, and indeed in the mode of an active latency that can cast its "shadows" or, better, its fore-light ahead. Ever since, philosophy has been fore-sight in the fore-light.

At the same time, Bloch eschewed his earlier conception of pre-appearance in favor of a multidimensional concept of haunting: on the one hand, this can refer to the prosaic daytime world's proximity to a world beyond that is full of spirits – the young socialist Bloch had no problem in speaking of metempsychosis, since he already understood, early on, that the spirit of utopia can only be vindicated if there is a principle that allows mortals to circumvent death, which is the absolute anti-utopian authority for non-believers. For him, as for Hegel, haunting also signifies the subject's vain attempt to revolve within its own interiority to stabilize itself in itself – it thereby experiences its own emptiness and continually slips away from itself, just as a ghost suddenly vanishes as soon as daylight reaches it. Lastly, Bloch recognizes a third shading of the ghostly, viz., as repercussion of capitalist abstraction and the fetishism of money – on this point, his reflections are not all that different from Alfred Sohn-Rethel's speculations on what the latter called real abstraction, which became prominent a few decades ago due to their influence on Adorno's work, only to fall back into present-day oblivion.

The effusive crudeness of Bloch's political ontology was always evident to his readers. On the one hand, it evoked a Gothic Empire and on the other hand had no problem defending the Stalinist regime of terror, its show trials and the absurd theater of lies supposedly necessarily "realize" the great thoughts of communism. This enthusiastic grobianism is without doubt the direct result of a Josephism inclined toward revolution, which the new interpreter of dreams wanted to use to directly intervene in the global political center of meaning in his time, the program of the Russian Revolution. If Freud hesitated to interpret the dreams of the aging lord of Schönbrunn Palace, even though he knew something of them, Bloch was resolutely determined not only to interpret the thoughts of Lenin and Stalin (something that other communist intellectuals such as Lukács and Kojève likewise wanted to do) – he first wished to teach the revolution itself and its leaders the right way to dream. He provided a spiritual superstructure for the crude implementation of the Red Terror by arguing that vulgar materialist Marxism needed to be enhanced with a metaphysical dimension, something that sounded plausible at the time. Hence he was an interpreter of dreams who also wished instantly to become a dream-teacher – something we can see at work in each twentieth-century praxis of dream interpretation. Evidently, the psyches of clients who are ready for treatment easily pick up on the categories of their therapists and in a short time begin to dream in the style of their respective school. While Bloch championed the daydream of a better world, he simultaneously turned into a bold advocate of illusion – by claiming that a kernel of truth could be extracted from even the most aberrant visions of a better world. This kernel of truth could be called "utopian" in the good sense of the term, while the regressive remainder of such aberrant visions would have to be strictly eliminated.

In sum, we can clearly identify a series of motifs in Bloch's work that recur in Derrida in an entirely different register and with different tendencies, under completely different auspices when viewed on the whole: the theme of the trace, the figure of the haunting specter, the logic of deferral, the concept of a messianism within or beyond Judaism, the thought of a fullness of self-possession perpetually to come or even impossible, and so forth. In the case of this last motif, we would have to show how Bloch's approach is diametrically opposed to his later colleague and closely akin for precisely this reason. In a typical, or perhaps telltale, passage, Bloch notes: "The final will is that to be truly present. . . . Man wants at last to enter into the Here and Now as himself, wants to enter his full life without postponement and distance."[17] If "Man" wants such a thing, then it is precisely because he is always already pervaded by the precedence of deferral, of distance, of the not-here and the not-now. It is obvious that Derrida would have disagreed with the author of such a statement. On his view, indeed, the metaphysics of presence was always merely a sublime fiction. But the law of deferral also applies for Bloch, because the world-process as such is not yet ripe – the world's maturation as a whole remains something that for the time being is merely to be posited and helped along with technological resources, political measures, and not least with philosophical explanations and evocations. Bloch would emphasize that virtually all human reflection is determined by the postponement of the "authentic." Indeed, in this regard, the misery of the *conditio humana* – as St. Paul already articulated and that Rilke still lamented in the *Duino Elegies* – has always shown us that we are not capable of presence, neither by thinking nor by living, neither in the sense that we would fully exist in being, nor in the sense that being would fully exist in us. For now, full presence is no real option for mortal beings. Moreover, Bloch would also define life [*Leben*] as survival [*Überleben*]. In a dramatic passage from *The Spirit of Utopia* he asks: "who or what lives life as a whole life, *as the broad, historical life granted to humanity as a whole*?"[18] According to Bloch, reference to the archive does not provide a convincing response, since actual traditions are easily broken and after a little while end up completely incomprehensible. Bloch chooses a quite drastic example: the score of Beethoven's Ninth Symphony will one day be as lifeless and incomprehensible to a later culture "as the Inca's knotted script[.]"[19] The guarantee of survival can only be found in the principle of hope and its bearer, "forward-moving matter,"[20] not in an archive, however extensive it may be. The contrast between Bloch's and Derrida's temperaments is informative, because it allows us to bring to light an aspect of philosophical psychodynamics that has rarely been explicitly noticed, one that is at the same time significant for the philosophical analysis of typological questions. If Bloch and Derrida shared a common interest in quite a number of motifs and elaborated these motifs in idiosyncratic ways, the enthusiast Bloch and the melancholic Derrida have irreconcilably antithetical basic outlooks. I do not know if Derrida ever read the letters of the young Bloch, or indeed if he was closely acquainted with the work of his antipode at all – it would be fascinating to imagine the deconstructionist's commentary on a passage from one of Bloch's letters to the latter's young friend Georg Lukács in 1912: "I am the paraclete, and the people to whom I am sent will experience and understand the God who returns home in themselves."[21] Comparison with Bloch's robust messianic mania clarifies a rather significant moment in Derrida's later work, one of the most remarkable and at the same time most poignant: how he worked his way from a fundamentally melancholic position to one that offered an approach to messianism.

In closing, I would like to offer a few remarks on what I called the third Josephistic offensive of the twentieth century. I am suggesting that we understand Derridean deconstruction as a kind of dream interpretation, and only time will tell whether it suffers the same fate as its predecessors: trivialization in the case of Freud, becoming obsolete in Bloch's case. Even the most recent version of Josephism inevitably results in a political interpretation of dreams – to put it more precisely, it results in a skeptical distance from every political ontology, or in other words: it results in a dream analysis of the kinds of dreams that imperial powers are used to dreaming about themselves. Derrida goes beyond Bloch's dream-hermeneutical approach, by sublating the dichotomy between nocturnal dreams and daydreams into a higher-order conception of the dream. This mainly occurs through his suspension of the boundaries between thinking and dreaming, or through his postulation of a reciprocal porousness between the two mental activities. Recent scholarly literature has particularly profited from this move by making a virtue of the removal of strict boundaries between thinking and dreaming, or in general from that between argument and fiction, in order to blur the genre boundaries between philosophy and literature.

At first glance, it might appear as though Derrida is initially merely concerned with a version of what in France was called the "return to Freud" – which as a rule meant the license to transform the Viennese master's ideas until they were unrecognizable. In reality, Derrida thought through the assumptions on which classical psychoanalysis rested – none of which he would endorse any longer, as he remarked in a conversation near the end of his life with Elisabeth Roudinesco – and furthered them, translating them into a philosophical (or semiodynamic) register.

What I am here calling "semiodynamics" is a concept that helps to translate the worn-out idea of "tradition" into more precise, more dramatic, and – why not? – into "more uncanny" [*unheimlichere*] categories. With this concept, we can show how everything hinges on phenomena that play a role in the formation of so-called "cultures." These "phenomena" perpetually concern the assimilation of an intellectual "heritage," they always involve the (more or less phallo-dynamic) adoption of prefabricated roles and positions in the cultural field, they deal with new materializations of messages, mandates, privileges, deliveries, and missions, with the unavoidable connection to existing languages, institutions, and disciplines, and with the openness of everything just mentioned to things not yet said, to relations not yet institutionalized, and to precepts yet to be put into practice, as well as arts yet to be plied.

With his contributions to the reformulation of psychoanalysis and his proposals for a general theory of the archive, Derrida belongs to a broader movement within recent and contemporary philosophy, which I characterize as the "mediumistic turn of the theory of the subject." As Hegel demanded that substance develop as subject, so Derrida – less *expressis verbis* than by his entire intellectual conduct – invites the subject to develop as medium. This is the only way fully to understand his talk of "specters," which many do not take seriously. It would be a gross misunderstanding to assume that terms such as *hantologie* (in layman's terms: a science of haunting) are merely metaphorical or parapsychological shenanigans. From Derrida's metapsychological perspective, subjectivity *per se* is only to be understood by recognizing that human beings have always been "inhabited" by texts. Thus the history of cultures and of the human being's formation must be understood as an event that could be called metemtextosis, a transmigration of texts, on analogy with metempsychosis, the transmigration of souls. Here we are concerned with pure this-worldly processes that engender the formation of "persons," or "psychical systems." Such processes require a logic of invasive communications – or, perhaps we could say that such processes require a theory of assimilations, of psychosomatic engrams and symbolic metabolism. Needless to say, this is all quite manifestly at work in Derrida's writings, although not as a positive theory, but mainly on a performative level and embedded in the *modus operandi* of his various inquiries, which have occasionally and justifiably been viewed as a kind of exercise [*Exerzitium*].

At a few points in Derrida's works, we can observe how he applied his mediumistic understanding of subjectivity to himself. Thus at the beginning of his speech in Frankfurt when he was awarded the Adorno prize in 2001, he said: "For decades I have heard voices in my dreams. Sometimes the voices have been friendly, sometimes they have not been. There are voices in me . . ." At one point, Derrida notes that the voices he hears invite him to acknowledge publicly the kinship between his own work and Adorno's. I consider this anecdote most likely to be an ad hoc device and do not believe that Derrida actually thought that he "owed" Adorno anything. Yet what he said is characteristic of his mode of thought. His allusion to the topos of the Socratic *daimonion* is unmistakable, a theme that inaugurated a tradition of philosophical mediumism in the days of the ancient Academy – though this tradition was silenced by the modern "subject-philosophy" ideology of self-determination, self-justification, and self-fabrication – only returning to the intellectual stage via the "philosophies of dialogue," the better media theories of the twentieth century, and the philosophical reflections of psychoanalysis.[22]

At first sight, Derridean dream interpretation seems to involve a rapprochement with the positions of the early Freud, since thinking the "trace" essentially entails understanding "dreamwork" from its tendency toward repetition. Thus haunting, again, seems to necessarily be a haunting-afterwards. Yet it does not merely signify the return of the repressed. Rather, it indicates the return of what has been left undone and incomplete, in the broadest sense of the term. This is hardly an innocuous thesis, because haunting and spectral beings that are bound to the past can also signify the return of illusion in the bad sense of the term. In concrete terms, they indicate an ongoing reluctance on the part of some to draw the necessary conclusions from the experiences of history, the implosion of the communist sphere in particular. Not for nothing did Derrida point out the dangers that arise from intractable "Marxist identities," in one of his most important political texts, *Specters of Marx* (1993), as well as in his response to the critics of this book, which was published under the ironic title *Marx & Sons*. To recapitulate this thought in a psycho-"spectrological" register: Derrida's specters, like the specters of postcommunism on the whole, are essentially loser-ghosts. They mostly manifest themselves in a melancholy way – they have lost sight of their utopian mission and yet stare further in the direction where just yesterday hope was still on the horizon. In their case, melancholy means nothing more than utopia minus aggression. But there remain furiously manic ghosts among them who cannot do without Marxism as a matrix of revenge fantasies.

As we have already noted, in his later work Freud extended the psychoanalytical paradigm and shifted from a theory of desire to a theory of compensation, with infantile needs for protection becoming increasingly prominent. In a comparable way, Derrida ultimately came to regard the philosophical dream of a knowledge fully present to itself as a compensatory phenomenon, although it initially seemed as if deconstruction wished to reveal the actual or merely supposed dream of metaphysics, of an ultimate closure in complete self-presence of mind, to be a case of intellectualized narcissism and thus wished to classify it as a libidinal phenomenon or autoeroticism. Derrida in fact shows that the dreams of metaphysics are uneasy fabrications that do not actually evince the self-enjoyment of knowledge or power, but are manifestations of an overarching self-concern and of a concern for the structures of the world and of knowledge – in a word, they represent compensatory phenomena that defend us against the dangers of ignorance and confusion. I consider this to be an indication that Derrida, as an interpreter of metaphysical dreams, had become increasingly convinced that such fabrications were inevitable and insurmountable – just as I am convinced that such compensatory phenomena are never fully able to believe in themselves. As I would put it, we need to discuss how the immunitary imperative becomes explicit, how each culture compels the creation and reform of, as well as instruction in, symbolic immune systems. We should note that Derrida's therapeutic approach did not aim to dissolve these phenomena (not for nothing did he emphasize the ethically significant difference between the cautiousness of deconstruction and the destructivity of "critique"), but to warn metaphysical dreamers of the dangers of hyper-immunization. Human beings lose reference to reality in the excessive *clôture* of imaginary self-presence and, under the pretext of self-preservation, end up in a vortex of self-destruction – echoing a leitmotif of the older Critical Theory in a foreign context. In psychological terms, this means that manias are far more dangerous than depressions. In this respect, deconstruction is always also a prophylactic against the dangers of mania.

Derrida's Josephistic offensive would hardly have been able to succeed had it ended by retrospectively engaging with the metaphysical thinker's logically shrouded dream activity at the center of the creation of power and meaning. Indeed, the aspiring dream interpreter not only wants to look down into the wells of the past and submerge himself in archetypes, he would just as much like to gaze into the future, to shape it with lucid anticipations. Just as the biblical Joseph read Pharaoh's dreams as cryptic prophetic signs, in which the future of the empire was at stake, so Derrida, the

Joseph of the post-communist world, wants to integrate Marxism's haunting remainder into a new legitimate dream function. In short, even here the dream interpreter has to admit that he is a teacher of right dreaming. On this point, Derrida is unwittingly close to Bloch, even if he was never familiar with the latter's conception of the utopian function nor with the concept of utopia in general. For the later Derrida, responsible dreaming for oneself and the world involves adopting a rationally filtered relation to things that have been impossible until now. In Bloch's system, this was precisely the function of the progressive daydream.

At this point, our author's final intellectual adventure can be elucidated – the connection of his rational dream-doctrine to the messianic tradition. As Derrida explained in the already mentioned Adorno-prize speech, "The possibility of the impossible can only be dreamed, it cannot exist as something that has been dreamed . . ." He adds that his own thought is perhaps closer to dreaming the impossible than to philosophy as such (insofar as philosophy, ontology in particular, exhausts what can be said about reality). At the same time, he claims that "The im-possible is the figure of reality itself." For Derrida, the mechanism that opens a window into the future is a paradoxical modal logic: the impossible determines the reality of the real. In plain talk: only the messianic event would reveal what can "really" happen in the world. The messianic dimension of the "event" that could come must be emphatically maintained, because, as a burnt child of the twentieth century, Derrida knows that a "revolution" that is merely resumed without allowance for the impossible would once again be nothing but another catastrophe – a monstrous bastard of the possible and the actual. "The point is to not become tired of watching over this dream, while waking up" (*il faudrait, tout en se réveillant, continuer de veiller sur le rêve*). Dreaming here means a new alignment of the relation between the actual, the possible, and the impossible.

In taking up this guard duty, Derrida again shifts his position. He sometimes feels obliged to be the dreamer himself, whose dreams were the point. The logic of the Josephistic offensive compels him to embody the Pharaoh in his own person, or better: to present a quasi-pharaonically extended self that dreams for the imperium and beyond the imperium, fully knowing that the fates of empires are decided on their peripheries and by their discontented classes. As Josephistic Pharaoh or pharaonic Joseph, he is tasked with dreaming and interpreting the great forward-looking dream, and he must do this fully aware of the danger that results from the poison of overambitious visions. Richard Rorty called attention to these kind of complications, when he insightfully noted in an essay on Derrida that "philosophy as a genre is closely associated with the quest for such greatness."[23] Yet such a quest is morally imperative here. It manifests itself as a function of disillusioned dreaming, which wants to be a messianism without messianism. "We are dreaming of another concept, of another set of rights for the city, of another politics of the city,"[24] as Derrida put it in a talk given in 1996 with the coquettish title (which brings to mind the Marquis de Sade) *Cosmopolites de tous les pays, encore un effort!* It is obvious that the later Derrida left the sphere of deconstruction behind here and moved into the unfamiliar territory of affirmation, judgment, decision, confession, and "positive thinking." Future readers will have to judge whether he finally sought harbor in naivety and became a useless goodwill-thinker.[25] Rorty is probably right, when in his already-mentioned essay he suggests an alternative to Derrida's endless and arduous deconstruction of metaphysics – but he is wrong when he claims that this alternative consists in "circumventing" metaphysics and simply doing something else, such as writing literature and engaging in union activity. A choice between deconstruction and circumvention (as Rorty puts it) is not really possible.[26] Deconstruction remains quite important because it responds to the immunitary imperative, with an elevated seriousness – traditional metaphysical constructs have been a brilliant, if often misunderstood, expression of this imperative. Metaphysics is a response to openness to the world [*Weltoffenheit*] – such openness can only be made livable by spherical safeguards. Safeguards, for their part, must always be oriented to openness *de novo*.

In conclusion, I would like to offer a prognosis on whether Derrida's philosophy will continue to return and haunt us. I thus proceed from the observation that, in the final analysis, the great Josephists of the twentieth century owe their partly abiding and yet partly temporary success to their interventions in the basic vocabulary of Western civilization. In this regard, Freud was unquestionably the most successful. He succeeded in associating the hypercultural primal word "soul" – "psyche" in its psychoanalytical translation – with the half-metaphysical, half-scientific concept of the unconscious. This association has probably become irreversible, regardless of whether a revival of Freudianism in the neuroscientific era succeeds or not.

The results of Bloch's messianic-utopian initiative are much more difficult to assess. His attempt to meld the technical-political term "utopia," frowned upon by the bourgeoisie, with the Christian-humanist term "hope" was only successful for a while and only within a certain domain. In contrast, it becomes evident with time that this linguistic-political offensive could not compete against the gravity of everyday anti-utopianism. Utopianism, on the whole, has regained its former bad reputation. The one hundred million dead from the Marx-inspired experiments in Eastern Europe and Asia testify to this. As is to be feared, this apparently minor semantic nuance will be the only remaining trace that bears witness to a holocaust in the name of utopia and the human lives annihilated in it. However, a telling reluctance to erect monuments to the victims of revolutionary ideology can be observed in Eastern and Western Europe. This is symptomatic, since the "Specters of Marx" are quite obviously engaged in preventing the erection of monuments to those murdered under Communism.

With that said, I can now also inquire into the likely fate of Derrida's fundamental politico-semantic operation. He also tried to associate a modern and idiosyncratic term with an ancient and deeply rooted primal term, in order to thus leave behind a trace in humanity's vocabulary. His main goal was to fuse the neologism "deconstruction" with the basic term "justice" – a concept drawn from the basic vocabulary of civilizations, without which both the advanced religions of the East or West and modern democracies are unthinkable. It seems obvious to me that this maneuver could be effective for one or two generations, at most, because it was encumbered in advance by its strong implausibility. What Bloch failed to achieve, Derrida too could not achieve in the end – a hope-lessly affirmative formulation such as "deconstruction is justice" changes nothing. Thus in Derrida's case it would be realistic to brace ourselves for a narrowing of the domain of haunting. While the Freudian association of the concepts "soul" and "unconscious" is holding steady, the Derridean association of the concepts "decon-struction" and "justice" has virtually collapsed and will not be convincing to anyone outside of a specialized niche.

This means that the Derridean power of haunting will remain strictly confined to the actual circle of influence he had in his lifetime. As a young man arriving in France, he already had the gift of con-sidering academia to be the entire world. He was inclined to believe falsely that his academic success would mean success in the world or for the world. He never corrected this pleasant category mistake, in my opinion. This explains why, in *Specters* (from 1993), he could make eyes at an academic Marxism in the USA and Europe that had been humiliated by the events in Russia in 1990 – yet the current managers of the firm Marx & Sons did not thank him: to be sure, they wanted to believe, with him, in a new international to come, but they wanted to shield such a belief from the impact of deconstruc-tion's cautious melancholy. After the debacle of 1990, they would have much more preferred to hear that Marx will be resurrected

– not that spectral remnants of Marxism will be preserved. With subtle irony, Derrida here touched on the difference between specter and resurrection, which Jews and Christians were supposed to sort out more clearly in the future. In resurrection, as with specters, something cannot die because it has unfinished business and for this reason does not depart from the world. In this sense, all those who would rather not hear that there is unfinished business in the world are unbelievers. Perhaps messianism is a title given to the feeling that unfinished business demands to be taken up again – no matter how extensive such business is. This kind of feeling particularly thrives in a highly refined culture, such as Jewish culture, which is based on the belief that God cannot possibly be satisfied with the human state of affairs – but perhaps one day the messiah will take care of unfinished business. In a roundabout way, Christianity has become the moral *a priori* of the West. Such observations can no longer be understood merely philosophically. Derrida's late interest in "religious" problems, as well as his turn to fundamental juridical questions such as problems with the death penalty, the right to asylum, or the prevention of cruelty to animals, lead us to believe that he recognized that it was necessary for philosophy to form new alliances with what is not philosophy.

In my opinion, we must proceed even further in this direction today. Academia will undoubtedly remain the haunted castle that Derrida's ghosts are fond of roaming. We should not hesitate to think beyond the limits of academic disciplines, thanks to his inspiration. The wide-ranging global crisis of our time should prompt philosophers who remain hidden in the bosom of universities to leave their hiding place behind. We must again take to the streets and plazas, to the *pages littéraires* and screens, to schools and popular festivals, if we are to make our craft, the most cheerful and melancholy craft in the world, relevant once more. When our craft is well-practiced, it remains relevant, even in non-academic life. Countless people will then no longer ask so urgently what they have been asking for a long time: what exactly is a good life, an examined life? If anyone thinks that they have an answer, or if anyone wants to pose a counter-question, they should now step forward and speak.

7

DEEP OBSERVATION

Toward a Philosophy of the Space Station

Classical philosophy of technology begins with the suggestive hypothesis that technological "devices" are essentially extensions of organs, allowing users of such devices to broaden the range of their senses and extremities. Thus the telephone increases our ability to hear to a marvelous degree, and shoes, streets, and automobiles dramatically augment our potential to move with our feet and legs. Hence one can speak of technology, in sum, as a dimension of the extension of man[1] – in which case the human being is imagined to be the ensemble of his or her organs, and technology the sum of prostheses, or functional extensions that aim to improve those organs. *Homo sapiens* would accordingly be the technological animal that from the beginning has sought to expand the radius of its action and to optimize its prosthetic organs.

At first sight, it might seem as if astronautics, as it developed beginning in the mid twentieth century, strongly confirms the validity of this approach. Anyone looking for new evidence to support this expansionist and extensionist theory of the human being might well find the reality of space travel to be quite impressive corroboration. From the beginning, human beings have been on the verge of bursting the age-old bonds that have tied them to the Earth and expanding their range of action into the realm of perigean outer space and beyond. Where else would human beings operate more "extensively" than in their expeditions into the universe? Where else would human beings more impressively realize their sensory and kinetic potential?

Yet if we look a little closer, we realize that space travel is much more than merely further proof that human organs can be expanded. The theory of organ-extension is no longer quite so plausible when we realize that the engineers of spacecraft and space stations, who consider perigean outer space to be a possible and actual site for human beings to dwell in, do not merely broaden the scope of our sensory endowment and of our kinetic range, although such broadening does occur. Rather, they create artificial islands in the universe that are designed to accommodate various inhabitants arriving from Earth, at least for a while. We immediately recognize why this is much more than merely the expansion of perception and movement on grander scales.

In fact, the creation of space stations represents a dramatic break in the history of human self-relation, provided we grant that perceptions of the environment and instances of self-knowledge converge in the human being. Indeed, as the history of ideas demonstrates, from time immemorial human beings have tended to soar above their natural state on the wings of idealistic evasion, yet modern anthropological thought has shown that they always require inclusion in a sphere that can sustain them, regardless of whether they are relatively emancipated from a given environment. Indeed, humans not only require a cultural sphere, as is to be expected for members of the symbolic species,[2] but also need to be connected to a natural sphere that permanently assures their vital functions.

Life's absolute dependence on a suitable environment is most obvious where there is no such environment – in outer space. Anyone who wishes to travel there has to bring their own environment along with them, if they would like to be able to *reside* somewhere. Although this might seem trivial at first, it nevertheless has far-reaching philosophical and anthropological implications. With space travel, humanity emerges from a stage in which the self is experienced through extension and expansion, and enters one in which it is experienced through transplantation and implantation. In the course of such a transition, organs are not transplanted from one body into another, as they have been in recent surgical practice. Rather, in the construction of space stations, we are confronted with ontological implants and transplants – that is, with the implantation of a world where there was previously nothing and with the transplantation of a suitable living environment for human beings into an external world-container. It is fair to say that, with these procedures, the art of constructing prostheses is spurred beyond the stage of replacing and extending organs to one in which the world is replaced and the environment extended.

Against this backdrop, we can philosophically articulate the space station's significance in the light of "world history." As soon as terrestrial human beings are able to install implants in the void of outer space and fill these implants with transplanted environments, they are also able to relocate temporarily to these off-center imitations of world and environment and to enter into a kind of ontological communication with those who have been relocated. If Martin Heidegger, in his epochal work *Being and Time* (1927), interpreted the human being's fundamental disposition as being-in-the-world, a philosopher on board a space station would accordingly speak of being-in-the-world 2. Through the actual construction of such a station, a hidden premise of being-in-the-world 1 becomes explicit: namely, the assumption that the Earth is the only possible site for accommodating the existence of those who inhabit technologically and symbolically produced world-constructs. As soon as the space station exists, the Earth ceases to have a monopoly on supporting environmental and cultural encasements. From now on, it must share this privilege with what has been implanted in outer space, even if this only requires an infinitesimal extension, measured in terms of the Earth's volume. What is called nature or the environment in being-in-the-world 1 is replicated by the space station's life support system in being-in-the-world 2.[3]

With the emergence of the space station, not only do we have proof that there is intelligent life outside Earth, but the ability to communicate with this external intelligence is also effectively demonstrated by the electronic transmission of data between station and Earth. In fact, this has world-historical consequences, since Earth-based worlds (which are also called cultures) can for the first time view a really existing shared world beyond. From now on, we are faced with a transcendence that Earthlings have themselves accomplished, and that can be distinguished from traditional, symbolically coded religious or metaphysical instances of transcendence by its allowing for reliable two-way communication. The metaphysical asymmetry between divine transcendence and terrestrial participation in such transcendence is replaced by the positional asymmetry between the space station and ground control. Under such an arrangement, the ability to hear voices from on high no longer has any ecstatic implications. It can thus be said that space travel has discovered the most elegant solution to the oldest metaphysical problem: it has solved the riddle of the ontological discontinuity between above and below by positing a continuum between being-in-the-world 1 and being-in-the-world 2. This is hardly speculation, and can be confirmed by what we already know with certainty on a practical level.

Even more important, however, is that the same intelligence regime prevails above and below in the new two-way transcendence. Thus the crew below can immediately take the crew above at their word, namely because the latter's view of Earth has the advantage of an off-center position, yet remains embedded in the same ontological continuum – the positions in this continuum are in principle reversible, in contrast to religious transcendence. If I am speaking with God, I am praying. If God speaks to me in a booming voice, I am schizophrenic. In contrast, if I hear Thomas Reiter or Hans Schlegel speaking German in outer space, I can conclude that all systems on board are running smoothly. Likewise, I can adopt the astronaut's view of the world, because, as noted, the perspectives in the ontological continuum are interchangeable – and even more importantly: there is a coherence of intelligence. What the astronauts know, see, and feel is also something that I can know, see, and feel for myself. If our witness up there, a rather matter-of-fact man, let us assume, is not able to conceal how deeply moved he is by the planet's phenomenal unity when he looks down on Earth, then his emotion is also valid for me.

At this point, the world-historical significance of manned space travel in the perigean realm has at least been suggestively outlined. Its implications are literally immeasurable, insofar as space travel dramatically enhances the human being's position on a globalized planet. It offers proof that technology has set a civilizing process in motion that will lead far beyond anything that might be established by cross-cultural and interfaith dialogues. While the advocates of monotheism will spend the next hundred years arguing over the convergences and divergences of their systems, astronautics has already provided a pragmatic form of universal transcendence, which orbits all Earth-based life forms and belief systems from an equal distance and surveys them equitably.

To understand this, we must remember that the fabrication or revelation of the gods in early Asian and Mesopotamian cultures served an extremely important psycho-political goal. The gods above came into circulation when human beings grew accustomed to thinking that their lives were continually being observed by an intelligence that was as all-knowing as it was all-watching, an intelligence that also had the power to present everyone with the moral balance of their activity *post mortem*. Every advanced culture is based on the idea that an external observing intelligence exists that is able to comprehend all life processes synchronously, even those that hide away in the darkness of ignorance or ill will.

The elevation of a divine observing intelligence is accompanied by the corresponding figure of an observed intelligence – since antiquity this has been called the soul or, in somewhat more modern terms, a conscience. To have a conscience means to know that one is observed from a deep off-center position and pervaded by it. God is traditionally a deep observer, for whom all facts lie on the same surface. He sees everything synchronously and from all sides, whether they are above or within. Incidentally, if the modern world has curbed religion, this is not least because individuals have reclaimed a right to privacy – that is, a form of the world in which even God, if there is a God, may only enter after receiving permission.

As to observation from above, space travel has obviously assumed at least this much of divine activity and transferred it to technological systems (observation satellites) and natural intelligence (human beings on board space stations). This act of transference partially explains their significance, which will last for centuries. Human entrusting of its off-center observation to its own intelligence based in outer space has allowed us to succeed in representing the external partner of conscience, overwhelmingly with technological means. This yields results that cannot continue to be entirely ignored for long. Education, both today and in future, aims to cultivate an awareness of the world that can in fact only develop if the authority of off-center observation is deep enough to be able to form a counterbalance to the egocentricity of local interests. Space travel thus attains a significance that can only be compared to that of the drama in which gods emerged, three or four thousand years ago, throughout the first regional empires.

Human beings in the global age are again looking up at the night-time sky. However, they do not merely believe that they are being observed, they know it, and in taking this knowledge seriously they become capable of acting as their conscience dictates. The images that our deep observer sends us speak a clear language. They speak to our conscience regarding the Earth. The unconscionable, however, must know that their lack of a conscience is already visible from outer space. Such images of the unconscionable can justifiably be presented as incriminating evidence in a trial against those who still wish to know nothing.

8

THE PERSISTENT RENAISSANCE

The Italian Novella and News of Modernity

For Hubert with love

Our excursion into the sources of the modern European awareness of happiness and misfortune should begin in the fateful and
auspicious fourteenth century, when the first indications of a still-
influential transformation in the mode of human being-in-the-world
were heralded. From this point on, there were signs that humans no
longer simply have a natural history in which the same things always
happen. But they are just as little able to exist as mere participants in
God's history with them, which left its mark on the Christian calendar. A third kind of historicity becomes evident here, which could be
called a humanized natural history – and that involves nothing less
than the integration of natural history into human history.

This third type of history obviously only came into its own in the
late twentieth century, and it is hard to see how it might end. The idea
of civilization's responsibility for the climate and indeed for global
environmental conditions is on everyone's mind, ever since human
beings in industrial nations became aware of their impact on the
Earth's ecology and on its biosphere and atmosphere, due to their
technological ways of life. And yet nearly everyone is also aware
that the discovery that human beings actively affect the climate – in
the broadest sense of the term – stretches at least as far back as the
fourteenth century. We fail to properly understand the so-called
Renaissance if we do not recognize the degree to which the oft-cited
"discovery of the world and of the human being" was connected to
steps that were taken in order to explicitly shape both symbolic and
natural environments. In fact, from this time in European culture
on, we find attempts to conceive a common history of morality

and atmosphere. My talk today will be concerned with this nascent awareness and with the traces that it left behind in documents of the time.

I would like to cite the poet and philosopher Giovanni Boccaccio (1313–75) as key witness to what I am calling the discovery of the environment from the spirit of the plague. In *The Decameron*, which was completed in 1353 and literally means "ten-day journal," Boccaccio sketched the outlines of what we have been discussing here as clearly as possible. In this opus, sometimes considered a frivolous book of anecdotes by those who are blinded by prudishness, he appeals to an audience of women with the explicit intention to heal them of the worst feminine illness, that of melancholy – which, according to him, arises from fixating on unattainable objects, and that can only be overcome by gradually redirecting our thoughts to amusing and achievable objects. The stories that Boccaccio calls the hundred novellas or novellettes are mainly intended for such women – they might even be called fables or parables or histories.

The frame story of *The Decameron* makes clear that Boccaccio has more in mind than a poetical gynecology. He is concerned with regenerating a society in ruins by using an exemplary cure, whose administration is supposed to allow us to again learn the art of living well – or as Pampinea, the beautiful and clever organizer of the main group in this book, puts it: We should not hesitate, even when confronted by the worst misfortune, to rationally avail ourselves of the remedy (*remedii*) that is suited for the preservation of our life (*alla conservazione della nostra vita*), according to the principles of natural law (*natural ragione*) that keep watch over the good life for all mortals (*il ben vivere d'ogni mortale*). The natural law of cheerfulness is here given pride of place. Morality and hygiene directly converge in such cheerfulness. Immunological ethics could never be more appropriate than in regard to the immense catastrophe of the fourteenth century that was known as the Black Death, a calamitous wave that originated in Asia and spread across Europe. There was widespread uncertainty regarding its causes, whether it was the result of the influence of celestial bodies or whether it should be attributed to the righteous fury of God, outraged by human misdeeds. Boccaccio makes clear that in the face of this calamity, human arts, medicine in particular, failed just as miserably as religious consolations. As a correspondent who ventured to the very front lines, he compiled a report on what happened in those days of horror:

> I say, then, that the years [of the era] of the fruitful Incarnation of the Son of God had attained to the number of one thou-

sand three hundred and forty-eight, when into the notable city of Florence, fair over every other of Italy, there came the death-dealing pestilence [P. S. – we should note the rhyming of the Italian adjectives that are here rendered as "fruitful" and "death-dealing" – *fruitiferra* and *mortiferra* – as though the author wished to indicate discreetly that the second event was enough to call the first into question] . . . many were the counsels given for the preservation of health nor yet humble supplications . . . made unto God by devout persons . . . this pestilence was the more virulent for that, by communication with those who were sick thereof, it gat hold upon the ound, no otherwise than fire upon things dry or greasy, whenas they are brought very near thereunto . . . one day . . . the rags of a poor man, who had died of the plague, being cast out into the public way, two hogs came up to them and having first, after their wont, rooted amain among them with their snouts . . . then, in a little while, after turning round and round, they both, as if they had taken poison, fell down dead upon the rags with which they had in an ill hour intermeddled. . . . And an infinite number of times it befell that, two priests going with one cross for some one, three or four biers, borne by bearers, ranged themselves behind the latter, and whereas the priests thought to have but one dead man to bury, they had six or eight, and whiles more. Nor therefore were the dead honoured with aught of tears or candles or funeral train . . . so great was the cruelty of heaven (and in part, peradventure, that of men) that, between March and the following July, what with the virulence of that pestiferous sickness and the number of sick folk ill tended or forsaken in their need, through the fearfulness of those who were whole, it is believed for certain that upward of an hundred thousand human beings perished within the walls of the city of Florence . . .[1]

Our correspondent's observations yield a picture of an urban society that was acutely disintegrating. Shops remained closed, field work was neglected, palaces were emptied and fell into the hands of plunderers and apocalyptic revelers, domestic animals were scared away, even the most loyal dog was left behind by its master. Even worse, parents abandoned their sick children, while panic and shamelessness reigned inside houses and in the plazas. Boccaccio's *bon mot*, according to which the healthiest people ate breakfast with their comrades in Florence only to then dine with their dead relatives in the next world, bears witness to just how much the human attitude toward life was in free fall.

Boccaccio counterposes his parallel novella-society to all of these calamitous events. Two miles from the plague-stricken city, on a hill with a panoramic vista of the Tuscan countryside, we encounter modernity's first aesthetic republic, in fact we even encounter the first counterculture,[2] composed of seven young women and three young men, all of whom were raised well and came from good families. In the church of Santa Maria Novella, they together hatch a plot to remain cheerful and courteous, and resolve to devote themselves to the regeneration of a life in ruins – which they achieve by obtaining a kind of nourishment [*Lebensmittel*] whose true significance is revealed when we see that the strange kind of nourishment they have in mind involves *narrating* – to put it more precisely: narrating novellas, *novellare*. The stories may derive from ancient sources, so long as the narrators give them a new point. They may be drawn from the present, provided that something remarkably stimulating occurs.

This revisionary [*novellierende*] activity should be more closely examined, since most of what, in later centuries, is characterized as "providing information" emerges from it (something that I can only suggestively indicate here). What Boccaccio presents us with is nothing more and nothing less than the emergence of modern information from the principle of reanimation. This virtually amounts to the discovery of mental immune systems. When these function as they are supposed to, they allow the morals of certain stories to be synthesized and immediately converted into an enhancement of a group's social and erotic fitness.

What is the relation between the stories we have mentioned and this revisionary activity? Ten of them are to be narrated each day, so that after ten days the number of stories reached would be one hundred. Did Boccaccio, as has sometimes been suspected, really wish to counterpose one hundred episodes of human comedy to the one hundred cantos of the *Divine Comedy*? Did he in fact embark on an intellectual adventure that centuries later came to be known as secularization – and did he perceive the risks of this endeavor so clearly that he thus interrupted the stream of narration on those days of passion, Friday and Saturday, in order to soften the contrast between the spirit of sacred stories and the principles of his earthly therapy? This would explain why the narrative framework of *The Decameron* comprises fourteen days in the country, with ten days of narrative, after which the young people dissolve their therapy group, return to Florence, and re-immerse themselves in the life of a society on the mend.

Boccaccio's sober perspective on the Florentine plague allowed him to see clearly the catastrophe's social and metaphysical implications: the epidemic tore apart the symbolic fabric that had previously held together the life of the Christian faithful. The world of pious legends, as Jacobus de Voragine had compiled them at the end of the thirteenth century in his *Golden Legend*, suddenly seemed as slight as dream-gossamer that had withered into dust. Familiarity with the Bible and Christian fables was quite evidently no match for the collapse of the real – as we have seen, praying was just as ineffective as fleeing, retreating inside to keep the infectious storm at bay was no more helpful than letting oneself go. The symbolic order as a whole teetered on the brink of collapse, the pillars of rational hope tumbled down, all at once we were confronted by a dim God, a God to whom one could no longer meaningfully pray, since in his nebulous wrath he had resolved to annihilate half of Europe's population within a single year. The Gulf Stream of religious illusion, which had to this point regulated the climate in our latitudes, came to a standstill, and anyone who was interested in promoting half-tolerable ways of life had to look around for alternative sources of inspiration to stimulate the will to live.

This very stimulus was precisely what was expected from the novellas that the young men and women were narrating to each other, in their civilized cloister on the hill in front of the agonizing city. Their apparent innocuousness belies the seriousness of taking total responsibility for the continuation and advancement of life. The poetry of the plague demands that we say *La vita è bella*, even if catastrophe-monks would not like to hear it. In one of the darkest hours in human history, in which even the gospel could no longer break through the onslaught of bad news, novellas take on a para-evangelical role. They disseminate the good news that, despite everything, there is always an art of life in the world that promises a new beginning – starting with a philosophical affirmation of the right to life (*la conservazione della nostra vita*) that is conveyed by a vital wisdom found in the inspiring examples we set for each other. Such wisdom culminates in a zest for life that is then propagated in the free and easy, uninhibited fellowship of societies. This is what the beautiful Pampinea has in mind, when she speaks of the *ben vivere d'ogni mortale*,[3] a formulation from ancient philosophy given a new resonance. On the hill above Florence, the earliest human right was articulated – the right to news reports that are better than what is actually happening, the right to stories that show us that we should never quit exercising our intelligence. It is the human right to poetry for creatures who require regeneration. Whoever demands to not hear news that is exasperating invokes this right.

We now understand that Boccaccio, who appealed to women shackled by domestic duties and menaced by melancholy, was actually speaking to future European generations. For him, *novellare* signifies an activity that will be essential to the European custom of life-giving stories. Their narration and retelling formed an alternate warming stream that has since proved to be crucial for our regeneration and reanimation. From the fourteenth century onward, this stream has continuously flowed through our civilization. If this continent has been devastated by recurrent plagues up to the present day, both literally and metaphorically, the warming stream that was then but a trickle now flows freely and, depending on the situation, can help determine the symbolic, aesthetic, and moral climate of Europeans and the cultures they have spawned.

A second distinctively European faith can be discerned in this stream, a faith that twentieth-century philosophy suggested we call "hope." It could also be called the will to culture. It expresses itself as a trust in reason that renounces proofs of God's existence, as long as stories and news reports can be found that prove that human beings need not remain impotent and foolish, without rights, if only they are properly encouraged. Every story told in this spirit is a gospel *en miniature*, a bit of good news from an open world in which human beings retain their claim to happiness with cleverness, cunning, and presence of mind. What is needed after the plague is not so much venerable formulas and rites, but glad tidings that report of discrete successes by those seeking happiness. These micro-gospels help survivors again lift their gaze to the earthly horizon. The Boccaccio-principle, as I would like to call it, makes this alliance against the threat of being pulled down in the mire explicit. Its practitioners not only brace themselves against the "dissolute temptations of regression and death," which later arose from a certain strain of German Romanticism, they tend even more to oppose discouragement in general, which is always already more than half the battle.

Boccaccio presumably did not know the circumstances under which the plague was able to arrive in Florence: it first spread to the Mediterranean, after the Tartars shot plague-infested corpses over the walls with heavy catapults while besieging the Genoese trade settlement in Kaffa in 1346. After the epidemic had subsided in Europe and trade resumed, a severe plague then erupted as lethal pathogens were introduced into Florence along with the commercial goods from Kaffa.

Our excursion into the fourteenth century can end on this note. We now understand that the Renaissance is much more than a stylistic change in the arts or an increase of interest in ancient authors. Renaissance is essentially an endeavor to sabotage resignation. Civilization after the plague is always on its mind. Its goal is overall regeneration. It leads to a concentration of skill against formlessness and of knowledge against confusion. It involves a revolutionary transformation of culture, which amounts to nothing less than a centuries-long plot whose avowed goal is to strike a blow against stupidity and to take the wind out of despair's sails – especially the despair associated with a submissive sympathy for disaster.

Admittedly, the Renaissance's significance can only be appreciated after the Enlightenment of the eighteenth century has kindled a second light – and the enlightenment has with good reason been called an endeavor to sabotage fate. The Enlightenment, for its part, can only be judged on its own merits after a third light has allowed us to see what can be carried over from its plans and brought into tenable civilizing projects, and what have merely been dreams of reason and ideological flashes in the pan. This light is shed on the logical space of the world system from the moment when human beings are compelled to realize how their own activity affects the climate – which does not happen on a mass scale until the last third of the twentieth century. At this point, it does not take much to see that human praxis, at every level of technology and the use of symbols, always also has eco-systemic and immune-systemic implications, which are not merely something to be wary of in the future, but must be managed and organized. I am arguing that we conceive the unity of the modern era as the educational context of globalization, in which we are not only faced with plague after plague, but also shipment after shipment, discovery after discovery, invention after invention, artwork after artwork, theorem after theorem, vaccination after vaccination, experiment after experiment, novella after novella.

Since 1348, Europeans have known that commercial cities are sites of infection. They are dangerous areas that include both welcome and unwelcome contact with others. Their inhabitants have to take a terrifying tutorial whose lesson is that wealth and infection are traveling companions. They must study the difference between revitalization and poisoning from the bottom up. One could almost say that, from this point on, Europe was transformed into an experimental space in which the unity and difference between what is life-saving and what is lethal is put to the test. In this sense, Boccaccio's Florentines were the first to learn the rules for playing the game of globalization. An urban society that does everything to obtain goods and to circulate them, without first clearly recognizing its own role, also makes travel arrangements for those unwelcome passengers that since the nineteenth century have been known as microbes – among which are not a few visitors that merit the title of *mortifero* to the highest degree. Since then, the distinction between welcome and unwelcome imports has been one of the most important tasks of civilizing acumen. In terms of lethal imports, Europeans discover what were later called side effects – the secondary effects of actions in particular and in general.[4]

It is indicative of the intelligence of Italian city-state administrations that they responded to the discovery of the dangerous alliance between plague and commodities by establishing quarantine stations at a remove from the commercial harbor. The quarantine island of *Lazaretto Nuovo* in Venice, which is still well known today, allowed that capable commercial city to reduce its death toll by a quarter in comparison with less-protected cities, from the fifteenth century on. Yet it was compelled to suffer a severe epidemic for fifteen to twenty years as the price of an unavoidable tribute to cosmopolitanism. Even in 1756 – when Goethe was already seven years old – approximately 10,000 people were sent into quarantine on the island, during one of the last severe epidemics. Death in Venice was for a while more of a business risk than an artistic choice. Yet, since the fifteenth century, cities in lagoons have been sought out so that we might consciously and deliberately expose ourselves to the invigorating agents that were to be found there at that time: new forms of knowledge, which require the wealth of metropolises, and of the arts, whose splendor is conveyed to the world. Thus it is no wonder if Jakob Fugger, known afterwards as "the Rich," was sent to Venice at the age of 19 not long before he was to go to monastic school, in the year 1478, the same year in which his older brother Markus succumbed to an obscure epidemic in Rome. He proceeded on his mission without concern for the fact that two other brothers of his, Hans and Andreas, had already perished from strange fevers in Venice, surely a bad omen. What the *Tedeschi* were able to learn in this city was the new written art of accounting and the new risky art of credit, which in any case made the trip worthwhile, if one survived it.

In these easygoing times where it was easy to lose one's life, it was unnecessary to visit Italy to directly experience the risks of the modern age: Jakob's fourth brother, Peter Fugger, also older than him, died at a young age in Nuremberg around this same time. The Frankish city turned out to be a place where the plague set up shop for a season. In 1494, the young Albrecht Dürer fled from Nuremberg while the plague ravaged the town, but because he had already been exposed to beneficial infections from the past century, agents that stimulate the desire for skill, artistic perfection, and sensational achievements, it is no wonder that even Dürer chose to head to Venice. He is probably not the last of those who came with vague hopes and departed ready for anything.

Having said this, I would like to argue for the following thesis: at the beginning of the modern era in Europe, which at the same time heralds the age of globalization, a structural transformation of belief occurs, through which modern activism supplants medieval passivism – despite every maneuver of the passivist party, today better known by its denominational name, Catholicism. Renaissance human beings did not yet know anything of the late-modern heresy in which the human being wishes to view itself as an autonomous subject. To them, the human being was and remained a creature subject to influence – not to say a plaything for supernatural powers, a medium through which various transpersonal factors operate. At the same time, they begin to realize that whoever allows himself to be played with also puts himself at stake. And as we learn from the philosophy of freedom in the twentieth century: everything hinges on making something out of that which has made us, thus among the first agents of the modern age the implicit maxim is formulated: it is up to us to play with what plays with us. In a similar vein, Shakespeare could say in *As You Like It* that all the world's a stage and men and women but players on it. However, so that contemporaries on this stage would get the right idea, globographers set to work, Waldseemüller, Apian, Mercator Senior and Junior, and all the rest. Imitation of nature in those days meant the depiction of the Earth as a clearly structured sphere. It is symbolically fortuitous that the world's greatest playwright wanted to show what happens when human beings play with that which plays with them, on a stage ironically called Globe Theatre.

We here touch on the deeper source of a term that has become common today, that of "global players." Since Columbus' voyage in 1492, there has been an intellectual avant-garde in Europe who understand that it is the Earth itself that wishes to play with us. Ever since its spherical shape was definitively established, human beings have had to inhabit a ball and play catch with it. This paradoxical task is not evident to everyone, and even today there are people who do not want to believe what the rules of the game have been since Columbus – they cannot see the ball coming, and they refuse to either catch or to throw it. But if the globe itself plays with us, we must play with the globe *nollens vollens*. In the spring of the fateful year 1492 the young Martin Behaim, returning from business in Lisbon, constructed his famous globe in Nuremberg, the first in Europe, to make clear to his countrymen that, if all the world is a stage, then in future the boards of this stage will be the planks of a seaworthy ship. Seafaring is now our fate. Only the seaworthy soul can still keep up with the demands of the modern age. Now the cry is raised: board the ships, you philosophers, and to sea, you believers! The ocean is the first internet, shipbuilding is its age comprehended in thought.

As we can easily see, these observations concern technologies just as much as mentalities. They thus have significant theological consequences. We are faced with nothing less than a shuffling of positions within the holy Trinity. The Middle Ages, not wishing to end, were devoted to an exalted *Imitation of Christ*, exemplified in the devotional book by Thomas à Kempis. In contrast, the modern age, wishing to begin, lapsed into thoughts that one could to some extent imitate even the Father. Whoever beholds the Son has a clear example of the power of the capacity for suffering – and since suffering is never over for human beings, anyone who is looking for help can find a master of suffering who will provide endless encouragement for one's own practice. In contrast, whoever orients him- or herself to the Father is watching a creator at work, and then it is enough to realize that creation, for its part, is never at an end, and to appeal to human beings with a new principle of mastery.

Such a principle aims at nothing less than the participation of creatures in creation. Now the ascent of the human spirit from pious impotence to a more hands-on shared creativity becomes the order of the day, becomes indeed the order of the epoch. Generally, this *imitatio Patris* is cloaked by a platitude that advocates the imitation of nature. The naive might like to believe that registering finished natural objects is what is meant, objects that the eyes then sensuously recognize. Those in the know, however, see that it is something much greater, namely that it is a matter of the generative power of latent nature, which is to be imitated insofar as it is the womb of all things. To invent now means to proceed beyond nature by means of nature. Ever since the principle of creativity took root in our civilization, the thought of a second nature has become technologically and aesthetically acute: this thought is no longer merely concerned with the cultural practices that are transmitted to us in flesh and blood, but constitutes a second creation. Whoever speaks the word "creativity" and actually knows what they are talking about means a civilizing cycle of innovation that will be accompanied by unforeseeable perspectives. If we were asked how we would date ourselves in the history of things, we would have to answer truthfully that, from this point forward, we have lived in an age in which the womb and production converge. We revise nature, we stand at the beginning of the second week of Creation, on the Monday of the human being.

Even the third member of the Trinity is subject to an equally subversive transformation. There is closer examination of the Spirit, of which it is said that it blows where it wishes. The wind directions of inspiration are studied, as the wind patterns over the Atlantic were studied, before we might venture so far that coasts were no longer visible. Indeed, a system of enthusiasm-currents is now discovered, governed by quite peculiar meteorological laws – in future, we will no longer be able to ignore such currents in our enterprises. We have now come to understand that the Spirit not only blows where it wishes, but blows where it can, and it can blow best where the human capacity for art, which for the most part can be learned, encounters chance, which wishes to be apprehended in passing – in fortune's blink of an eye, which only looks at you for a second to examine whether you are able to return its gaze. Over the course of this inquiry, the hidden Trinity of the Renaissance takes shape: it will henceforth consist of the Father, Son, and Fortuna.

Perhaps the best way to explain Renaissance culture's internal propulsive drive is to think of it as a change of meaning for that Roman goddess who, in the early days of the Empire, kept watch over the military campaigns of emperors and the victories of gladiators. The Middle Ages inherently aimed to disabuse human beings of their belief in Fortuna – with its all-too-human wavering between magic and fatalism. Instead of such faith, human beings were to be oriented to the values of a stable and just heaven. Hence the chronic insulting of Fortuna as a fickle and unjust mistress who derisively leads her admirers around in circles. According to medieval authorities, only fools would wish to ride on her carousel. At the beginning of the modern age, however, the winds change course, and we now see beautiful goddesses maintaining an equilibrium in their cosmic spheres, equipped with one of the oldest symbols of the merchant's fortune, the wind-swelled sail – as one sees in the Punta della Dogana in Venice, where the nude woman exposes her rear end to the doges in St. Mark's Square for reasons that are not entirely clear. We are now in the age in which Machiavelli can teach that Fortuna is a woman who likes to be handled roughly,[5] which is why she is fond of favoring the one who grabs her forcefully enough at the right moment.

The fact that wealth is still known today in Europe as "fortunes" (in French and English) is one of the lasting results of modern Fortuna-theology – such fortunes do not refer to a fixed family inheritance at all, but recent wealth that has effervescently accumulated, acquired in its owner's lifetime and by its owner's efforts at the fortune-goddess's gambling table. *Fortunatus*, titular hero of a widely published German chapbook that first appeared in Augsburg in 1509, is one of her most popular supporters. This chapbook provides an answer to the question of how the novella north of the Alps was doing. Jakob the Rich liked to ironically skim through it and shake his head from time to time. We immediately see how a bit of fairy-tale morality is here smuggled in: we are supposed to believe that the hero, a young man from Cyprus who was lost and in distress, encountered the maiden Fortune in a forest clearing in Thuringia. It is an ancient custom of ours to encourage people to believe that all you need to do is get lost in the right forest at the right time, and then the treasures of the world will be yours. Six virtues are granted to the young woman from the "influence of heaven," so she says, from which her protégé may choose between: wisdom, wealth, strength, health, beauty, and a long life – and in opting for wealth, he points out that even life in this country, scarcely 15 years after Columbus' voyage, prefers to hustle down here in a world that has been extended and opened up, rather than to keep trying to enter the beyond through self-denial's eye of the needle.

In light of these speculative suggestions, we can now more clearly state the significance of the Renaissance belief that human beings exist in a field of influences held permanently in tension. Fortuna is the president, as it were, who stands before the modern parliament of influences. Under her presidency, ways of life develop that need to cleverly handle uncertainties if they are to survive. They are thoroughly based on the axiom that the human being is neither free nor unfree. In an absolute sense, human beings are neither masters nor servants, they are neither omnipotent nor impotent, they continually oscillate between forces that help and ones that harm. The human being is always the third party in fate's coalition, and always remains caught in a net of powers and tendencies – and pulls itself out of its entanglement more or less energetically, thread by thread, in order to weave its own garment from what had ensnared it.

Insights such as these sound very familiar to present-day humans, since after the remission of the Enlightenment delirium in the eighteenth and nineteenth centuries we have become increasingly accustomed to the idea that we are not masters and owners of the world, after all, neither as individuals nor collectively. When everything goes as it is supposed to, we are mainly users of confusing devices that extend the scope of our action and that oddly enough often function as we wish and expect them to, even if they do not always function this way. Hardly anyone today can still imagine surveying the world as a whole from a sovereign vantage point – we are satisfied if we have instruments that allow us to navigate in conditions of poor visibility and in stormy seas. We have set aside the great maps of the history of philosophy and enrolled in a course on Chaos theory. All of this leads to us feel that Renaissance human beings were our immediate predecessors. In fact, they were the first to understand that human beings can learn to negotiate with their own stars. Thus one should not misconstrue the early modern fascination with astrology as a sign of increasing passive fatalism. It rather very much bears witness to the emergent sense of a kind of thought in which we must recognize constellations in order to intervene in them with our own maneuvers. Thus it could justifiably be said that stars have their own tendencies, but do not compel us. We know that this is actually true, because this is precisely the case with conjunctures of fortune and business.

At this point, we can now return to the idea of the novella. It should be clear by now that we are no longer merely concerned with a new literary genre among others. The novella's eclipsing of legends certainly represents a victory of the interesting over the edifying, the triumph of curiosity over piety. But this is only part of the story. The novella is actually the mother of the news. As the new Monday is a human creation, so is the human being's Tuesday devoted to the publishing of novellas. These publications do not merely report on the small triumphs of everyday intelligence over circumstances. Rather, they view the entire world that is to be discovered and culti-vated as a source of revitalization from which enlightened recipients will never cease drawing creative inspiration. The modern world is a workshop for lightening up. Whoever reports on it, or pub-lishes reports on it, is connected to a gospels-generator that gives off sparks of innovation – assuming that the world does us the favor of confirming the archetypical prejudice that we harbor as participants in modernization: that the new is simultaneously the good, that what is newer is better, and that what is newest is best.

Of course, the world only does us this favor at remarkable moments, which is why modern human beings must get used to the fact that good and bad news arrives on our doorstep without having been sorted out. This even applies to the novella of novellas, the news of the discovery of the new world, which after 1507 was known as "America," due to a cartographer's error. Columbus' ships had hardly returned to Spain in March 1493 before a severe epidemic of syphilis broke out among the soldiers who besieged Naples shortly thereafter, including some members of Columbus' voyage. After the decimated army had disbanded, the epidemic overwhelmed all of Europe until the end of the century. Albrecht Dürer carved the first precise depiction of a syphilitic on a wooden engraving from the year 1496. The bad news was that a (virtually) new plague had entered the world – the good news was that the art of depiction was not going to stop, even for syphilis. Whoever lives in the modern age had to wait for more good news: from 1910 on, the horrors of syphilis were alleviated by Paul Ehrlich's Salvarsan, and from 1942 on, Alexander Fleming's penicillin was developed for controllable use.

The play of good news and bad news,[6] which travel on the same freighter and are broadcast on the same frequency, has defined modern life ever since. Anyone who releases news reports must know that he or she creates a human climate with them. Our moods are produced on the catapults of information. The true news report, daughter of the novella, is a message that has the right to be disseminated, insofar as it represents the unity of information and animation. Novellas will no longer be proclaimed from the pulpits – they are disseminated through their own networks and owing to their intrinsic qualities.

It is no accident that the sixteenth-century Reformation succeeded after the invention of a printing press with movable type. The dissemination of the gospel into various vernaculars is the prototype of benign symbolic epidemics, whose proliferation becomes the responsibility of enterprising humans themselves. Yet now the Bible itself can be seen in a different light. Was the New Testament not the novella of the suffering son of God, which provided support to others who were suffering? As soon as we realize that creation is not over, and feel the mood that corresponds to this realization, do we not then obviously infer that the editing of works and texts that are necessary for human salvation cannot be concluded? After and alongside the venerable Old Testament and the salvific New Testament, must not a third, Newer Testament be written that would discuss the events of the second week – all the wonders of ongoing creation and the adventures of burgeoning arts? Does it not then seem even more astonishing if new publishers, who know how to trigger epidemics of the wonderful with tiny letters of lead, began to look for stimulating materials where they were to be found, under the circumstances – in the stories of human beings who experienced something remarkable and worthy of thought as they negotiated with their own stars?

We can venture a definition for all this: Renaissance is the Newer Testament's age of editing. Its manifest symptom is the quarrel between the ancients and the moderns, which was only apparently decided in the latter's favor. As we now understand, it is impossible to conclude this quarrel on its own terms. In reality, a second quarrel is at issue – that between partisans of what is here called the Newer Testament and those who profess older revelations. Traditional accounts of the relation between reason and faith fail to adequately explain this friction – and however much we would like to welcome Benedict XVI's Regensburg address on the rationality of faith, owing to its conciliatory overtones and its reasonableness, it is nevertheless beside the point.

The persistent Renaissance, which defines the modern era's implicit calendar, develops into a network of infectious stories, animations that deserve to be repeated, and expansive endeavors that are articulated by the age of globalization's knowledge of the world. This testament – forever informal and open – is composed of a host of micro-gospels set against a dark background. With their turbulent streaming, these micro-gospels announce that new intelligences and animating energies, new artificialities are in the world, so as to bring human beings under their influence. The first providers of this network were royal, bourgeois, and academic libraries, which housed everything that could be known and disseminated. Their readers formed a new nation of the faith, who essentially wished to become a new nation of the novella, a nation of knowledge, a people engaged in endeavors. They founded the Republic of Better Knowledge, whose legacy we have inherited. What is more, these knowledgeable predecessors of ours never nurtured the illusion that they were autonomous subjects. All of their knowledge began with the realization that human life meant existing in streams [*Flüsse*] and under influences [*Einflüssen*].

As we have noted, the figure of the player who even negotiates with the influences to which he or she is supposed to readily and willingly succumb could only emerge in this climate. The figure of the publisher who invests his own financial resources into the business of influence, by publishing novellas and news reports, is one of the first manifestations of such playfulness. Publishers thereby use their own financial resources to increase playfulness and channel their readers' wishes toward participation in worldly miracles. The vital figure of the artist who creates marvels and new natures now emerges. These marvelous prodigies are supposed to shine like the stars of a second heaven into contemporary life and into the lives of future generations. After preludes that stretch back to the thirteenth century, the figures of the wholesale merchant and the banker then emerge, whose significance primarily consists in the fact that they hone influence into a precise technique. Anyone investing in commodities has to recognize that they are merely hypotheses on which influences might captivate potential shoppers. Anyone providing credit must bear in mind that gold is nothing more than an abstract and universal influential energy, which circulates through human calculations and wishes, converting them into concrete and discrete influence.

These patterns all merge into the figure of the enterprising prince, who embodies the modern age's human ideal, *uomo universale*. His combination of power and intellect bears witness to the possibility of new possibilities. He allows us to anticipate what a complete life would look like. Lorenzo de Medici, who was already dubbed *Magnifico* by his contemporaries, exemplifies such a player whose moves raise the game to a higher level. He did this by making his own existence into a forum where intelligences and talents of all kinds could meet. He talks to intellectuals and engages in the business of his time, establishing himself as medium, as host, as matchmaker, and as a patron of the arts (we would today call such a person a networker) who would like to construct a playing field on which the best can play with what plays with them.

9

HEIDEGGER'S POLITICS

Postponing the End of History

The politicization of Heidegger exegesis has reached a point that is unparalleled in the history of ideas. And because the political interpretation of Heidegger is no longer content to treat what happened in 1933 as an episode, but often considers it to be the key to his oeuvre as a whole, this isolated incident is supposed to be proof of a total philosophical catastrophe. After the upheavals of the twentieth century, philosophy has lost the privilege of existing in a realm that was somehow above politics. Anyone presuming to speak of "Heidegger's politics" can assume that it is a real issue and that it has been properly identified, although the findings call for careful interpretation, now more than ever, after the studies of Alexander Schwan, Pierre Bourdieu, Silvio Vietta, Dieter Thomä, Philippe Lacoue-Labarthe, John Caputo, and Peter Trawny, to mention only a few of the many commentators. Even so, such an approach is at odds with testimonials from numerous colleagues, students, and others who were associated with Heidegger, who have assured us based on first-hand experience that he was "fundamentally" apolitical. To decide that Heidegger was apolitical is not entirely implausible, since we otherwise attribute an inappropriately commonplace or pragmatic conception of politics to him, and because explaining Heidegger's behavior *ad personam*, as a typical case of "fallibility in matters outside of his expertise,"[1] would have us believe that he was similar to Plato, the failed philosopher-king and reformist pedagogue. On such a view, we would not be surprised if Heidegger were one day to be asked "Back to Syracuse now, my friend?" In what follows, I will explain why we do Heidegger no favors if we try to defend him by claiming that he was "apolitical," as if a philosopher's errors or poor decisions should not even be taken seriously, indeed precisely when such errors and poor decisions are suspected to have not been simple oversights, but are rather to be understood as essential elements of his thought.

In what follows, we should read the formulation "Heidegger's politics" in a threefold way: First of all, it characterizes Heidegger's own approaches to the political sphere – approaches that could be characterized as actually quite extreme, if not antipodean, which is why a "German mandarin's" wildly inept attempts at political intervention will here be expressed in the profane dimension of national and ideological conflicts. Next, Heidegger's role in a scenario from the history of philosophy will be described under the same heading, which includes the qualifications necessary for a philosophy to assume an official position in political theory. Finally, "Heidegger's politics" also signifies his occasional interventions into political theory in the 1930s, as well as his resignation from a position that he unsuccessfully tried to hold. The concept of politics is thus being employed in a polysemous manner and on a number of levels, in keeping with its contemporary usage, since it includes a programmatic dimension in addition to its practical sense in everyday conversation, so that we finally reach what we might with good reason call its metaphysical and meta-political significance.

9.1 Boredom and the Authentic Collective

The term "Heidegger's politics" initially indicates that a young Roman Catholic intellectual from the post-First World War era, marked by his origins in the countryside and his academic studies, participated in a great event in the history of mentalities, which I have suggested we call the "apocalypse of the real."[2] This event obviously began long before 1918: we could even say that it became acute after Hegel's death, when, in a quarrel over the master's legacy, a metaphysical left was formed, which aimed to popularize philosophy's profoundest mystery. The Young Hegelians' overt rejection of religion divulged the best-kept secret of ancient wisdom to a bourgeois audience: the esoteric realization that neither God nor gods exist and that the only true world is the actual one we live in yet fail to properly recognize, because our gaze tends to overlook reality in favor of the transcendental. For millennia, the masses and those who were educated but naive allowed themselves to believe that this supposedly true world was to be found in a higher beyond; but now it was time for the real to reclaim the true. Against this backdrop, post-idealists could make a realism from below the order of the day. The names of the four "dysangelists" (as they were called by Eugen

Rosenstock-Huessy) – Marx, Darwin, Nietzsche, Freud – designate the most important positions of the young-realist literature of exposure: when these authors speak of material production, human animality, the will to power, and the masks of the libido, they teach modern minds to believe in the omnipotence and omnipresence of a reality that is built from the bottom up – and is indeed always built so that subtler superstructures remain more or less directly dependent on massive underlying forces. Physiologists, pragmatists, and anthropologists are teachers of descent and retro-scent: they indulge in doctrines of origins and lines of descent, in genealogies that deem us to have come from hirsute ancestors, and forms of pragmatism that bring us down from false heights. The goal is always to reach the terra firma of facts and forces that establish the new era's authority. The reality of what is real will henceforth be derived from bodies, money, and the will to power, as well as movements drawn from these fundamental forces.

Perhaps we should trace the "apocalypse of the real" back to the French Revolution, because after the long Christian intermission we once again find a pragmatism clad in neo-Roman fashion as Europe's prevailing *modus vivendi*. Its occult center was the naturalistic esotericism of the Marquis de Sade, for whom the ultimate truth of pleasure-giving matter is only revealed to uncommonly free spirits who are willing to become media of nature by professing crime as the most advanced technique for happiness. There is no need to explain why the great majority of new realists avoided such excesses, even if they aspired to be "radical." What nevertheless links them to de Sade is the basic anthropological view that human beings, as creatures of desire, need help to achieve their worldly satisfaction.

It is not our task here to explain in detail how Heidegger became associated with this young-realist trend. We need not concern ourselves with a young scholastic's transformation into a young radical. Biographers have pointed to the deep impression that the works of Luther and Kierkegaard made upon the Catholic Heidegger during the First World War. In addition, it seems certain that he benefited from reading Dostoyevsky in the 1920s and borrowed certain motifs, such as anxiety and boredom, from him.

For us it is enough to note that the entirety of Heidegger's early work, when he left behind his ecclesiastical and scholastic origins, is permeated by a quite idiosyncratic pathos that is both extreme and yet in keeping with the times: he is never closer to the creative source of his conceptual power than when he maps out his exodus from the pseudo-eternity of scholastic knowledge into the turbulent temporality of contemporary existence – an existence entirely lived out beneath the dim light of its own bewilderment [*Ratlosigkeit*] and restlessness [*Rastlosigkeit*]. While engaged in this project, Heidegger develops a powerful explicitness that is a striking proof of his genius. The term "existence" seemed to offer a powerful cutting-edge awareness of time, from early on: because the young-realist notion of existence displays a counter-transcendent turbulence and because it pursues de-eternalization with great dedication, coming down from the de-realized heights of disinterested theory, intent on merging with the present moment (in the sense of Lenin's "becoming concrete"), it is impelled by its own momentum to affirm its belonging to the onward rush of time.

The pathos of de-transcendence [*Ent-Jenseitigung*] leads to a heroic disquietism – a feature that not only marks the culminating phase of Heidegger's thought, but is also a prominent character-istic of European philosophy and artistic work between the world wars.[3] A thinker who wishes to become the medium of his avant-garde work and transforms into the mouthpiece of an apocalypse of the real embraces his "own time" in two ways. First, he declares himself ready to be pervaded by the epoch's unrest. Second, he sinks into a solitary disquiet that emanates from an awareness of his own mortality. What makes an existence exposed to this disquiet unique is thus marked by two exercises in expropriation: The first happens through the loss of a firm standpoint toward or outside of the flux of time, a loss that is affirmed, since realism requires that we flow along with such time. The second comes into play with the thinker's acquiescence in a protracted final self-expropriation that will result in his death. In the course of this self-expropriation, the avant-garde philosopher exchanged the bourgeois academic self with its motto of "I-think-therefore-I-am-I-know-I-exist-for-as-long-as-I-think" for an artistic-heroic self with its attitude of "I-am-dying-but-not-right-at-this-moment-and-want-to-do-some-thing-that-I-deem-thought-provoking." As the earlier young realists of the nineteenth century had helped to engineer the apocalypse of labor and animality, Heidegger, in his own stormy young realist period, distinguished himself by his apocalypse of existential tempo-rality, in which the meaning of existence is disclosed above all from the standpoint of being-toward-death.

Admittedly, Heidegger struggled to convincingly relate the indi-vidual temporalization of being-toward-death (and the completion of the period-of-time-before-death by a project that necessarily includes me) to the collective temporalization of the individual's membership in historic collectives roused to act. Simply put, his thought begins with precisely this problem, an approach that can with some justification be called "Heidegger's politics." Here we are only ever concerned with the question of how I, the individual who has been thrown into a tumultuous world or held into nothingness, "transition" from lapsing into my own death, from my death-span, to the life's work of an overarching collective world history.

The discoverer of the equivalence between being and time is forced into this kind of transition, because he could not limit the existentialization (one could even say the ekstatic qualification) of being-in-time to individuals. In this regard, *Being and Time* has merely a preparatory function, as has often been noted. Yet how to think the history of existence's inclusion in a history of being, indeed how the latter is even to be conceptualized, is something that was by no means clear to Heidegger at that time. In order to make the same decisive opening move (to qualify temporality with the self-enactment or "project" of an ekstatic existence) when thinking through transpersonal historical processes, it was necessary to identify a complex or a collective that would be able to bear essential temporalization on a large scale. This would have to be a collective (in other words, a cultural complex) whose actual existence made it possible to carry out a massively indefensible and undeniable historical task. Having read Dilthey, who pioneered the critique of historical reason, Heidegger knew why the transition from a time of individuals to world-time could not be directly implemented: such a transition can only ever be accomplished indirectly. This is because an individual autobiographical kind of knowing, which illuminates one's own life story as a "context" that understands and projects itself, inherently has the potential for such a transition. In contrast, no single person can experience, recount, and plan for world history as his or her own biography. One would have to be the world spirit to intuit the whole of being as it has unfolded through history into its current state.

Thus it was necessary to find another route to the key process of trans-individual history. As is well known, Heidegger tried out a number of quite distinct, even contradictory, positions and formulations for determining the bearer of collective temporality – beginning with the German people's time of awakening and upheaval, to the ripening time of the artwork (which constructs a world), all the way to the quiet countryside's waiting time, which looks forward to a new revelation or a final god – a god whose manifestation or "passing by" [*Vorbeigang*] will bring the series of apocalypses here below to an end. In each case, Heidegger tries to bridge both qualitative temporalities: if they are to be linked, they must form a plausible passage from the existential temporality of the individual, who has been appointed to die his or her own death and who has constructive, responsible work to do in advance of this, to a collective's ontological temporality, which is needed for bringing about or preserving a historical truth, or a world-formative work.

We will note right away that this transition is ironic. To be sure, existential ontology has made it unmistakably clear that individual mortality has a peculiar temporal structure, which, precisely as existential, distinguishes it from physical and cosmological time, as well as from capitalist time *toto coelo*, no matter the particular civilizing situation (even modern medicine has yet to make very great strides in increasing the natural lifespan). Yet whether similarly clear results will emerge from the temporal structure of historical complexes and collectives remains to be determined. It remains an entirely open question whether further historical missions or "movements" can be formed under all circumstances – or whether "history" as a whole might not have come to an end along with the tasks assigned by it. Who can rule out the possibility that history might at some point transition to another phase that would again be closer to the cyclical temporalities of natural and economic processes than to being tensely stretched to the end in existential-linear fashion? Should this happen, we would lose the "objective" pole of temporal occurrence, and the transition we are looking for, the passage from individual to collective time, would no longer have its bridgehead on the other shore.

In what follows, I would like to argue that all of Heidegger's logical and political troubles are in fact connected to the decline of the public and collective pole of essential temporality. As early as 1928, he recognized that present-day humans cannot even be sure that they are still living in "history," however much they are convinced that they will always be mortal. My claim is that the master from Todtnauberg discovered his own version of the "end of history" or at least the possibility of its end (as Alexander Kojève also did, a short while afterwards), and I will indicate how he tried to avoid the consequences of this discovery.

If something like "Heidegger's politics" really exists, then it would initially refer to the fact that he was a very unconventional participant in the young-realist exodus from the captivation of old Europe by metaphysics, as we have already pointed out. If we recall that philosophy has always aspired to expose the reality of the real and to conceptually articulate it, we can better understand why modern thought must embrace this mission more explicitly than ever before. With unprecedented ferocity, it enters the battle over realism that is just getting underway. Heidegger's avant-garde temporo-logical realism turns out to be more radical than its competitors because, with his unwavering view that existence is being-toward-death, he restored time's position as mistress of being in motion, which had otherwise been completely downplayed and marginalized, had indeed been intentionally denied and humiliated by thought's preference for eternity. A sovereign consignor of fates and a stern transmuter of things, time was thrust into the role of that which is most real of all. Indeed, even all-consuming time, the fury of destruction, now appeared to be even more tragically dark than in Hegel's talk of history as Calvary.[4] Initially, because of time's authority, only the role of a heroic accomplice was open to the philosopher: what he calls resolute existence [zu sich entschlossene Dasein] designates a way of knowing how to be consumed and transmuted. Yet because, as we have seen, existential time cannot be reduced to the span between the not-yet-now and the terminal now of our own death, Heidegger's task is to reconstruct a collective temporality superordinate to, and yet integrating, one's own suspension before death – the very time of "history," from which it is supposed to follow that history does not merely prove to be the transmuter and destroyer of individuals and generations, but also a creator and a project manager, and even the vessel for a wide-ranging eventuation of truth [Wahrheitsgeschehen]. His later conception of the "history of being" [Seinsgeschichte] helps articulate this desideratum.

It is a testimony to Heidegger's conceptual creativity during his most advanced lucid phase (which should probably not be dated much past 1930) that he began to work on a dramatic ontology of reality, after the conclusion of Being and Time. Heidegger discovered a striking feature of any present moment in time, which he went on to call moods [Stimmungen]. A mood is a vat for dyeing, into which existence is immersed, so to speak, and indeed so early on, in such a pervasive manner, and in anticipation of everything further, that the mood that is here absorbed will pre-emptively anticipate any other object that later appears to be objectively given. Anything later encountered as a single object, state of affairs, or situation can only come to light tinged by the operative anticipatory mood. Anyone who wishes to address human beings more profoundly than was typical in traditional philosophy and its development into Enlightenment must start at the pre-objective level and there begin to work on moods. This also brings us close to the great pole of historical eventuation, since only a mood can shed light on the state of history (though not on its course and its goal).

In discovering the topic of moods, Heidegger the academic philosopher changes into Heidegger the metapolitical clinician, or more precisely, he changes into a psychagogue and trainer, whose main task is to prepare his patients for treatment by drawing attention to their most extreme and deepest-rooted preconceptions of existence as a whole, their existential moods. The procedure is based on the quasi-homeopathic principle that patients' symptoms must be intensified to paroxysm before a crisis brings about an end or a recovery.

To put it bluntly, his diagnosis is that contemporary human beings suffer from a generalized diffuseness – a malady that manifests itself in the incapacity to be really convinced by anything, accompanied by the tendency to follow every public uproar and lend an ear to all manner of nonsense. In his new discourse on moods, Heidegger discovers the ontological version of hyperactivity and multiple personality disorder, as it were – which is a rather cursory way to characterize the significance of his findings. Ultimately, moods are only philosophically important because they articulate the first positive link between the individual's being-in-his-own-time and his being-in-the-epoch. First, moods build the bridge (or at least provide support for a possible bridge) from the individual to the collective, insofar as moods well up in a group of people existing at the same time. Second, they provide an orientation that precedes all theory, as well as every "thou shalt" [*Sollen*], insofar as moods are supposed to imply a deepening of prescriptive guidelines from what is "merely" logically and ethically evident to what is pervasively evident in an existential sense, in other words, to being gripped [*Ergriffenheit*]. The term "being gripped," which becomes more significant for Heidegger beginning in the late 1920s, refers to how we are supposed to conceive of an existence that is carried away by the pole of being. Being consciously overcome by a mood, or being gripped, is knowing how to submit, as it were, to what a situation makes evident, something that can be traced from the past into the future.

By 1928–9, Heidegger begins to believe that his work on the temporalization of being by the world-pole has advanced far beyond the preliminary achievements of *Being and Time*. He now has a conceptual framework that allows him to offer a promising articulation of existence in the collective space-time complex of the present. Tellingly, it always comes down to concepts that can describe how we inhabit a drab epoch. The first items to be discussed in his own present day are emptiness, boredom, ambiguity, and a dearth of actual events. If we consider Heidegger's formulations at the end of the 1920s to be fundamental for characterizing the collective milieu, he would have to be considered the genuine discoverer and author of the theory of *posthistoire*. His descriptions of inauthentic existence in the notorious *das Man* chapter of *Being and Time*,[5] as well as his analyses of boredom from the *Grundbegriffe* lectures,[6] leave no doubt that we are presented with a superlative diagnosis of time. This diagnosis charts the existential disposition [*Befindlichkeit*] of human beings who have lost any meaningful history. Heidegger the philosophizing young realist teaches that anyone who exists today is confronted with sheer facticity and ends up in the "haziness" [*Diesigkeit*] of being as a whole.

In what follows, we can draw on the observations that Heidegger shared in his lecture course during the winter semester of 1929–30, titled *The Fundamental Concepts of Metaphysics: World, Finitude, Solitude*. This lecture course undoubtedly forms the most fascinating advertisement for philosophy since Boethius. At the same time, it contains a quite daunting account of the reasons why Heidegger's contemporaries will in all likelihood be unable to come close to undertaking what has been advertised without fear and trembling. A dictum of Novalis, which Heidegger approvingly cites, reveals the reason why such an undertaking is virtually impossible in present-day philosophy: "Philosophy is really a homesickness, an urge to be at home everywhere."[7] According to Heidegger, philosophy's urgent basis has been completely undermined because the contemporary way of life wishes for nothing more than the ubiquitous production of relaxation and satisfaction: thus emerges the progressive human being, without homesickness, who "has raised some mediocre aspect of himself to the status of a god."[8]

Under these circumstances, the new introduction to philosophy is condemned to make a strategic detour, in order to first restore the human capacity for the basic metaphysical mood – which can only happen by sending human beings to a preschool of the uncanny. This evocative therapy constitutes the lecture course's second stage – which may well have lasted until the run-up to Christmas 1929.

This scathing opening salvo sets the stage for a psychagogic maneuver that for the first time can be reasonably called "Heidegger's politics," although the term "Heidegger's exercise" [*Exerzitium*] would be more apt. Anyone wishing to here emphasize this procedure's implicitly political or, even better, pre-political or proto-political dimension would have to speak of a politics of awakening – though we have to be careful regarding the connotations of such a term. What is supposed to be roused is the opposite of a political impulse. The philosophical wake-up call "Existence arise!" has nothing to do with typical wake-up calls for mobilizing national or proletarian might. From §16 of his lecture course on, Heidegger is devoted to awakening a philosophical mood that does not aim to reveal the identity of something latently or manifestly resent-at-hand (to reveal the identity of a collective ressentiment or of a national pride, for instance), but to "*let* whatever is sleeping *become wakeful*."[9]

The irony of this exercise becomes evident as soon as we realize that what is here referred to as "sleeping" is not something valuable, nor is such "sleeping" in anyone's interests. It is a profound unease, and awakening to it is inconceivable without appealing to the courage of whoever is waking up. To awaken, Heidegger says, means to let something present itself anew by allowing what is "in a peculiar way absent and yet there" to come into the foreground.[10] Heidegger's conscious awareness that awakening is related to the development of a collective, and *eo ipso* to a proto-political procedure, is revealed by his cautious use of the pronouns "we" and "us." "The question immediately arises as to *which* mood we are to awaken or let become wakeful in us. A mood that pervades *us* fundamentally? Who, then, are *we*? What do we mean here in referring to "us"?"[11] Are we speaking of ourselves as academics? As agents in the history of ideas? As concerned parties in a German, a Western, or, in a wider sense, a European event? From this moment on, Heidegger evidently recognizes that, in future, philosophy must become a discussion of our situation [*Lagebesprechung*].

If we grant this, then it stands to reason that previous contributions by others in interpreting the situation would be cited in an expedient and collegial manner. With animated abstraction, Heidegger brings order to supposed chaos differently than Karl Jaspers, who mainly emphasizes the impossibility of gaining an overview of the situation, in his 1931 overview of *Die geistige Situation der Zeit* [Tr. – "The Spiritual Condition of the Age"], published two years later. Four main positions are to be distinguished at present, according to Heidegger. First, that of Oswald Spengler, whose thesis in *The Decline of the West* essentially diagnoses the decline of a life that had been lived in and through spirit, yet does so in such a way that this decline is to be accepted with a Stoic attitude and lived through as unavoidable fate. A similar diagnosis is offered by the next position, that of Ludwig Klages, whose slogan "Return to life!" advocated the liberation of spirit. Third, we have the position of the later Max Scheler, who preferred to view present-day humans as having already reached an era of balance between life and spirit. Finally, we come to the position of Leopold Ziegler, who proclaimed an imminent new Middle Ages that would end the opposition of spirit and life.

Heidegger does not fail to note that all four positions are rooted in Nietzsche's account of the antagonism between the Apollonian and the Dionysian. He brushes aside these majestic attempts to define our situation by objecting that their authors were talking past the actual condition of contemporary human beings – he thought that they had missed and failed to grasp the fundamental mood of the epoch's operative "we," because their statements "*do not attack us,*"[12] but merely provide superficial views of who we are. Cultural diagnoses and grand prognoses of this kind merely provide a snap-shot of us strolling like passers-by along a broad avenue on which the drama of world history is supposedly being acted out. According to Heidegger, such philosophy exhausts itself in presentation and observation [*Dar-stellung und Fest-stellung*], without ever getting through to *Da-sein*, existence or "being-there." Such philosophy speaks "from where we stand" and forgets to ask, *"How do things stand with us?"* All of these inspired and interesting philosophies, which confer grandiose roles upon us in world history, relieve us of ourselves by scripting us into a scenario in which we find ourselves very interesting without having to understand ourselves.

But why do we need to make ourselves interesting in this way? Heidegger asks this question (suggestively), and goes on to answer it himself: because, in the core of our existence, we feel that we are empty, not wholly convinced of anything, and not really gripped by anything, either. When we hearken to the authentic fundamental mood of our time in our own existence, we become profoundly bored with ourselves and with our circumstances. The fundamental feature of our age, which marks us most profoundly, is the absence of every authoritative orientation. We are paradoxically gripped by the fact that nothing that tries to take hold of us really grips us. Awakening to boredom means grasping what it means to not be gripped as such. According to Heidegger, we live in an age where nothing is evident, that is, we live in an age that lacks an authoritative purpose. The arrow of history has overshot its mark and vanished into a post-historical haze. What remains is a confused mixture of agitation and indifference. At bottom, historical time is already at a standstill – and its standstill is reflected in our existential mood.

We thus end up with a bizarre definition of the age's real collective: to begin with, it consists exclusively of a few honest and bold contemporaries who give our profound boredom the chance to surface in our consciousness – that boredom that we have long felt, even if only in an inauthentic way. The psychagogue Heidegger can initially only invoke this collective of the heroes of boredom with a lyrical question: "Have things *ultimately* gone so far with *us* that a profound boredom draws back and forth like a silent fog in the abysses of Dasein?"[13] To ask this in another way: are we not beings who are only strung along and ultimately remain empty, regardless of everything that happens with us or through us? Do we not "ultimately" feel condemned to pass the time since, no matter how far we look, we can see no project that seizes hold of us, engages us, and carries us away? These are initially just rhetorical questions, meant to be affirmed (even though an ontological second wind will be speculated about afterwards – when this second wind sets in, such admissions are downgraded into preparatory exercises for more serious and positive things). By affirmatively replying to such questions, we *de facto* enter our epoch's essential collective, which has yet to assemble. This collective consists of those who, at present, have not been effectively gripped by an imperative necessity. We may only authentically say "we" for the first time when we include ourselves in this collective of the essentially and knowingly un-gripped. We meet in the silent fog for our constitutive assembly. The historical avant-garde consists of those who are honest enough to admit to each other that history no longer speaks to them.

In this way, what was referred to above as the building of a bridge between the existential temporality of mortal individuals and the historical temporality of a collective that shares the same mood can finally be achieved: the individual resolved for him- or herself, who preserves his or her resolute mortal cogito, from now on can join an authentic collective. They can be recognized as *socii* by the fact that they have woken up to feel the mood of their deadly boring existence – or, better, they have been subjected to the "strange or almost insane demand . . . not to let boredom fall asleep."[14]

It is not enough to merely realize this, we need to also recognize how bizarre it is: the anonymous collective of the truly and profoundly bored is the prototype for a collective that a short while later will be encapsulated by "National Socialism." As was to be expected, this encapsulation fell apart relatively quickly. Thus a second, less embarrassing encapsulation soon had to be attempted. It is obvious that we cannot identify those who are aware that they are bored with a nation, neither with the Germans nor any other people. Epochal boredom does not fit the pattern of a national mood, but is rather a kind of world mood – though a philosophically inclined nation such as the Germans or perhaps even the Russians might well be more open to this feeling of boredom than others. Those who bear this boredom form an authentic avant-garde that is called upon to advance into the new and unfamiliar. What is most unfamiliar is admitting to ourselves that we are only still connected to the grand narrative of history to the extent that we feel that history no longer has anything to say to us. In particular, this means that we accustom ourselves to orienting a specific present moment that exists within a greater present time to the characteristic features of not being convinced and not being gripped. There is every indication that an avant-garde of being-with-history-at-the-end here took shape, an unstable avant-garde, admittedly, which due to its untenable position was condemned to regress to some form of ploughing ahead with history.

Having said this, we can now consider the odd question of how this quasi-metaphysical avant-garde International of the empty soon afterwards took on the features of a national movement that was officially represented in the Berlin *Reichstag* by a party that rhetorically mixed populism and socialism, and violently disseminated their message.

9.2 Dostoyevsky, Heidegger, and Kojève: Projecting the End of History

"Heidegger's exercise," though not his "politics," would have already been able to achieve its goal by mobilizing the collective of those who are not gripped. He wanted to do more than merely appeal to us to take up boredom, and indeed for a number of reasons. For one thing, he was not entirely sure of his own evocation of the true mood-collective, because he had been influenced by the nineteenth century's heroic conceptions of history, and thus still expected the actions of great men and of states from real history – even if they begin by negating their own possibility. For another, he intuitively understood that mobilizing the psycho-political collective of the authentically bored, those who feel empty and not-gripped, does not at all result in a transition to a historically concrete collective, regardless of whether it were to take the form of a party, a nation, or of the "West." Finally, it would have been clear to him that even his audience would expect more of him than being drafted into a disoriented mood-collective.

We will have to see how a supposed German elite of the profoundly bored in 1930 could turn into the national revolutionaries of 1933, whose slogans the philosopher began to project his ideas onto soon after the conclusion of this lecture course (only to become disgusted by them a short while later when he learned more about his odd allies). Before we do this, however, we will have to explain how the fundamental mood of boredom could have become a general European, and German, state of affairs.

I would like to take up the above-mentioned thesis, according to which Heidegger may be considered the actual founder of the *posthistoire*-theorem. In view of Heidegger's reputation as the ontologist of historicity, this claim is outlandish enough to require some explanation. Such an explanation will have to show what premises are necessary for us to be able to think of history as something that can come to an end at all – and how the difference here between end and goal comes into play. The concept of a time "after history" is initially associated with the theological idea that God will one day reclaim the world he created and *eo ipso* cast into time – and indeed at a moment that is humanly inconceivable, namely when he is finished with the world. If one translates these ideas into the language of secular logic, we find the assumption that history as a whole is pursuing an end, or an estuary, to put it more cautiously, in which the historical process is finished with itself. It could reach such a point if the energies that had impelled it forward until now were used up or if the conflicts that had hitherto rendered it dynamic were completely resolved. Such an end would be humanly conceivable and ascertainable, in distinction to the transcendent conclusion brought about by God. As is well known, these kinds of ideas had previously been part of the Hegelian tradition, which had suggested the establishment of the constitutional state in the Napoleonic era, the cessation of class conflict following the Russian Revolution, and the satisfaction of the human striving for recognition (or rather its hedonistic miniaturization), as possible criteria for admission into post-history.

With that said, the claim that there was also a non-Hegelian route to the *posthistoire*-thesis should now be plausible, although this was hardly mentioned in the corresponding discussions. According to our interpretation, Heidegger, with his powerful intuitions about the diagnosis of time, followed this alternative path to establishing the end of history, before he was compelled by his neo-heroic imperative to take a detour in order to devote himself to the creation or letting happen of supposedly decisive world-historical actions, works, or events.

The real father of the non-Hegelian theory of the end of history (it would be better to call it a vision or a daydream), which Heidegger occasionally espoused, is acknowledged to be Fyodor Dostoyevsky – particularly in his short novel *Notes from Underground*, published in 1864. This work has to be recognized as the founding charter of modern ressentiment-psychology, as well the founding charter of anti-globalization sentiment, if such an anachronistic back-dating of the term is allowed. The narrator of the virtuous monologue in the first part of the book (a bitter and comic prelude to philosophical anthropology offered in the first person) is a figure whom we would today call a modernization-loser. He represents a neurotic version of Nietzsche's last man, a character whose motivation has been undermined, who can only satisfy his desire for self-respect by deviously taking pleasure in his own humiliation. He is someone who contrives his own misfortune and flirts with it. He settles into a "cold, loathsome half-despair," into a "half-belief," into an "assiduously produced and yet somewhat dubious hopelessness,"[15] which serves as an Archimedean point that he can use to unhinge the world of progressive minds. The narrator in his squalid hole (which is described as a deliberately chosen dingy subterranean dwelling on the fringes of St. Petersburg) presents himself as a vehement critic of the Western way of life,[16] an opponent of globalization, in the parlance of our times. He also professes himself to be a man of the present day and argues that the "man of the nineteenth century" is morally obligated to be a "characterless creature" – almost the only claim in the subsequent cascade of words that he really seems to believe in.[17] It gives him the greatest satisfaction to act like an anthropologist who marshals evidence that the predominantly pro-Western ideologists of the market, of relaxation, and of universalized humanitarianism have made their calculations without reference to actual human beings or, to put it more precisely, without reference to the ungrateful and rebellious freedom of human beings, which amounts to little more than continually taking it into one's head to oppose every given order, even one promising universal happiness. In this context, the well-known neo-Cynical thesis is formulated according to which the human being is an ungrateful bipedal animal.[18] Nietzsche could rightly remark that Dostoyevsky's "terrible and cruel work" presents us with the sharpest mockery of the Delphic inscription "Know Thyself!"[19] The author of this confession clearly and intuitively understands himself to be a creature of boredom – a witness to an existence without beliefs, responsibilities, and obligations. His stream of words reflects whatever enters its author's mind, without reaching a standpoint or a truth worthy of being repeated. The rambling talk of the voice from underground thus demonstrates just how impossible it has become to participate in a meaningful history.

> I swear to you, gentlemen, that I do not believe a word, not one little word, of all I've just scribbled! That is, I do believe, perhaps, but at the same time, who knows why, I sense and suspect that I'm lying like a cobbler. "Then why did you write it all?" you say to me. And what if I put you away for some forty years with nothing to do, and then come to you in the underground after forty years to see how you've turned out? One cannot leave a man alone and unoccupied for forty years, can one?[20]

It is crucial to note that this man without commitments continually refers to those opposed to his own *modus vivendi* with the clairvoyance of the evil eye: he finds such opposition in the secular anthropology of progressive Western parties. Such progressives, whether liberal or socialist, believe that human beings have needs that can in principle be satisfied. They derived various policies for satisfying needs from this view, but the strategic differences of their policies could not conceal the fact that they were basically after the same thing.

The Crystal Palace of London, erected in 1851, the greatest structure in architectural history at that time, was a public symbol of this belief. It was triumphantly erected in a mere ten months to accommodate the first world's fair in Hyde Park. It was set up again on an even larger scale in 1854 on Sydenham Hill, near London, as a popular indoor theme park. The Crystal Palace's articulation of the nineteenth century's civilizing tendencies had a significance that can only be compared with the World Trade Center in New York, whose collapse in September 2001 was symbolically on a par with it. The megastructure of Sydenham gave the citizens of that time a World Satisfaction Center, in which the ultimate aims of the progressive way of life were completely revealed for all to see. The underground man is quite obviously a contemporary of the Crystal Palace, since he understands why the superb construct was erected: the temple of satisfaction is a house of worship for the anti-metaphysical project of modernity, which aims to dissuade satisfied human beings who have been accounted for, made equal, and discreetly animalized, from the further use of their freedom. Historic tensions [*Spannungen*] are supposed to achieve a post-historical equilibrium in this grand overarching receptacle [*alles überspannenden Behälter*].

The Eastern observer is opposed to such pretension and intervenes, drawing upon Christian anthropological motifs to claim that desire is insatiable:

Shower him with all Earthly blessings, drown him in happiness completely, over his head, so that only bubbles pop up on the surface of happiness, as on water; give him such economic satisfaction that he no longer has anything left to do at all except sleep, eat gingerbread, and worry about the noncessation of world history [P. S. – i.e. to have sex] – and it is here, just here, that he, this man, out of sheer ingratitude, out of sheer lampoonery, will do something nasty. He will even risk his gingerbread . . .[21]

This challenge to the politics of happiness reveals two clearly distinct modes of post-historicity. In the first mode, human beings participate in systems of satisfaction, but from time to time escape the crystal palace to preserve their honor as human beings, that is, as those who are free to break with given conditions – in the most extreme case, on a whim, they opt for madness and self-destruction.

In the second mode, human beings indeed remain excluded from the benefits of existing in the sphere of comfort, but find their own satisfaction in despising the contentment of the palace-dwellers. Even the idle despiser lives in a post-historical situation, though with a twist, namely that such post-historicity contains elements of pre- and extra-historical existence, since it never participated in the struggles for historical satisfaction – and is not subsequently inclined to struggle, either. The first mode results in the comfortable *posthistoire* of a freedom reduced to absurd whims (half amusement-park culture and half bloodbath), while the second mode results in the uncomfortable *posthistoire* of ressentiment, which remains condemned to self-satisfaction and otherwise to lethargy, due to its supposedly (or perhaps genuinely) greater depths. While suffering and doubt are eliminated in the system of comfort, or are at least continually reduced (". . . what good is a crystal palace in which one can have doubts?"),[22] only partisans of ressentiment have the option of intentional suffering.

> And yet I'm certain that man will never renounce real suffering, that is, destruction and chaos. Suffering – why, this is the sole cause of consciousness.[23]

The observing despiser of the crystal palace does not have an alternative project, as is to be expected. Yet he remains parasitical on the faded historicity of others and shares in their end, insofar as his contempt depends on it. Either human beings in the crystal palace are deluding themselves, and history is not really at an end even for them, or it is in fact concluded, but then its being-at-an-end and the satisfaction provided by the crystal palace would not amount to much, because the human resolution to suffer and to impose suffering has not been extinguished even under post-historical conditions, as the underground man tries to demonstrate. With his will to suffer, he fends off the unreasonable demand that he should admire the accomplishments of the party that has triumphed in history. In his masochistic authenticity, the first opponent of globalization deflects the progressives' claim to superiority – though he seems to be susceptible to envy. He objects to the world of happiness with the thesis that another world is possible, a world in which there is still enough suffering to give the cold shoulder to history and its tranquillization by universal satisfaction.

Before we explain how Heidegger pursued a similar line of thought fifty-six years later, although with a shift in emphasis and a more profound grasp of the metaphysics of history, we should recall a second Russian thinker, whose work is inextricably associated

with the motif of the "end of history." As early as the beginning of
the 1930s, only a short while after Heidegger's foray into the mood
of post-historical boredom, Alexandre Kojève had concluded from
his studies of Hegel that human history was in fact over. Along with
Dostoyevsky, Kojève shared the anthropological view that human
existence represents a series of struggles that arise from the striving
for satisfaction. Yet while the novelist interpreted satisfaction, in
light of his religious doctrine of freedom, as a narcissistic enjoyment
of rebellion that is always on the move and never leads anywhere,
Kojève interprets satisfaction to be an attainable goal of the struggle for recognition by the other. The concept of recognition thus
becomes the political, psychodynamic, and spiritual key to world
history, because the striving for recognition, if unsatisfied, is the
main reason for the noncessation of historical struggles. In contrast,
if this striving is satisfied, it is reason enough for the cessation of
hostilities and thus the conclusion of history. The fulfillment or non-
fulfillment of the human demand to be recognized as free subject
and sovereign source of negativity determines the difference between
the happy and the unhappy consciousness. Historical movement
resumes in conflicts in which the unhappy consciousness is utterly
eliminated and turned into the happy consciousness.

Kojève views two fictional warring factions as world-historical
agents in this drama, the figures of lord and bondsman, whom we
are familiar with from Hegel's *Phenomenology of Spirit*. A completely anthropologized history begins with the initial stages of their
contention. Starting with an imaginary primordial duel in which
two freedoms grapple with each other, as representatives of a surreal
pride, the human realm is divided into victor and vanquished, with
the former taking on the role of lord, while the latter ends up in
the position of bondsman, who in future must see to the material
bases of the lord's freedom. Here begins the era of labor, with its
heteronomy and its struggles against this heteronomy. At the same
time, this is also when the unhappy consciousness befalls both sides:
The lord's desire for recognition remains unsatisfied, because the
bondsman, with his servile attitude toward the lord, cannot possibly
provide equal recognition. Likewise, the bondsman is condemned to
non-satisfaction or a substitute gratification in religion, due to the
grim realities of his condition.

In describing this struggle, everything hinges on the final position:
it is thus characteristic that the bondsman (or the third estate, to put
it in historical terms), trained and empowered by the labor he has
performed for so long, finally obtains the means to successfully rebel
against the lord. These means are systematically codified in the civil
constitutional state. And as soon as this state were to reach its uni-

versal form, history would arrive at its immanent end as a sequence of struggles for recognition; an era of satisfied consciousness would have dawned. The phrase *tutti contenti* from the end of Mozart's and Da Ponte's *Le nozze di Figaro* (after Beaumarchais) is the first word of post-history.

From this point on, human beings must exercise their freedom by laboriously negating the given, that is, they must modify nature through their own labor, in revolting against the lord as an exploiter of servile labor. Human beings are constituted as the fortunately unemployed, that is, as proprietors of a power of negation who no longer find any objects with which to seriously engage, thus becoming the post-historical *Homo ludens*. The substantive content of post-history is either contemplative or cheerfully animalistic. With the exception of work that is no longer servile (in other words, aided by machines), we are left with art, sexuality, and nonsense to fill the long afternoons of post-history.

Kojève's model has history come to a standstill in the awareness of achieved satisfaction. Yet the philosopher pays a high price for his blithe thesis: splitting the meaning of the phrase "end of history" into theoretical and empirical versions necessarily leads to ambiguity. If history is to end in theory, whether with the end of Hegel's *Phenomenology*, while the thunder of cannons from the Battle of Jena booms in the background, or whether following the Russian Revolution and its violent consolidation by Stalin, we cannot but be embarrassed that the universal and homogenous (socialist) constitutional state has been taking its sweet time arriving on the world-historical stage. History would accordingly come to an end, to be sure, but not reach the goal. Thus Kojève can get no further than a semi-post-history, in which much remains to be done empirically, although everything has been done, in principle. This situation is reflected in the irony of the philosopher's happy consciousness as he comments on the disturbing fallout from the world's remaining misfortunes. A philosophical irony that is neither Socratic nor Romantic, but rather post-historical, leads Kojève's to rely on the concept of the sage, in order to re-legitimate provocatively the ancient fatalistic division of the human collective into the wise and the ignorant. Only in a truly universal state would the sage's irony be transformed into humor. If end and goal were to coincide, avant-garde sarcasm, which displays elements of impatience with those lagging behind, could be resolved into contemplation and benevolent retrospection.

9.3 Affirmation of Danger: Back to History!

In conclusion, we will show how Heidegger's seriousness, by adopting a non-Hegelian theory of the end of history that traces back to Dostoyevsky, develops an alternative program to Kojève's irony. In fact, Heidegger takes up a position that in many respects is quite close to that of the underground man. The phenomenologist of inauthentic existence and profound boredom is also to some extent an observer of the crystal palace, although he does not call it by this name, instead describing it with such terms as enterprise, mediocrity, inauthenticity, ambiguity, machination, and technology. He is likewise convinced that the lifestyles of a technological, analgesic world oriented to happiness allow "human metaphysical potential" to lie idle, to put it bluntly. In contrast to the Hegelian ironist, Heidegger cannot settle for a politics of the cheerful re-animalization of the human being that would then send the latter off to find amusement: the reason for this is to be found in an interpretation of satisfaction that allows Heidegger to move beyond Dostoyevsky and Kojève. In Heidegger's world, to be satisfied requires more than merely offering evidence of the inexhaustibility of human negativity, or delighting in occidental and vesperal wisdom. Here it is necessary for you to wake up from ontological complicity and change yourself into a messenger and an outpost of being.

Heidegger ontologizes avant-gardism, by tying the possibility of satisfaction to the possibility of a calling by which you can be sent ahead as a vanguard of being into its own affairs. We have already seen above that temporalized being, which in a mood's timeliness addresses our respective contemporaries, initially wishes to be immersed in an enveloping boredom-bath. From this bath emerges the bizarre figure of an avant-garde that is called upon to push forward into the heart of boredom, that is, into a most profound having-nothing-more-to-do. At the same time, Heidegger does not want this to be understood as a calling for the Oblomovization of the West. To those who can and wish to hear it in the dialect of boredom, the being of the 1930s says something of this sort: I need you for my newest project, to prepare existence to cease with its previous history-making. You should occupy yourself in our resigned elite by exposing history as, essentially, a collective flight forward and by helping turn it against itself!

To make a long story short, we now wish to show how Heidegger accepted this paradoxically coded assignment and wrongly deciphered it. He succumbed to a misunderstanding, because he obviously had a second voice in his ear that gave him conflicting instructions. What we are here calling a second voice is an ensemble of anthropological concerns that pertain to the human being's transformation in technological civilization – we find this articulated in the only slightly later anthropological work of Arnold Gehlen. The young Heidegger is involved in a discourse on the essence of modernization as a process of relief: with the utmost presence of mind, he grasps that progressive relief is undermining the basis for its own métier, philosophy as metaphysics. If philosophy is supposed to entail the urge to be at home everywhere, the manner in which this urge is presently diverted into other directions is nevertheless unmistakable: due to its satisfaction with enlightened, touristic, and informative expedients, in Heidegger's time as well as today, it leaves the stream bed of philosophy behind and trickles away into the institutions and activities that assure existence's modern welfare. From this perspective, so-called globalization, which has characterized world discourse for decades, forms only the most current mode of the non-philosophical redirection of the urge to be at home everywhere. On this analysis, present-day humans tend to want to be relieved of metaphysics and self-reflection. Heidegger is not prepared to stand back while that happens, without formulating an oppositional manifesto.

This manifesto is rooted in a grand diagnosis of time, in which Fichtean and Kierkegaardian motifs converge: if, in his lectures on *The Characteristics of the Present Age* (1804) – the birth certificate of the philosophical diagnosis of time – Fichte had defined the present moment as the "age of complete sinfulness" (in other words, as rock bottom, after which we can only proceed upwards),[24] and if Kierkegaard, in his polemics of the 1840s against the conformism of the zeitgeist, had portrayed the "public" as a collective non-person – and as the source of all irresponsibility (from which the later portrait of *das Man* [Tr. – the "they"] in *Being and Time* is supposed to have come) – then Heidegger, in the era of the *Black Notebooks* (1931–1948), was devoted to an increasingly in-depth inquisition against the activism of modern technological civilization.

Research into the sources of evil in the world culminates in a serious philosophical reconstruction of communism: as an oligarchic party (that is, as rule by the few), communism embodies the innermost tendencies of modernity. The Russian contribution to an all-consuming techno-pragmatism consists in launching this still-reigning "machination."[25]

Ubiquitous "machination" is common to the British Empire, the French Republic, Americanism, Bolshevism, and National Socialism, and sometimes even the Jewish contribution to the mobilization of all things through the intention to use them is evident to the diagnostician. It is also obvious from a few embarrassing reviews of the *Black Notebooks* that they can easily be reproached for "antisemitism." It would be wiser to determine the soundness of Heidegger's diagnosis that the accomplices of machination, metaphysics and technology, really lead fatefully to the devastation of all things, whether the agents of devastation bear the names of concrete historical collectives or not.

The second voice that Heidegger hears demands that he connect philosophy's concern to that of the burden – and indeed, since relief already represents a *fait accompli*, that he connect philosophy's concern to a repeated and reconstituted burden. Thus repetition is also the soul of thought: it aids the thinker in the task of encountering the issues that thought is engaged with, which are always difficult, without false ease. If modern relief *per se* includes the temptation to forget philosophy, then it is to be identified as the enemy, with the battle against it determining the fate of philosophy. Since it has undeniably occurred and hence radically transformed the premises of thought (even if academic philosophy misses this entirely, due to its prevailing ignorance), it is now a matter of thoughtfully considering the issue of burden. Burden after relief amounts to re-burdening.

I would like to argue that "re-burdening" is essential to what may be called "Heidegger's politics." Even the evocation of boredom in the lecture course *The Fundamental Concepts of Metaphysics* can only be appreciated if we understand it to be part of a procedure of re-burdening. The new avant-garde collective will not convene in order to be bored until the end of time, as an elite of the empty (in the manner of a certain Asiatic misunderstanding of Heidegger), but to prove that even today there are still human beings who do not take the easy way out, although most succumb to the temptation of ease. Since the folly of being open to the mood of present truth is the hardest thing to expect of contemporary human beings, the way for "us" to reach our own epoch leads through just such a gauntlet. Being initially requires us to be there and to be willing to bear the burden of the absence of evidence or of being gripped. The reward for this is revealed in "our" awakening to the sense of homesickness for forgotten being. But because our present time is not able to formulate a task in positive terms, the historical project that could grip us must lie ahead of us in a future that is still unclear.

The crucial onto-historical questions are thus: What really lies ahead of us? What will have enough force to carry us away, inspired by a new belief? What exactly is happening today, that we are needed as media? A hint of great things to come is suggested by the pronoun "us" here. The searing advent in the Freiburg lecture hall in 1929 is formally linked to an ontological advent through which we are supposed to allow an imminent sense of being happen to us in positive terms. Of course, Heidegger is just as unsure as anyone as to how a new imperative of being might manifest itself, but he is confident that he has understood how we need to be prepared to go through such an advent – namely, we must be ready to be re-burdened. Hence it is just fine with him if "All that is great stands in the storm,"[26] as he puts it at the end of his rector's address, thanks to a questionable translation of the ancient Greek. Anyone who has joined the avant-garde of boredom and already exposed him- or herself to the truth of the present has met the prerequisites for making a stand at the front line of the raging storm, ready for assignments from the future of truth.

With that said, we should clarify that Heidegger's interest in introducing the so-called "leader principle" into academic life, which forms the nucleus of his rectorate, was mainly to introduce the principles of trainer and training into existence. Training means structuring our life into a series of exercises that increasingly burden us, and this is precisely how the principle of re-burdening is disseminated among the relieved and disoriented.

"Heidegger's exercise" remains inscrutable as long as we do not also recognize the entry of sport into post-historical politics. Sport is precisely the form of exertion in which nothing is really at stake and that we nevertheless engage in to restore a sense of what is ultimately engrossing. The political field, too, in its own way makes this turn toward sportification [*Versportlichung*], whether as democratic "fair play,"[27] or as recent forms of serious political sport that demand dictatorship in order to drive off those who have been relieved of burdens.

Mussolini was not entirely wrong when he identified the source of *fascismo* to be a feeling of horror when confronted by a comfortable life. This should unquestionably be interpreted as the key term for Europe in the 1930s: it articulates the Western-Catholic and martial-sportive response to the objections of the underground man against distracted existence in the crystal palace. In fact, even relieved Western human beings rebel against being surrounded by offers of happiness, but their rebellion does not quite reach the state of willful destruction, as Dostoyevsky suggested, although a few such examples are not lacking. Rather, Western rebellion occurs as an act of freely burdening ourselves, that is, as sport.

By 1933, Heidegger's idea of leadership already implied a dictatorship of the trainer, who ensures that *we* remain in shape, as the team for history's next chapter, although it is quite unclear what particular match history will require us to play. The way in which the ontological advent takes on the atmosphere [*Stimmung*] of a finals match, in which the team of discomfort is matched against the team of comfort, should now at least be evident. From Heidegger's perspective, what happens here is always solely a match for the truth of being, which is played in the arena of current universal time. He is now ready to interpret "we" as a national team and thus comes to be associated with Hitler, to whom he is prepared to offer a role as assistant trainer of the national team – although, incidentally, it is clear that Hitler, too, only represents a subordinate medium who can have no idea of how he might contribute to the team effort.

Heidegger actually uses the specific example of the Nazi movement to articulate his expectation that history might not have ended in the silent fog of boredom. He wagers everything on the hunch, indeed the claim, that while those of us who are honest continue to keenly feel that history is at standstill, being is gathering itself in preparation for an epochal leap. And this leap needs *us*, since it is the gesture by which *we* collaboratively make history, understood existentially. The leap is precisely the act of moving forward, which is an essential part of mediumistically collaborating with what is coming. It needs *us* because it will not happen without *our* boldness. Our boldness follows from the realization that when we are in danger, the only way out is to keep moving forward. Thus to conceptually formulate "Heidegger's politics," we would have to demonstrate how a post-historical re-burdening that turns life's struggles into a kind of sport merges with being horrified by the end of history, which at the same time was interpreted as the end of philosophy.

This convergence does not need to be described in detail here. Its strategic purpose, to compel progress or a new start to history, is all too clear. Anyone who has interpreted being as time would have concede the annihilation of being, if he or she wished to acknowledge the end of history, and this was not something Heidegger could do. He insisted on claiming that he stood in the midst of an advent that was about to reveal something compellingly new and great. History must thus remain open, and its end, although present as a current possibility, is to be postponed again and again. *Tant pis* for those affected, if nothing more attractive than National Socialism is currently on offer to promote the advent. Yet when was history ever very particular in recruiting its agents?

We should now be able to see that Heidegger's doctrine of the historicity of being is not intrinsically connected to his membership in the National Socialist movement. As is well known, similar ideas have characterized the behavior of militantly leftist authors such as Merleau-Ponty and Sartre. Like the master from Meßkirch, these thinkers were convinced that we do not stand over and against a world that is historically in motion, but that "the world . . . in fact

... envelops us."[28] At the time, all that Heidegger's thought could do was to relate to a sufficiently heroic "movement" upon which it could project its positing of recurrent history. This could just as well have been something like Roosevelt's "New Deal" or the Russian Revolution, had the thinker's fate been to exist as an American or a Russian in those days. Like so many who were scandalized by that epoch, Heidegger felt compelled to raise the question: Where is great history going here? And when he received the answer that it was heading "for the Brown-Shirt Revolution," he was ready to devote his energy to that promising hypothesis. Though we repeatedly find the claim that his thought must be National Socialist because he was a member of the party, this position is unjustified, as irksome as his rectoral address must seem in critical hindsight. In any case, we learn more about the intentions of interpreters from such interpretations than we do about the author in question.

What really matters is that Heidegger revised his onto-historical over-interpretation of the National Socialist movement shortly thereafter, because he was able to realize the true nature of the company he was keeping, based on his own experience. He even had to make an objectively ironic about-face when it became evident to him that this very movement represented an explosive form of the world of boredom. It was impossible to see it as a turning point in the history of being. Rather, the will to power's assault on everything quite clearly revealed an essential feature of a subjectivism that is forgetful of being. If one complements this with the view of the underground man, then the irony of Heidegger's attempt to participate in the opposite of what he intended becomes quite pronounced: Hitler's politics, seen from underground St. Petersburg, were simply an attempt to bring the crystal palace under German control and to guarantee the new masters' comfort by adding a new deck onto the eastern wing. Instead of a new dispensation of the occurrence of truth, what followed was a return to slavery and manhunts as a kind of post-historical power sport. What was supposed to be an escape from the comfortable life turned out to be the cruelest possible establishment of a secure perimeter around the crystal palace.

By 1934, Heidegger knew that he had failed to become a catalyst of the advent. From that point on, he was careful not to further dabble in forced attempts to help along epochal turning points. He began to emphasize the necessity of waiting and to look around for new allies with whom he could form another "we" and make alternative arrangements for a deferred epoch. Poets now become important to him, Hölderlin in particular, because they provide key information on the problems we face in forming the avant-garde of a wretched future. Because emphasis is now placed on the poetic disclosure and arrangement of the world, the concept of the *work* becomes significant, indeed it occasionally takes center stage in Heidegger's reflections during the middle stage of his "path of thinking" [*Denkwegs*]. As hollow as it may have appeared to its first audience, this concept can help us bear in mind that the occurrence of history in a collective is not merely constituted by moods, but even more by works to be accomplished, whether they are works of state or works of art. Both should be thought of as vessels for truth's emergence-into-the-light. The poetizing of state, the poetizing of art, indeed *ex negativo* even the poetizing of the crystal palace and its anticipated renovations shifts to a truth-historical perspective through works.

There is a high price to be paid for this alliance with poetry. Heidegger has to acknowledge that even metaphysical philosophy, which he initially wished to advocate, has reached its end. According to him, the epoch of the forgetting of being continually proceeds as the age of technological development. This is the focus of the later Heidegger's view – an extremely abstract view, in which Bolshevism, fascism, and Americanism amount to merely three versions of the same assault on beings as a whole. We need not emphasize that views like this cannot remain at such lofty heights: what is supposed to be prepared for with anticipation for the future is not only another epoch of being, but also another era of formative thought. Other thinkers are supposed to replace the exploitation of beings with an ethics of conservation. Heidegger's political excursion comes to an end with his quietistic turn. The rest is damage control.

I would like to conclude by observing that the question of whether we can or should somehow associate ourselves with Heidegger today is no longer urgent, as it was for those who worshiped him in the 1950s and those who condemned him in 1964 (the year in which Theodor Adorno's polemical text *Jargon of Authenticity* appeared) or 1987 (the year of the uproar around Farías' work).[29] This is mainly because what used to get people worked up about the philosophy of history is now a distant concern to us in 2015. If a philosopher in 1933 allowed himself to be gripped by the imperative "Forwards to history!," this hardly still seems to matter to contemporary intellectuals. Philosophy today has little more to say about the phenomenon of history other than that it cannot be completely over. Incidentally, we no longer really know what "history" is supposed to mean when we abandon its narrative form. In any case, we dread the "grand narrative." The *status quo* is expressed in the rallying cry "Back to morality!," which has since come to dictate the agenda – sometimes also in the form of "Back to religion!" The new situation offers the advantage of rendering the seduction of philosophers by an opportunism that goes-along-with-the-times powerless. There cannot be another Heidegger. Outside of the guild, it turns out that opportunism no longer needs the pretense of history and its metaphysics. Office hours and business practices have absorbed so-called being and its history. A post-ontological and post-historical *modus operandi* is virtually ubiquitous.

The only connection we still have to Heidegger's era and its agitated forms of thought can be appreciated with a figure of speech: "Time gives us problems, and we have to solve them." That is the small price we must pay for an engaged life. If Heidegger wished to overpay, we see that as his problem, but no longer ours.

The real cause for concern today is the fact that the current politics of the United States are an alarming sequel to the European and German drama of the 1930s. Having considered Heidegger's case, we can now better understand the dangers of a forward-charging regression into a time when history was not the right history for the course of the world to come. If Europeans today consider it anachronistic that America is regressing into an avant-gardism that is also at the same time unilateralism, this very regression seems to be the historical mission of the ideologists at work in Washington. A certain speechwriter wrote the following statement for George W. Bush to read in 2001: "The call of history has come to the right country . . ." And additionally: "We meet here during a crucial period in the history of our nation, and of the civilized world. A part of history has been written by others – the rest will be written by us."[30]

Europeans should know that not much can be said to people who want to make history. Given this, we should try to explain to those of our American friends who can still be reached by arguments that neither God nor being have dictated Bush's speeches and wars, but rather speechwriters. In light of our experience, we must demand an explanation from these writers and compel them to tell us what exactly they mean.

10

ODYSSEUS THE SOPHIST

On the Birth of Philosophy from the
Spirit of Travel Stress

10.1 Polytropos – The Man of Twists and Turns

Anyone who uses the word "odyssey" nowadays generally means nothing more than wandering around. Such wandering can lead to a safe and sound homecoming – thus the comfortable and circumspect way of thinking, which does not wish to hear about roaming around unless the story ends with the reminder that there is no place like home. But wandering around can lead to distant horizons, and this corresponds to the modern sensibility that generally mistrusts arrivals and praises those who keep going – because all places seem in principle to be equally good or bad. Thus I can tell whether you are a conservative or a modern if you tell me whether you prefer for an odyssey to end at home or whether the name "Ithaca" only refers to a stage on a journey that continues further, to a familiar destination or to parts unknown.

If we open the *Odyssey*, attributed to a poet by the name of Homer, who is supposed to be the same person responsible for the *Iliad*, a book about the rage of Achilles and the fall of Troy, then simply reading it will convince us that its famous stories of wandering have merely an episodic function – they constitute just four of the twenty-four books that form the corpus of Odysseus' tale (although this way of arranging the text was a late addition by an Alexandrine editor). The other twenty books have a single theme: how it could happen that Odysseus, the man who for a long time could not find his way back from Asia Minor to Ithaca, still finally arrived back home after a twenty-year absence, by the will of the gods and in keeping with his own heartfelt desire? Thus any actual reader of the *Odyssey* – or better, any listener who allows him- or herself to be enchanted by the rhapsodic recital as though at a concert – will be quite certain that it is a story of coming back home after a war, even more: an apotheosis of the return to domesticity. What the *Odyssey* celebrates in twenty of its twenty-four books is the ability to put a monstrous ten-year war on foreign soil behind one, and to then suffer ten years of nautical and erotic catastrophe on various islands and at sea, and yet to be able to once more become a Greek among one's own kind at the end, a friend among friends, a man of the house with his wife, in a word: a man who returns home to peace. Only in this way is the story structured in a decidedly Ithaca-centric manner. And this was the only way to convince all post-Homeric generations of Greeks, initially listeners but later readers of the songs, too, that a Greek is someone who succeeds in returning from a foreign war to once more devote himself to the binding powers and dynamic vital energies that are to be found in a place of his own – and even to the tragedies that not seldom follow the homecoming.

In short: Even today, when we open the *Odyssey*, we read the greatest story of re-civilization in Western literature. It provides an answer to the existential question of Greek culture: "Is there life after the Trojan War?" It can affirm that there is, by showing how the process of the heroes' return home tends to end up subtly disarming the heroes – along with a tragic local politics and endless dramas having to do with relationships.[1]

So let us turn to the much-read beginning of the *Odyssey* once again and listen to how the singer provides a framework and perspective for his subject-matter:

> Sing in me, Muse, and through me tell the story
> Of that man skilled in all ways of contending,
> The wanderer, harried for years on end,
> After he plundered the stronghold
> On the proud height of Troy.
> He saw the townlands
> And learned the minds of many distant men,
> And weathered many bitter nights and days
> In his deep heart at sea, while he fought only
> To save his life, to bring his shipmates home . . .
> And when long years and seasons
> Wheeling brought him around that point of time
> Ordained for him to make his passage homeward,
> Trials and dangers, even so, attended him
> Even in Ithaka, near those he loved . . .[2]

We have said enough for now about the epic plot. In fact, the *Odyssey*, from the thirteenth up to the twenty-fourth and final book, only recounts the details of Odysseus' difficulties after he returns to Ithaca – he has come home and yet is far from reclaiming his property. In his formerly wealthy home, a host of parasites have established themselves and gotten used to enjoying the delights of a freeloading life, in some ways comparable here to a modern society of those who live off the interest from their trust funds while devoting themselves to amusements. The homecoming hero must avoid their murderous intentions, and the former ruler of Ithaca must match his own sense of wounded honor, which must be made right, against their exploitative impudence, even if the price to be paid is a massacre.

The epithet that first provides a closer description of the story's hero is key to the issue under consideration. We find the first instance of Odysseus' name in the forty-eighth verse, yet the first verse already introduces his winged epithet: *polytropos*, a word whose adequate translation has racked the brains of Hellenists and Homeric experts since the Roman era. Livius Andronicus, whose rather loose translation *Odusia* inaugurated Roman literature around 200 BCE, decided on the Latin expression *virum versutum* [Tr. – "well-versed man"]. In 1781, Voss, for a long time the most successful of the German translators of Homer, rendered it in a philologically faithful manner as "*der Vielgewanderte*" [Tr. – "he who has wandered much"]. The translation used above, by Robert Fitzgerald from 1963, uses "that man skilled in all ways of contending."[3] Earlier English Hellenists used expressions such as "much-traveled" or "crafty" for this passage, while more recent ones, provide a free poetic rendering, such as Robert Fagles' "the man of twists and turns." The French poet Lecomte de Lisle adapts *polytropos* in his translation of the *Odyssey* from 1867 with: *l'homme subtil qui erra si longtemps* – which is unquestionably quite a stretch from the spirit of the original. Ippolito Piedemonte, the author of the classic Italian translation, renders the critical passage with the phrase *l'eroe multiforme che tanto vagò*. If we realize that Homeric epithets are the soul of rhapsodic movement, we know that translating them is anything but a minor issue. Just as Hegel will later speak of "the labor of the concept," so we must speak of "the labor of the epithet" in the world of Homeric formulation. On this critical question, I believe that we should award first prize to the translation of old Voss, with second prize going to Robert Fagles, who caused a furor in 1990 with his new translation of the *Odyssey* – in which he risked breaking up Homer's epithet too much with his "in twists and turns"[4] – harming the authentic rhapsodic tone quite a bit, which requires the eternal return of concise stock phrases.

Anyone wishing to know who Odysseus is must start with the fact that from the very first line he is *polytropos*: the man of many paths, who has been put to the test by his detours, a sufferer of setbacks, someone who has been storm-tossed, a man who is played with in many ways and yet who always manages to ensure that the moves made by circumstance ultimately lead to a single result on which everything hinges, the completion of his return home. Because his difficulties in returning home can be traced back to a divine grudge, his wanderings are to be understood as a punishment. They are not an endless sentence, but rather an assignment that he can complete in a certain amount of time with the assistance of Athena and a good deal of his own ingenuity. Thus ten years of divinely sent obstacles are added to ten years of absence caused by war. A large part of the second decade is spent by the hero on two different islands under the spell of women who are skilled in magic, first with Calypso, who demands seven years of love-bondage in her grotto, and then with Circe, who claims an additional year for herself and her marvelous bed. A shorter part of the journey's time is spent in actual sea-faring, facing storms, shipwreck, and the famous adventures with the oblivious lotus eaters, the one-eyed man-eater Polyphemus, the eccentric Laestrygonian giants, and finally the fairy-tale-like friendly Phaeacians, to whom he relates his adventures one long evening as thanks for their hospitality – the odyssey within the *Odyssey*.

The *polytropos* is thus the hero of delayed movement toward a goal. This predestines him for all manner of metaphorical reinterpretation and spiritual appropriation, since Odysseus is directly or indirectly a factor any time the structure of the complicated return voyage is taken up again in later European culture. For early Christians, paradise is an Ithaca of the soul, for Augustine the human heart is always restless and is storm-tossed by exercises until it finds rest in God, while in Novalis the correct Romantic answer to the question "Where are we going?" is "always back home," and even for Hegel the *Odyssey* is a symbol of spirit's journey around the world, which after its long exile in externality finally returns as the reflective arrival of the idea at home with itself.

As *polytropos*, Odysseus is a man who is stretched on the rack of delay. Hence his maneuverability is only the flip side of his constant suffering. In truth, he is a passion-hero, a man of sorrows who encounters obstacles on his return home, even when circumstances seem to ensure that his delays are enjoyable. He is not just a passion-hero when he is tossed about in the flood sent by Poseidon, which lasts for days, with death seemingly right around the corner, or when barbarians eat his traveling companions while they are still alive, he is also one when he takes a year off to rest in the arms of the nymph

Calypso. As the goddess's nightly lover, he sits on the shore of the island of Ogygia by day and weeps bitter tears, feeling homesick. He heroically perseveres in sleeping with the goddess, of course, but his heart is not really in it, since his home and his wife are always on his mind. He only analogically shares a bed with another woman, insofar as she is a respectable surrogate for his wife. He agrees to pay tribute to femininity at another point, since from his distinctly faithful perspective every attractive woman is more or less created in the image of Penelope. Thus he can never be entirely unfaithful when he is attracted to other women – traveling around the world has its price. But since Odysseus' love, in the final analysis, is bound to his native soil – *patrida gaia* – and to his marital furrow, he must be disappointed by every woman that makes him weak in the knees but cannot provide him with that great feeling of finally arriving home and seeing his herds in the fields, when the wandering traveler comes back for his own. Even the incredibly voluptuous Circe finds this out and has every reason to say to the reluctant hero: "Hale must your heart be and your tempered will. / Odysseus then you are, O great contender . . ."[5] – we again hear the key word, *polytropos*, which characterizes the hero's being tossed back and forth. Odysseus climbs into the bed of the witch of Aeaea after she makes a solemn vow to not harm him. Otherwise, he would have to fear that: "now it is I myself you hold, enticing / into your chamber, to your dangerous bed, / to take my manhood when you have me stripped."[6] After Circe's pledge he is nevertheless ready to give it a try, even if the homecoming temporarily fades from view here.

The much-wandering hero's frequent movement even includes an encounter with his own epic shadow. Odysseus undergoes a primal staging of the encounter with the self, indeed of self-reflection, near the half-way point of his journey, when he attends a banquet at the court of the Phaiacian King Alcinous, where the blind rhapsode Demodocus (whose name literally means "honored by the people") performs in the midst of the festivities. Incredibly, Demodocus sings of the very events in the war from which our hero has escaped not long before. At the Phaiacian king's table, Odysseus hears the song of the fall of Troy and of the unspeakable suffering of the heroes who died there, indeed he even hears the story of the Trojan Horse and the sack of the city: this is more than he can bear, and he loses his composure. To conceal his distress, he draws a veil over his face and freely weeps tears that his host cannot see: "And Odysseus / let the bright molten tears run down his cheeks, / weeping the way a wife mourns for her lord / on the lost field where he has gone down fighting."[7]

In this moment of emotional reflection, he first fully becomes *polytropos*, a man who got around so much that he had to stumble across the reflections of his own past. Here reflexivity emerges from maneuverability, an encounter with the self emerges from being tossed about. In this staging of subjective memory, the oldest in European literature, the epic reunion with his own fate still initially seems to be a superficial coincidence, and yet here memory is already linked to emotional pain – centuries before tragedy and millennia before psychoanalysis. Catharsis immediately follows anamnesis. If even tears must somehow be learned, then we could say that Europe has learned a beneficial kind of crying from Odysseus and first realized how stories and tears belong together by observing him, a storm-tossed man. Of course, Odysseus weeps to himself over everything that has happened, everything in which he was actively involved and everything that he suffered, and sheds ecumenical tears for friend and foe alike.

Many centuries later, Virgil still adheres to this principle that depiction and storytelling renew pain, when he has the Roman Odysseus, Aeneas, a refugee who is on his way from the old Troy in the East to Rome, the new Troy in the West, encounter ornate images that immortalize the Trojan catastrophe, shortly after landing on the coast of Carthage – images before which he stands stunned, "sighing often the while, and his face wet with a full river of tears."[8] Though in convulsions, Aeneas manages to say *Sunt lacrimae rerum et mentem mortalia tangunt*: "Even things themselves have their tears, and mortal fates touch the soul."[9] Virgil provides a formula for how the realist art of narration functions in Aeneas' subsequent telling of the story to Dido, when it occurs to the hero to say to his listener: *Infandum, regina, iubes renovare dolorem*, or "Dreadful, O Queen, is the woe thou bidst me recall."[10] Theodor Haecker was probably right when he remarked that Virgil here managed to write one of the most sonorous lines of all time with five of the most ordinary words in Latin.[11]

10.2 Polymētis – Someone Who is Never at a Loss

The epithet most used by Homer for Odysseus is *polymētis*, which literally means "of many counsels" or "the powerful schemer" – since in Greek *mētis* refers to good counsel and the ability to cleverly ensure that things turn out well; it means the stratagem, the simulation, the hunter's trap, the feint, and inspired wit. Hence it is the quick-witted man's virtue *par excellence*.[12] At the same time, *Mētis* is the proper name of a goddess of intelligence, whom Zeus pursues in his usual manner. He fathers a child with her, whose birth he fears, since it had been foretold that the child would be his equal in intelligence – which prompts him to devour the pregnant mother. He winds up with a very difficult brain-pregnancy as a result. Hephaestus relieves the headache by striking Zeus on the skull with a double axe, so that Athena can leap out of his head armed with a lance and wearing a full suit of armor. Zeus later comes to terms with his exceptionally wise daughter, and when Athena offers candid opinions during the gods' council, he contents himself by saying to her in a paternal tone: "My child, what strange remarks you let escape you."[13]

In what follows, I would like to make a case for my basic thesis that ancient Greek intellectual culture, informed by *mētis* as it appears in the *Odyssey* and is reflected in various Hellenistic myths about cunning, represents a distant prelude to what in our view is the most Greek of all phenomena – the Sophistic movement, which led to the secession of philosophy in the fourth century. In contemporary German, a society animated by sophistic arts would be called a *Streitkultur* [Tr. – "agonistic culture"] – we can see here that even though Germany has a word for this phenomenon, it lacks the thing itself, because, instead of a *Streitkultur*, we have an accusatory culture [*Hetzkultur*], a culture of denunciation, a culture of disparagement, in which things are decided in advance, before they have a chance to become controversial. In contrast, the Greek polis was organized on an agonistic basis. Not only were there organized interests and divergent classes in every city, there was a ubiquitous pluralism of claims to nobility and excellence that could not have been made without a rhetorically articulated competition between the claimants.

To truly understand the Sophistic movement in its original sense, we must rid it of the bad name given to it by the Academy, a reputation it received partly on valid logical grounds, and partly from dubious strategic motives. One of the positive effects of Nietzsche's epochal emergence in the recent history of ideas was that even academic philosophy was compelled to reevaluate the Sophistic movement. In our present context, we can resume this reconsideration by observing that the Sophistic movement signifies precisely the continuation of the Odyssean praxis of intelligence with urban means. The homecoming hero's capacity to negotiate a viable future for himself with every power in the world, with the gods, with human beings, indeed with the sea itself, recurs in the polis as the capacity of orators and lawyers to navigate the sea of disputes within the city and between cities and to conclude their mandates successfully.

If Homer often endows the storm-tossed voyaging hero with the epithet *polymētis*, he is not merely labeling a specific person, but

characterizing a type of masculine existence in which renowned
heroic vigor (in other words, the ability to make an impact) for the
first time concludes a new kind of compromise with cunning – with
a purely navigational or operative cunning. Such cunning thought
still remains entirely bound to current situations. This early version
of cunning is still a long way from abstract theory. The characteristic
feature of Odyssean intelligence is that it understands itself to be
dealing with the challenges that fate has posed for it from day to
day, from port to port, and from case to case. The challenges to be
overcome by the seafarer on his delayed journey home are proto-
types of what will one day be called "problems" – but there can only
be "problems" at all, if homecoming heroes have turned into argumentative citizens and if they have they transformed the monsters at
the ends of the Earth into mere legal adversaries. In urban space, a
free-ranging intelligence forms concepts that are gradually detached
from the level of given cases and concrete examples. The desire to
have and to solve "problems" begins to flourish when the cunning of
polymētis Odysseus changes into the maneuverability of the urban
or "political" rhetoric that distinguished lawyers and orators at the
peak of Hellenistic culture. There is a moving episode in the *Odyssey*
that is a powerful example of *polymētis* Odysseus' art. I am thinking
of the shipwrecked sailor landing on the beach on the island of
Phaeacia, after a storm has destroyed the raft that was supposed
to bring him home when he left the nymph Calypso behind. More
than half-drowned, with his last bit of strength he saves himself, and
after several days of floating around on the tempestuous sea ends up
on the beach, where, stumbling into the bushes, he falls into a deep
sleep, concealed by a hedge. On the following day, Nausicaa, the
daughter of King Alcinous, and her maids head to the shore to wash
their clothing and discover the unkempt shipwrecked voyager, who
emerges from his hiding place at that very moment.

Homer sets the scene, showing how the unclothed foreigner winds
up in the young women's view:

> Odysseus had this look, in his rough skin
> Advancing on the girls with pretty braids;
> And he was driven on by hunger, too.
> Streaked with brine, and swollen, he terrified them,
> So that they fled, this way and that. Only
> Alkínoös' daughter stood her ground, being given
> A bold heart by Athena, and steady knees . . .[14]

Odysseus is now faced with a fateful choice: he can either throw
himself at the feet of "this beauty" and clasp her knees – or stand

away from the young woman and appeal to her from afar with flattering words. After deliberating for a moment, he realizes that he prefers the second option, because he is mindful that a daughter from a good house might become easily annoyed if he were to presume to touch her knees without permission. This consideration leads to the shipwrecked voyager's speech on the shore – or, as Homer puts it, he "let the soft words fall."[15] In terms of the history of rhetoric, this can be viewed as the first plea ever made by a lawyer *pro se* on European soil. The naked speaker mounts the rostrum that his need has erected, and devotes himself to the task of winning the harshest public in the world, the bold heart of a young woman, over to his side.

> Mistress: please: are you divine, or mortal?
> If one of those who dwell in the wide heaven,
> You are most near to Artemis, I should say –
> Great Zeus's daughter – in your grace and presence.
> If you are one of Earth's inhabitants,
> How blest your father, and your gentle mother,
> Blest all your kin. I know what happiness
> Must send the warm tears to their eyes, each time
> They see their wondrous child go to the dancing!
> But one man's destiny is more than blest –
> He who prevails, and takes you as his bride.
> Never have I laid eyes on equal beauty
> In man or woman. I am hushed indeed.
> So fair, one time, I thought a young palm tree
> At Delos near the altar of Apollo –
> I had troops under me when I was there
> On the sea route that later brought me grief –
> But that slim palm tree filled my heart with wonder:
> Never came shoot from Earth so beautiful.
> So now, my lady, I stand in awe so great
> I cannot take your knees. And yet my case is desperate:
> Twenty days, yesterday, in the winedark sea,
> On the ever-lunging swell, under gale winds,
> Getting away from the Island of Ogygia.
> And now the terror of Storm has left me stranded
> Upon this shore – with more blows yet to suffer,
> I must believe, before the gods relent.
> Mistress, do me a kindness!
> After much weary toil, I come to you,
> And you are the first soul I have seen – I know
> No others here. Direct me to the town,
> Give me a rag that I can throw around me,

Some cloth or wrapping that you brought along.
And may the gods accomplish your desire:
A home, a husband, and harmonious
Converse with him . . .[16]

But the white-armed maiden, Nausicaa, says: "Stranger, there is no quirk or evil in you that I can see."[17]

We can clearly see that Odysseus on the shores of Phaeacia does not have what we would call a "problem" at all. He is in need, in a tight squeeze with only one way out, precisely where the young woman is standing. The man whom Homer calls *polymētis* is a warrior who has learned to transform every hardship into a challenge. From his nakedness he makes an argument, and he forms a project out of his destitution. He is literally someone who is never at a loss. We should never forget that at the inception of European rhetoric, we find a sea monster making its plea and frightening off young women. Only one brave maiden holds her ground to form an audience. A miracle occurs in her ears – the salt-encrusted monster opens its mouth and reveals itself to be the most human of all human beings. The *zōion logon echon*, as defined a half-millennium later by Aristotle, the living being that has speech – here stands on the beach, with his irresistible flattery, his musical declamation, and his ability to make a virtue, that of beautiful speech, out of the most urgent necessity. It then occurs to Nausicaa that she might fall in love with a man who speaks to her this way, not so much because of his quite forward compliments, which drift past her like a warm breeze, but because she feels and suspects that a good and clever man stands before her. She has experienced a logophany – proof that language, as soon as it comes into its own, elevates the human being. If the disheveled foreigner is not a god, he has provided proof of his humanity by speaking as no beast, no fool, and no villain could.

From here, we can proceed further in an almost direct line to a scene that played out centuries later in Athens. In one of his dialogues, Plato tells us how a father brings his teenage son to Socrates the sophist, who was known for his ability to educate youth. Socrates turned to the young man with a single request, "Speak boy, so that I may see you."[18] The belief in the logophanic revelation of the human being's essential nature reaches its culmination here. At the same time, Odysseus' plea on the beach also leads directly to other fifth-century sophists who were famous for their ability to argue any position. Isocrates, the prince of Greek lawyers, demonstrates how significant this influence was in his notorious *Helenē Encōmion* (*Encomium of Helen*), which is supposed to prove that a good lawyer can win a case that seems lost in advance. What case could be more hopeless than the one against the most fatal woman of antiquity, the unfaithful beauty for whose sake the Trojan War must be fought?

We learn of Gorgias that, in his case, the ability to speak about anything at all degenerated into his really being a know-it-all. In one anecdote we read: "For coming into the theater of the Athenians he had the boldness to say 'suggest a subject,' and he was the first to proclaim himself willing to take this chance, showing apparently that he knew everything and would trust to the moment to speak on any subject."[19] Only one aspect of this story is of interest here: Gorgias has walked every step of the path that leads from a distress that still can find words to playing with mere "problems" – this can be observed in the word he uses to challenge the Athenian public to propose a topic for him: this word is *proballete* – from the verb *proballein*, meaning "to throw something" at him, "to suggest" something to him, "to pose a topic," a word from which both ancient and modern *problemata* derive. The "problem" that Gorgias wanted to "solve" in the theater was simply a random topic for an expert to develop a thesis on or for a virtuoso to use as a basis for extemporization.

If the Sophistic movement is supposed to involve the translation of existential hardships into a kind of relaxed playing with topics, then Odysseus is not yet a sophist in this sense. Odyssean intelligence is still bound to the harsh necessities of the struggle for survival, and cannot claim the privilege of relaxed observation for itself. Nevertheless, we can trace a line of descent from him to the Sophistic movement, since we discover in *polymētis* Odysseus the first signs of a general craft consciousness that is an essential feature of Classical Greek civilization. From a distance, the *Odyssey* already heralds that great event in the history of thought which can only be called the Greek miracle: the birth of problems from the proud awareness of being able to deal with them. The brilliant words of an Austrian essayist, written before the First World War, seem appropriate for fifth-century Greeks: "Culture has a wealth of problems, and the more mysteries it discovers, the more enlightened it is."[20] We could even say instead that culture is the sum of relief efforts [*Entlastungen*] in response to primal needs. Decadence sets in the moment that the recipients of such relief forget why they needed culture to relieve them in the first place.

10.3 Polytlas Dios Odysseus – Odysseus, a Man Who Endured Much

If we advance further in our examination of Homeric epithets, which make the hero into a man with qualities, we come to the most dramatic epic formula of all: the oft-recurring expression *polytlas dios Odysseus* – godlike much-enduring Odysseus, or *der göttliche Dulder Odysseus* [Tr. – "the divine sufferer Odysseus"], to make use of Voss' translation once more, while English translators here introduce phrases such as "much-suffering brilliant Odysseus" or "long-suffering godlike Odysseus." Thus readers of the *Iliad* naturally recall the analogous expression *podarkes dios Achilleus*; godlike swift-footed Achilles. This stock figure of speech, which according to expert philologists surfaces 37 times, always in the nominative case and at the end of a verse, as needed to maintain hexameter, once more reminds us of the connection between traveling and suffering, which is essential for understanding the epic psychology of the *Odyssey*. For ancient Mediterranean cultures, travel – or sailing – and suffering are indissolubly linked. A stormy sea with the obligatory shipwreck strikes them as a universal metaphor for existence. The statement attributed to Pompey: *navigare necesse est, vivere non necesse* – "to sail is necessary, to live is not necessary" – suggests that suffering is necessary and that we lose our lives in any case, even if we remain on land, but more quickly at sea. Prior to the Romans, the Greeks thought the same thing, as indicated by their saying *plein anagkē, zēn ouk anagkē* [Tr. – "to sail is necessary, to live is not necessary"], and even in the nineteenth century the narrator of *Moby Dick* is of this opinion – which is why, on the very first page of his book, he explains to the reader that when a cold November arrives in his soul and he really finds himself feeling suicidal, he simply climbs aboard a ship.

Polytlas dios Odysseus – with this solemn stereotypical figure of speech, the narrator invokes an existential position that broadly characterized the Greeks returning from Troy. Anyone who believed that the city's fall meant that the heroes' battle was over saw his hopes dashed – the battle is never over, even when confrontations shift from the battlefield to the high seas and from an epic distance to the home front. The battle is not even over when arguments replace weapons and local rivals step in to take the place of foreign enemies.

Yet this Homeric phrase already expresses a tendency to interpret the endurance of suffering in active terms. If Odysseus is often addressed as the man of much sorrow (*polypenthēs*), of many tribulations (*polytlēmōn*), and of much endurance (*polytlas*), the purpose of these epithets is not to depict him as a victim – a modern type of victimology is the last thing on the mind of the author of the *Iliad* and the *Odyssey*. Rather, such epithets serve to characterize the hero as a man whose suffering never made him wretched and whose constant ordeal never made him weary of himself and of life. In the language of later philosophy, we would probably say here that the hero's many sufferings are mentioned because he constitutes a substance whose attributes are suffering. Incidentally, we can trace the development of thought in this formulation: classical philosophy no longer has any place for heroes and heroism, because it is trying to carry out thought's task of dissolving subject into substance – in contrast, modernity proclaims the counter-formulation: substance is to be developed as subject. Substance is the only hero of metaphysics, whether it is called God, *physis*, being, or matter. Once this logical monstrosity is conceived, the only thing left for brave human beings to do, in their vile individuality, is to get rid of themselves for the sake of this colossus – to be a wise human being thus means to be very good at imitating lifeless substance, but wisest is he who obliterates himself, like Empedocles (the Etna diver), to abolish the troubling difference between self and absolute fundament.

Such reductive measures are not alien to the epic interpretation of the world. An epic hero is a determined adventurer who repeatedly passes the test and in doing so seems to be on the way to a certain kind of "substantiality" that would be synonymous with a certain kind of "subjectivity." Yet the epic hero always remains utterly enveloped by particular struggles, he is always involved in an ongoing adventure, and even his thoughts are entirely related to some current conflict, though he has occasionally been celebrated as the protagonist of a nascent inner life. To again put this into philosophical terminology: he is only alive to the extent that he bears attributes – the establishment of a permanently stable Odysseus-substance or the preservation of a permanently stable Odysseus-subject is the least of his worries.

Odysseus does not yet need to either establish such a substance or preserve such a subject because what endures [*das Bleibende*] in him is concealed in another mode of lasting. The epic world requires that he hold on [*Bleibe-Leistung*], and he is able to do so precisely because he is distinguished for being *polytlas*, someone who endures much suffering. His endurance of suffering cannot simply be equated with passivity, it has *a fortiori* nothing to do with the metaphysical and religious forms of masochism that later flourished in fatalism, mysticism, and dolorism. The performative character of heroically enduring suffering is unquestionable to the narrator of the *Odyssey*, and if Homer repeatedly calls him *polytlas dios Odysseus*, someone who has suffered much, someone who divinely perseveres, he is simply emphasizing that Odyssean suffering is a skillful kind of suffering that has little or nothing to do with the way we are ordinarily overwhelmed by circumstances that render us passive.

The relevant *locus classicus* for obtaining a picture of the hero's endurance of suffering can be found in the story Odysseus tells at the Phaeacian court. He there recounts how he and his companions had already seen the shepherd's fire on the coast of Ithaca and were about to rejoice over their successful return home, when a catastrophic storm drove them back to the island of Aeolia, from which they had embarked not long before. The storm seems all the more ominous since it was provoked by Odysseus' companions. While Odysseus was dozing at the ship's helm, they found what they believed to be treasure that he had concealed from them, and opened the closed bag that the wind god had given to the hero to take along on the voyage. The crew's lack of trust in their captain was the source of the catastrophe. At this point, we hear what Odysseus thinks of the situation:

> Roused up, despairing in that gloom, I thought:
> "Should I go overside for a quick finish
> Or clench my teeth and stay among the living?"[21]

Endurance of suffering is the practical ability to avoid becoming impatient enough to lose all hope. This is precisely what we observe in the *Odyssey*'s most famous episode, when Odysseus would like to kill the sleeping Polyphemus with his sword, after the cyclops has eaten a few of his companions, but refrains from giving in to this initial impulse because he sees that the cave's exit is blocked off and only the giant can open it. Philosophically inclined readers of the *Odyssey* have long celebrated this as the first depiction of having "second thoughts."[22] This episode suggests a link between thought and hesitation that will eventually culminate in Shakespeare's *Hamlet*, at the inception of the modern era. Twentieth-century sociologists call this link "the inhibition of action by reflection." We observe something analogous after the hero's return to Ithaca, when he has the appearance of a ragged beggar and one of the suitors gives him the kind of kick that would have sent any other man reeling.[23] Odysseus pauses for a moment to consider how he should avenge himself: should he strike the man with a club from behind or lift the man up and slam his head into the ground? Restraint prevails: "Then he controlled himself, and bore it quietly."[24]

The spectrum of the endurance of suffering in the *Odyssey* is quite broad. In the first place, as noted, the hero must put up with the hardships of sailing, already mentioned in the fourth (of twelve thousand) verses: "harried for years on end."[25] We are thus programmatically given notice that a good number of the tests the hero will face will occur in the maritime realm, where education, *paideia*, happens on the high seas, before it becomes the business of schools.

The frequent loss of companions while underway is an additional hardship that must be suffered – as is the price the hero must pay for the stupidity and outrages of those same companions, whether they are slaughtering the cattle of Helios or opening up Aeolus' wind-bag. Odysseus is not a solitary hermit, he is rather collegial, and he puts up with and may well even enjoy being together with his companions (or *hetairoi*) for long stretches of time. And if such men are not available, even women companions do not seem to be unwelcome to him. The name for such feminine companions has been better understood in its more than two-millennia-long voyage into the modern lexicon than its masculine form was – we merely have to look up the word "hetaera" to see how unconcerned the Greeks generally were with gender when thinking about companionship. We have already discussed Odysseus' two time-consuming feminine companions on the islands of Ogygia and Aeaea, and we have also already noted that these erotic evasions could fall under the rubric of endurance – embraces are to be counted as tests when the embraced would prefer to pursue another agenda.

Finally, misrecognition is yet another misfortune that must be endured by Odysseus after he returns to Ithaca, when he first goes unrecognized, if not unnoticed, as he reenters his own house in the guise of an old and ragged beggar. There, lying on the steps like a proto-Diogenes, he is fed on the leftovers that the suitors toss his way. Indeed, to experience complete degradation, he fights with another beggar for a food prize that has been offered as a reward by the cynical suitors. Modern social philosophers would undoubtedly say that Odysseus must undergo alienation from his true self in order to preserve himself. Admittedly, such thoughts would be anachronistic in an epic context, since the singer has no interest in either substance or subject. The singer is merely concerned with the hero's transformations according to the law of the situation. If the situation demands that the hero be incognito, this happens without self-pity – with a wave of her wand, Athena changes the homecoming hero's outward appearance so that even those most closely related to him no longer recognize him. There is no mention of alienation when this occurs. Even as a beggar, *polytropos* Odysseus is no one but himself – yet he is himself precisely in the endurance of suffering. He accepts the basic law of life, according to which enjoying ourselves is an exception and suffering the rule in a harsh world. Endurance is the hero's cunning and resilient ability to hold on through an entire range of situations, to become what the situation demands of him, beyond identity and non-identity. The author of the *Odyssey* has a special epithet for such resilient prudence:

talasiphronos, which Anton Weiher reliably and precisely translates as "*standhaftklug*" [Tr. – "cunningly firm"].

There is no final exam in the Homeric world. Yet the homecoming hero will be severely tested one more time – a tougher test than dodging the volley of spears heaved by the suitors, when he later engages in a life-and-death battle with them. Odysseus' ideally faithful wife Penelope is the next to last person to recognize him – his father, the aged Laertes, is last – and her obstinate failure to recognize him, her incredulity, her refusal to believe the words of the wet-nurse who had recognized Odysseus after noticing his scar while washing his feet, forms the key obstacle that must be overcome before the hero may trust that he has really arrived back home. Worried that she might be disappointed, she is unwilling to recognize him, although he completely reverts to his old form after the bath and stands before her fully ready to be recognized, saying to her: "Strange woman, / the immortals of Olympus made you hard / harder than any. . . / Her heart is iron in her breast."[26] So he must pass the final test that Penelope's cunning has devised for him: she insists that their old marriage bed should be moved from its present location to another spot – and as soon as his answer proves that he has seen through the riddle (having built it with his own hands from a massive, ancient olive tree that could not possibly have been uprooted, Odysseus knows something that only he can, namely that the bed is immobile), Penelope relents and is ready to believe and to recognize him. Now, after the homecoming hero has given the "sign" and provided intimate proof that he is Odysseus, the spell is broken, and what generally follows an *anagnōrismos* then occurs, when those who had been inseparable finally recognize each other after so long a time apart – composure is overcome by tears, until dawn finally breaks, though not as early as usual on this occasion because *rhododactylos Eōs*, the rosy-fingered goddess of dawn, is deliberately a bit late on this special day so as to allow the magnificent couple some time. Tears of recognition tell their own stories – as we already know. The reunited couple, already sharing their bed, do not fall asleep before Odysseus has recounted his entire story one more time.

Odysseus told
Of what hard blows he had dealt out to others /
And of what blows he had taken – all that story.
She could not close her eyes till all was told.[27]

We can again trace a path from this scene of recognition to nascent dimensions of Greek thought, in this case to the quite marvelous,

suggestive, and fateful Platonic hyperbole that all cognition is essentially remembrance and recognition – namely, glimpsing the ideas
that were present in the soul prior to its birth. What the *Odyssey*'s
ancient editor called Penelope's *anagnōrismos* is the original depiction of everything that comes to be known as *anamnēsis* in the
Platonic tradition. It is obvious that Homeric recognition follows
entirely different laws than does Platonic memory. While *anamnēsis*
is guided by eidetic constants and grounded in the alignment between
a priori formal archetypes and *a posteriori* manifestations of those
formal archetypes, Homeric *anagnōrismos* stems from the discovery
of a distinctive feature. Neither his wet-nurse nor his wife recognize
Odysseus from the way he looks, or from how his outward appearance resembles the formal-archetypical self that we would find in a
universe operating according to Platonic rules of the game. Instead,
they determine his identity by means of a discrete distinctive feature
– Homer explicitly says: *sēma*, just as with modern passports today
there is talk of "unalterable distinguishing features" – in the case
of the elder Eurycleia this is the scar from the boar's tusk on his
foot, while in Penelope's case it is the secret of the bed made from
an olive tree. Nevertheless, Odysseus' return prepares the Greeks
in advance for Platonism and its subtle logic of returning. Even
later Gnostics, who were interested in the soul's return home to its
ancestral world beyond, did not fail to note the edifying analogies
to the Odyssean nexus between recognition and returning home.[28]
Incidentally, Plato memorialized the sublation of the epic ethos into
a philosophical and non-tragic attitude, when in the tenth book of
the *Republic* he expounded on the myth in which Odysseus' soul, at
its reincarnation, chooses the life of a private individual who minds
his own business: "remembering its former sufferings, it rejected
love of honor [*philotimias*]."[29] Plato knows his conceptual terminology: where *philotimia* was, there *philosophia* shall be. The motif of
homecoming first really comes into its own in philosophical leisure –
as true retreat into the contemplative life. Philosophy is the mother
of the idyll and utopia its granddaughter: reckless, like all heirs, it
would like to send the entire human race to Ithaca.

The clearest trace that leads from Odyssean motifs to later positions in Greek thought begins with an image of divine endurance of
suffering and perhaps inevitably brings us close to Stoicism, that is,
to a philosophical movement that could be summed up as a general
system of being-in-the-world-enduring-suffering. There are two
essential elements to Stoicism: the theoretical conviction that the
world is a place where human beings are exposed to burdens, and
the practical resolution to harmonize with this belief by performing
daily exercises that involve burdens. Thus *sapientia* and *patientia* are

slowly fused together. So it is no accident when Odysseus, in Roman stoicism, is stylized into the archetype of the wise philosopher – yet we also find a contrasting tradition in Rome, which elaborates a disagreeable image of Odysseus, not least in Virgil, who transfers the radiant virtues of Greek seafaring heroes to Aeneas, so as to leave only dubious qualities for the original. Among Stoics in general, as a metaphor for life, seafaring remains as self-evident as it is indispensable, and philosophy was considered by them to be a preschool for foundering. We thus read in Seneca: ". . . who sails this sea that has no other shore but death." In which case, to philosophize means daring to cross the sea of life, and, indeed, not on the raft of emotions and bad habits, but on the carefully constructed boat of practice and tranquility.

10.4 Polymēchanos – The Versatile Teacher of How Not to Be Helpless

None of Odysseus' frequently recurring epithets is as sonorous and full of prescient undertones as the word *polymēchanos*. It brings to mind the connection, already evident to the Greeks, between cunning, guile, and contrivance [*Maschine*]. If, in the parlance of our times, we speak of "machines" [*Maschinen*] (a term that can be traced back to the Latin *machina*, the equivalent of the Greek *mēchanē*), we ordinarily do not still have this term's basic meaning in mind. Originally, a *mēchanē* or *machina* is just a ruse, a subterfuge, a trick, hitting an opponent below the belt. Its "setting in life" (as Biblical philologists put it) is initially only to be found in the way that human beings deal with rivals and adversaries who are considered to have violated the rules of the game. Only with the concept's extension to complex instruments do we arrive at a machine from what was originally a ruse. This extension occurs with good reason, insofar as we are ready to define machines as devices for the circumvention of nature, whose assistance allows human activity to sidestep a problem that cannot be directly resolved, in order to handle it indirectly.[30] As is well known, the lever is the paradigm for every cunning mechanical effect in antiquity. With levers, human beings are able to transport loads that would otherwise be impossible to move. In ancient times, levers were often used to operate a theater crane, which allowed tragic poets to have the gods float down into a scene from above – something still familiar to us today as *deus ex machina*, the first special effect, which can be traced back to this technological device. A while later, we find something comparable in the Church Father Ignatius of Antioch, when he declares in his *Letter to the Ephesians*, about 100 years after Christ, that the cross (*stauros*) is a *mēchanē* of Christ,[31] an expression that has to be translated as "rope attached to a hoisting crane." This device's usefulness in constructing the realm of God must be acknowledged – which is precisely what Ignatius means when he says that such machines of Christ first make it possible to erect a temple for the Father's glorification. In contrast, until the eighteenth century, every use of the word *machina* was subjectively characterized by strategic orientation, indeed sheer cunning and making a move was so present in the term's usage that one can only decide on a case-by-case basis whether a given discourse is concerned with a ruse or with a machine. In Lorenzo Da Ponte's libretto *The Marriage of Figaro* from 1786, we find the semantically and musically crucial passage: *tutte le macchine rovescerò* [Tr. – "All your plots I'll overthrow!"] in the aria "*Se vuol ballare, Signor Contino*," and it is here evident that the word *macchine* here does not mean "machines," but rather "machinations," by means of which the Count would like to enforce his feudal privilege with the lovely Susanna – the very woman with whom Figaro is head over heels in love.

If Homer frequently describes his hero as *polymēchanos*, it is not enough to translate this word as "cunning," "resourceful," "deviser of intrigues," and so forth, as though we were simply confronted with a sly character's incidental features. We must bear in mind that the machine's triumphal procession through the human sphere had already begun in Homer's time. *Polymēchanos* is thus not merely an attribute that adorns a single clever hero, at a basic level it can already be used to broadly characterize the civilizing work environment of that era – including metallurgy, navigation, urban planning, and epic poetry. Because war has always involved the polytechnical education of engineers, it is no wonder that the epithet *polymēchanos* is initially attributed to a warrior. It has often been noted that Odysseus represents a new type of hero, who, very much in distinction from the purely thymotic and violently raging type (exemplified by Achilles), can be described as a cognitive hero, proficient in delay. The defining feature of the character Odysseus is not merely a more advanced operation of reflective qualities, but more importantly his quite pronounced manipulative attitude toward human beings and things, from a strategic perspective.

This shift of perspective already defines the conclusion of the *Iliad*. It is well known that Achilles' wild raging power does not decide the Trojan War, but rather Odysseus' war machine, the sinister hollow horse, in whose belly some of the best Greek warriors are hiding – and, incidentally, we should note that we have traditionally been provided with more names of passengers than there were spots available in the horse's interior. With the apparent retreat of the Greek fleet from the Trojan shore, the strategic aspect of this *mēchanē* is emphasized, namely that it makes the gift seem plausible. The horse-machine not only outwits the Trojans, at the same time it plays the gods off against each other, since while it is an apparent offering to Poseidon, who was favorably disposed toward the Trojans, it is really intended as a tribute to Athena, who was favorably disposed toward the Greeks.

Yet the cunning of polymechanical Odysseus does not celebrate its greatest intellectual-historical triumph in Troy, but on the high seas, when he constructs the first machine of self-inhibition while his ship subtly sails past the treacherous rocks on which the Sirens perched, which has since become legendary in the European tradition. The technical simplicity of the hero's fettering should not deceive us – even here we have a genuine case of mechanical engineering. Odysseus constructs a *dispositif* by building a functional ad hoc wax-rope-mast-machine. Stoics were already able to easily expand on this image, by interpreting the fettered sailor as a prototype of the sage, who traverses the temptations of the world bound to the mast of exercise and reflection. The mast symbolizes the fundamental Stoic distinction between the things that are up to us – these, of course, are our own thoughts, feelings, and judgments – and the things that are not up to us – in other words, the colossal remainder, which with explicit disparagement is referred to as the external world or *adiaphora*. Only someone tied to his or her own mast has the chance for a happy life, insofar as such a person will be happy in a philosophical sense by keeping to what falls within their own sphere of power, a life that has found refuge from temptation.

The analogies between the mast and the cross obviously did not escape the early Christians. Maximus of Tyre is the clearest example of this when, in the first half of the fifth century, he writes that "Christ . . . was bound to the cross so that we can be drawn through the tempting dangers of the world as though with closed ears." The Christian community is here interpreted as a group of *hetairoi*, who row through the world under the command of their crucified captain, with the wax of the gospel in their ears.

Over the last two millennia countless authors have assimilated the episode of the sirens into their own respective frameworks, drawing on this kind of unscrupulous reinterpretation. Not too long ago, the unorthodox Marxist Theodor Adorno showed us where such reinterpretation can lead: he seriously thought that we could recognize Odysseus as the first citizen, who, bound to the mast of delayed gratification, misses out on what he desires, yet does so in a conscious and culturally enlightened way, while the rowers represent the unconscious proletariat, who have the wax of mass culture in their ears and never experience what he is able to avoid. Had Adorno not speculated from memory, but consulted the original, he might have noted that the sirens are not prostitutes who offer their charms for free and feign erotic socialism, nor are they singers in a Wagnerian opera who glorify the love of death. Their lethal charm is based on their ability to charm the hero sailing by into believing that he is experiencing his apotheosis, so that he feels transported from their mouths to the realm of myths and gods – this divinization while alive is what drives men out of their minds, leading them to jump overboard only to perish at the foot of the transfiguring rocks.

Bazon Brock has more likely adopted the right approach, when he would like to recognize Odysseus as the father of "artists of self-captivation," or, in other words, of the rare species of artists, at least to this point, who are ready to shield the contemporary social world [*Mitwelt*] from its own delusions of grandeur and from its fury for self-actualization. On this reading, we find ourselves back in Stoic territory, since Stoics not only learn to be on their guard against external distractions, but are also cautious when it comes to the ambivalent tendencies of their own internal states. The sirens would thus be accomplices of the megalomaniacal dispositions that are so easy to arouse in the souls of warriors and artists – and that today provide the cues for the art market and celebrity complex. That Odysseus resists the Sirens' temptation should ultimately not surprise us, indeed we might even ask whether he would have made it past them without rope and mast, since he had already refused private immortality at Calypso's side. But since the Sirens' overtures concern great or popular immortality, it was perhaps sensible to avail himself of rope in the case of such temptation.

Nevertheless, I do not think that the Stoic appropriation of the figure of Odysseus should have the last word here. If we take the epithet *polymēchanos* seriously, it once again leads us to the Sophistic movement, which had a much higher potential for genuinely philosophical content than might have been apparent after Plato's lethal denunciations. We can see that the Sophistic movement had an indispensable and unparalleled spiritual and philosophical significance, as soon as we acknowledge its fundamental ethical figure. It puts all of its best energy into a single gesture – supporting the revolt of human beings against helplessness, which has proven to be an essential element of the adventure of European civilization.

Helplessness had a name among the Greeks: *amēchania* – which literally means the complete absence of cunning, guile, and contrivance, the lack of an art or wits that would show a way out, to be without the resources that could help those in need avert what is

ailing them. It is the condition human beings descend into when the
spirit of *mēchanē*, the *polymēchanos*-attitude, is dormant. They then
sink into a stupor, or become resigned to their lack of resources,
falling into a kind of contented misfortune. They succumb to dejec-
tion when faced with the challenge of finding ways out and ways
around adversity to something better. Thus if we are unwilling to
translate *amēchania* as "helplessness," we could perhaps instead
render it as "oblivious to resources" or "refusing to see that there is
a way out" – phrases that horrifyingly sum up what most of humanity has actually accomplished throughout history.

Among the Greeks, as we know, divinity easily emerges from a
general concept, and thus they recognized a goddess or *daimōn* by
the name of *Amēchania* (Helplessness), the sister of *Penia* (ragged
Poverty). The latter – as we may recall – is the goddess of not-having,
who is depicted in Plato's *Symposium* as the mother of the demigod
Eros – that forceful rogue who guides human beings toward what
they are lacking. Both *daimones*, Helplessness and Poverty, played a
role in a famous diplomatic dispute that is recounted by Herodotus:
when Themistocles wanted to impose a tribute on the Andrians with
the argument that Athens had two powerful and obliging gods on
its side, Persuasion (*Peithō*) and Necessity (*Anagkē*), the Andrians
are supposed to have replied that this alliance might well explain
Athens' good fortune, but that, in contrast, they were the homeland of two less obliging goddesses, *Penia* and *Amēchania*: ". . . the
Andrians being possessed of these deities would not give money; for
never could the power of the Athenians get the better of their inability."[32] Today it would appear that the Andrians have the upper hand
nearly everywhere. Incidentally, it is a testament to Sigmund Freud's
classical education, when, shortly before the publication of *The
Interpretation of Dreams*, he remarks in a letter to Wilhelm Fliess
from September 1899: "I have made the acquaintance of helpless
poverty and am constantly in fear of her" – he is thus quite aware of
how *Penia* and *Amēchania* go hand in hand, and moreover knows
that speaking and being allowed to speak can help us against both
of them. To be sure, money earned by the psychoanalytic sophistic
is a still greater help to him, and not for nothing does Freud say in
the same passage: "Money is my laughing gas," since where money
flows, helplessness has lost the game.

In making these observations, we touch on the dynamic of Greek
cultural life and approach everything of concern to Europe via a
detour through Greece: if we find the struggle between ability and
inability at the basis of our culture (and ultimately at the basis of all
other cultures), then philosophy should take a stance in this primal
dispute. As long as philosophy is well-disposed to knowledgeable

and proficient ability, it reveals itself to be partisan. It only comes
into its own when it sets to work to expand the initially still small
island of ability out into the ocean of inability. However, as soon
as philosophy separates knowledge from ability, only to pursue
impotent theory, it is eaten away by ressentiment – precisely as
happened in the theoretical tendencies of later Platonism, with
its grudge against rivals who could also address themselves to the
masses, and which is also prominent in more than one present-day
school of philosophy, when we find polemics against authors who
are attempting a philosophical conception of the world in terms
their contemporaries can actually understand.

To advocate the vital unity of knowledge and ability was the
Sophistic movement's sole historic mission, insofar as it represented
the first educational system and first training ground for capability
in general. Yet since Greeks of the classical era considered being able
to speak well to be the most dazzling of all abilities, the sophists put
great stock in the rhetorical training of human beings so as to equip
the latter with the necessary quick-wittedness for any situation in
life. Seen in this light, the Sophistic movement is something like a
shipping company that wishes to make human beings seaworthy in
the broadest sense of the term – it thus has the right word for every
storm and an impressive conclusion anytime there is foundering.

True sophists are utterly convinced that succumbing to *amēchania*
is never advisable for human beings. The living being that has speech
never seems entirely at a loss, is never entirely inept, without any
counsel, and lacking in techniques that can provide a way out. And
because the Sophistic movement unprecedentedly and unforgetta-
bly validates the fundamental human claim to not being helpless,
polymēchanos Odysseus is on board every enterprise that involves
this clever praxis. Athena once said of this pre-Socratic from Ithaca
that he was the cleverest of all men – the Oracle of Delphi later
says the same thing of Socrates, so that the seafarer and the sophist
are thus subtly associated with each other. From this perspective
and despite Plato's objections, the Sophistic movement is the better
philosophy, both before and after Socrates, because it much better
supports the human emergence from self-imposed helplessness than
does the exclusively obstinate and perpetually offended Academy.

Helplessness, which may initially be blameless, is self-incurred
from the moment when the poor and less able for some reason
refuse to learn what is necessary from those who are more capable
and wealthier, so that they could become their rivals. Who could
deny that this temptation today puts half of humanity on a slippery
slope? If nothing else, Europeans, who are about to be transformed
into a nation of lotus-eaters, are in peril as they willingly break with

their own tradition. Anyone who wishes to offer a new explanation of Europe to languishing Europeans, who would like to motivate them to return to their former glory, should again open ancient books, the European testaments to necessary sailing, travel stress, tests, crosses, cranes, masts, and contrivances for clever living. The great homecoming hero remains an indispensable, paradigmatic, absolutely exhilarating ally, the versatile teacher of how to not be helpless: *polymēchanos, polytropos, polymētis, talasiphronos, polyphronos, polytlas dios Odysseus.*

11

ALMOST SACRED TEXT

Essay on the Constitution

11.1 The Moment of the Constitution

With the thesis that "sovereign is he who ensures normal conditions," the artist Bazon Brock corrected the constitutional jurist Carl Schmitt's dictum. Schmitt, in his *Political Theology* of 1922, had wished to locate political sovereignty in the person who makes the decision on the state of exception. Thus – after correcting for Schmitt's one-sided decisionistic emphasis – sovereign would be he who provides the conditions for the possibility of political and social normality. On this view, the *Parlamentarischer Rat* [Tr. – "Parliamentary Council"] that had been commissioned to develop a West German constitution was a credible sovereign, when, although still under the oversight and guidance of the three victorious Western powers, it decided to hold an opening ceremony on September 1, 1948, in the vestibule of the Alexander Koenig Research Museum in Bonn. The choice of this site to open the most important convention for facilitating normalization in recent German history occurred for mostly practical reasons (at the time, the city of Bonn did not have any other suitably prestigious spaces), yet it was not entirely pointless to choose it as the *genius loci*. The building had once before been a site for dealing with the consequences of war – shortly after it was completed, it had been seized in 1914 by the German state and functioned as a military hospital until the end of the First World War. The fact that the momentous process of authoring a constitution was begun in the presence of a stuffed giraffe, whose removal from the hall had proven to be impossible, is to be considered one of the symbolic oddities of the ceremonial gathering – which is why this mute representative of the animal world was covered with cloth for the duration of the opening ceremony.

What sovereignty can mean under constrained conditions was apparent even in the choice of locale for the subsequent work sessions of the plenum and of the committees of the *Parlamentarischer Rat*: postwar German democracy was launched in a *Hochschule* for the education of teachers, the Bonn *Pädagogischen Akademie*, founded between 1930 and 1933 according to designs by Martin Witte in the post-objectivist style. It was a building that from 1949 on became the oft-renovated and frequently extended *Bundeshaus* [Tr. – "federal parliament building"]. Even here we should note a powerful expression of political symbolism: a striking feature of the nascent German understanding of the state then articulating itself was to conceive of democracy as a process of continuing education and self-instruction open to correction and unable, in principle, to be concluded.

Sovereign also is he who decides on the date when the will to normalization is proclaimed. It was anything but an accident that the vote on the adoption of the "Constitution of the Federal Republic of Germany" – which, deliberately provisional, was not yet to be understood as a constitution for the entire nation – was held on May 8, 1949.[1] On this day, after numerous amendments, the Constitution was passed about five minutes before midnight with a majority of fifty-three votes for and twelve votes against. (Four days later the Western military governors gave their consent to the Parliaments of the federal states to approve the plan in the subsequent days, so that it could be proclaimed and implemented on May 23. The only exception was the Bavarian state, which was hoping for a stronger federal emphasis.)

The choice of May 8 as the date for the deciding vote was supposed to indicate that the day for the unconditional capitulation of Hitler's Reich to the "founding fathers of the Constitution" – as well as four women (out of 65 people) convened at the constitutional convention – should be not merely thought of as a day of defeat, but even more as a moment for a new beginning under radically different auspices. The politically symbolic dimension of adopting the Constitution in the final minutes of May 8, 1949, can hardly be overstated. It expressed a binding mandate for all Germans to realize that the collapse of the previous dictatorial regime was a moment of liberation, that indeed it was the beginning of a political and civilizing rebirth.

The preceding remarks make one thing clear: if constitutions are documents of a sovereignty that aims to make civilized normality possible, then sites of the debate over the structures that do make civilized normality possible are just as deliberate as the times of decision-making are. If we examine the relevant historical documents of other nations in this regard, it becomes evident that sites and times of constitutional processes nearly always exhibit significant relations to prior upheavals. The idea of offering a constitution to the commonwealth bears *per se* an affinity to political change in itself. In fact, as a rule, new constitutions do not follow the repudiation of earlier forms of political rule that have become intolerable – whether absolute monarchy, tyranny, dictatorship, or a colonial regime. This is not to say that existence's will to order under a democratic or republican constitution necessarily leads to conflicts. Rather, in many cases the creation of a constitution involves the cessation of historical conflicts that precede the emergence of a commonwealth in democratic states or republics.

In this regard, the circumstances under which the German Constitution came about are comparable to the convulsions that led to the two paradigmatic constitutional projects toward the end of the eighteenth century, the American and the French, at least from a typological perspective. In the first case, turbulence preceded the American Revolution, in which the War of Independence (began in 1775) ended with the British defeat in Yorktown in October 1781 and was finally concluded with the Treaty of Paris in May 1783. The political-juridical result of the fierce conflict was the Constitution of the United States in 1787, which has remained in force until the present day, and was supplemented by an additional catalog of civil rights, the so-called Bill of Rights. The fate of French efforts to produce a constitution for the post-absolutist state assumed an entirely different form: far from moving the nation out of its revolutionary unrest and into normalized relations, the development of the French Constitution was continually swept along by the storms of revolution, civil war, imperial adventures, and restoration. The country went through twelve constitutions between 1791 and 1852, none of which were able to extricate themselves from their connection to the vicissitudes of France's national history, both internally and externally. Some of the constitutions were only in force for a short time or were never really effectively implemented. Yet even the temporary dictates of imperial flights of fancy and monarchic restoration helped ensure that the quasi-sacred, timeless core of these new types of basic texts for the formation of a commonwealth, the guarantees of basic civil rights, would never be completely eclipsed. From this one can gather that the speech act that founds political modernity in the most profound sense of the term consists in proclaiming a catalog of civil rights, which can assume the form of a declaration of human rights. Such proclamations are no longer the

crowning achievement of guaranteeing civil security, wrested from
the established order, as was the case with the older British Bill of
Rights: rather, the declaration of human rights is the performative
act – in idealist terms, the "fact-act" [*Tathandlung*] – by which civil
society, also known as the people [*Volk*], grants itself autonomy.

If we proceed by observing the German case in 1948–9, we should
note that the remarkable moment of formulating the constitution
points to a "thereafter" in the most eminent sense of the word. To
be sure, the new Constitution could not put an end to the preceding
chaos of an unjust regime, war, and terror all by itself, although it
was able to shape conditions after the chaos. This might generally
be the case for situations in which communities, after a period of
upheaval due to oppressive rule and inner strife, learn to seek a
local formula for an existence of self-determined freedom. Because
constitutions are typically formulated in the shadow of war and
catastrophe, they generally have a clear "antagonist" [*Wogegen*].
The more clearly pronounced the memories of intolerable relations
that have been overcome are in a population, the easier it is to
generate the fundamental consensus of citizens on the "spirit of the
laws." If the founding moment has receded into the past, the constitution's guiding principles must be reconstructed and reanimated
by interpreters – even and precisely when the latter no longer have
direct access to the horrors of former wrongs, because normalization has since come to prevail. In fact, the fundamental gesture of
producing a constitution – in Germany more than anywhere else – is
associated with an act of reconsideration or, to put it in religious
terms, with an inner and outer gesture of conversion, of metanoia. It
is a characteristic feature of the art of a post hoc interpretation of a
constitution to empathize with the meta-noetic spirit of formulating
a beginning and of repeating the gesture of conversion to a new and
good normality under the unpredictable conditions of a subsequent
situation [to avoid repetition of "conditions"].

11.2 The Generation of the Democratic Sublime

If sovereign is he who provides the conditions for the normal state
of affairs, then the implementation of the decree on that remarkable
8th of May, 1949, was in the hands of a twofold sovereign: On the
one hand, it was up to the American, British, and French military
governors, who had given the necessary permission to their German
partners for the development of a constitution for what was at that
time the "Western zones," in the spirit of Western liberal democracies. On the other hand, it was to be found among the members

of the *Parlamentarischer Rat,* whose consultations over nearly nine months – based upon the preliminary formulations of the *Herrenchiemsee* convention in August 1948 – produced the version of the German Constitution that is still in force today, although it has been amended more than fifty times in the interim.

Nevertheless, the actual authors of the preliminary German "constitution" or, more precisely, its 53 proponents on May 8, 1949, rejected the assumption of sovereignty for their own council, wisely limiting their power. They granted full sovereignty to the "German people" [*Deutschen Volk*] – who here step onto the stage of international law with a capital "D," thanks to a mistaken capitalization of the adjective *deutschen.* With this gesture, the Fathers and Mothers of the Constitution are integrated into the history of political modernity: since the proclamation of the American and French Constitutions, the characteristic feature of such a constitution has consisted in the transfer of sovereignty from an absolute monarch appointed by God to a nation appointed by nature, or by history, to rule itself. The Preamble of the "Constitution" attributes an authority to this sublime collective by virtue of which it is designated as the genuine author of the document that was adopted: this authority is referred to as "constituent power" in the Preamble. To be a people in the modern sense of the term accordingly means: to be sovereign. On the other hand, to be sovereign means to have the authority to adopt a constitution that is conducive to self-rule. Constituent power moves within this sublime circle: the people must already be sovereign in order to be able to adopt a constitution, but they only become sovereign after they have exercised their constituent power. The German population becomes the German people through the practical construction of this circle.

The organ of the sublime circle is the constitutional convention. In its representation of a new sovereign, the people, it institutes the latter in their sovereign role. In instituting the people, it legitimizes itself as the people's authorized representative. While an ordinary parliament is no more than a transparent instrument of the "electorate" that is manifested across a spectrum of votes in favor of political parties and individual candidates, a constitutional convention is something that is inconceivable without an element of the politically mysterious. Like the Church Fathers, the authors of the constitution are indeed themselves delegates of organs that already have a limited democratic legitimacy (in this case, they have such legitimacy in the federal states) – yet the task of producing a constitution is nevertheless of a higher order than trivial delegation. They are "ordained," as it were, by their delegation to the sublime organ: they become delegates of the potential sovereign, who after an appropriately lengthy phase of consultation and reflection will be named the current sovereign by these very same delegates. As soon as they take their place in the midst of this council, they are no longer merely partisan representatives. They are expected to change into agents of that ominous *volonté générale,* which would better be termed *intelligence générale* or *compétence générale* – that is, they are expected to change into personified media of the spirit of democratic laws.

The mystery of representation is never to be more intensely observed than in the emphatic moments of the political history of ideas, in which a few delegates have the task of formulating the institutional framework of relations under which the sovereign collective, for whom they speak, is supposed to reach its politically vital optimal condition. The fulfilment of such an office is inconceivable without an element of elevation. The delegates of a constitutional convention must convincingly embody the mandate to select the best practices and to draw the most important conclusions from the sum of their own people's political wisdom to this point. In addition, it behooves them to learn from the experiences of their own history and to incorporate every precautionary measure into the constitution that will immunize the community's vital new political endeavor against breakdown and abuse, insofar as this is possible.

As is well known, the *Parlamentarischer Rat* of 1948–9 was two-thirds composed of civil servants, with half of its members lawyers – reason enough to ask why a circle of such persons were possibly thought qualified to function as the clear and selfless media of universal interest, to the extent humanly possible. The dominance of the juridical factor in this sublime council is retrospectively justified by the fact that the future democracy was supposed to be entirely arranged as a nomocracy: the *Parlamentarischer Rat* heeded the advice of Montesquieu, by seeing to the rule of law with a strong and independent judiciary. In contrast, the large presence of a civil-service element was indicative of the understanding that democracy is condemned to fail without loyal public officials and a credible implementation of legal procedures – although a potentially problematic preponderance of government structures over and against the intransigence of civil society is already heralded by such a disproportionate presence.

That sixty-five delegates are supposed to put the rational will of seventy million (or fifty-two million, if one does not add the population of East Germany) members of an entire nation [*Staatsvolk*] into words, and codify it with supreme authority, is a clear indication of the predicament of representation. Numerically speaking, every single member of the *Parlamentarischer Rat* bore the mandate to represent approximately one million human beings. This relationship is inconceivable without a certain mysticism of condensation. The constitutional convention is similar to a political distillery, in which the essence of the best moral and juridical institutions is supposed to be extracted by a population that has been rocked by dictatorship, war, and defeat – along with the best knowledge obtained since 1787 of the institutional structure of a democratic commonwealth.

Looking back over the work of the *Parlamentarischer Rat*, it is no exaggeration to observe that it perfectly justified this challenging mandate. It succeeded most impressively in crafting a document of the democratic sublime, which has passed the test of time *summa summarum*, with flying colors, through changing circumstances and fluctuations of the zeitgeist. This is especially true for the excellent statements in the Preamble and the first nineteen Articles, which can virtually be characterized as a solemn atrium leading to the pragmatic sections on the state's structure. With deliberate pathos, the Fathers and Mothers of the Constitution began with an impressive catalog of civil rights. In this way, they expressed the quite costly recognition that respect for individual rights and the protection of such rights must form the state's paramount goal. The sovereign constitutive people should never again be thought of as a total collective, least of all a genetically determined collective substance, as nationalist ideology would have it. Above all, the *Parlamentarischer Rat* justified its historical mandate by establishing a bulwark of sublime protective formulae around the individual citizen – in recognition of the evident fact, which was palpable at the time, that citizens must continually be protected from the encroachment of autocratic collective organs.

In Article I, the Constitution forcefully stipulates in a dogmatic manner that human dignity shall be inviolable – the word "dogmatic" should here be understood in its best sense. In making this statement, the authors claim the prerogative to not merely publish a fundamental theorem that is legally axiomatic, but to accept nothing less than an anthropological teaching position in which they distill the quintessence of old European humanism from its Greek, Roman, and Christian sources. Their declaration includes an individualistic confession. From the very first lines, the German Constitution confesses to perpetually leaving unresolved the conflict between the principle of the people's sovereignty and the principle of the sovereign dignity of the individual. What we now refer to as "the people" is already of its own accord an inevitably polyphonous, occasionally dissonant concert of micro-sovereignties, each one of which is supposed to be endowed with the highest of all the attributes of immunity – inviolability.

The German example is a powerful reminder that the art of writing a constitution requires us to balance two tendencies of exalted pathos: the pathos of founding a commonwealth and the pathos of protecting the rights of individuals. This balancing act is drawn from a bipolar anthropology that characterizes human beings as empathetic and cooperative, but also egotistical and antisocial. The very first word of the Constitution's first sentence, which reads "Human dignity," remains incomprehensible if we do not recognize an air of compromise between enthusiasm and realism: the dignified human being can only develop its dignified status through the indissoluble assumption of dignity. The human being confirms the lofty assumption of such a status by developing into someone who merits it. Thus the concept of "human dignity" always includes futuristic elements. This concept evocatively possesses the dynamic of a predicate that makes good on its own claim to truth – otherwise it would merely be an empty formula for idle talk on Sunday afternoons. Although formulated in the present tense, the phrase *ist unantastbar* [Tr. – literally "is inviolable"] is simultaneously operative in the future tense, that is, as "shall be inviolable." Although expressed in the indicative mood, it also implies a solemnly discreet optative mood. And just as the concept of "democracy" only makes sense when it does not merely describe a given organizing framework, but also provides an orientation for the commonwealth's further development, so the term "human dignity" does not merely signify the axiom of an already established legal system but also includes guidance on how to assert the basic principle more broadly. We should thus always be mindful of a temporal tension in the concepts "democracy" and "human dignity." Everything seems to suggest that the much-cited "eternity clause" in Article 79, paragraph 3 of the German Constitution – which protects the catalog of civil rights and the federative structure of the state from new amendments that would alter the constitution – should not merely be understood as a gesture that provides an additional immunizing bulwark for the constitutional inner sanctum. Rather, the eternity clause can be interpreted as a formal trace of the mandate to forever keep open the tension between what has already been and what has yet to be, a tension that makes democracy possible. This tension is the logical place for what is called political freedom.

We could thus say: sovereign is he who decides on the first sentence of the constitution. We are faced with a fundamental decision from the very first moment. With admirable resolve, the Constitution for the Federal Republic of Germany declares that the human being him- or herself is the exception whose conditions for possibility, within the enclosure of protecting laws, can never be struggled for too much nor prove too costly. This act proclaims that the will to make the improbable into the normal state of affairs is essential to real civilization.

12

THE OTHER LOGOS, OR THE REASON OF CUNNING

On the Intellectual History of the Indirect

The fact that a profoundly radical climate change occurred in the Greek intellectual domain, and among the Athenians in particular, as the fifth century BCE ended and the fourth began, is a well-known, if seldom appreciated, part of old European cultural history. It is usually associated with the negative effects of the Peloponnesian War – that thirty-year ancient conflict that led to Athens' ruin and the loss of its hegemony in the eastern Mediterranean. After the Spartan invasion in 404, the infamous dictatorship of the Thirty Tyrants was established and provoked a democratic countermovement whose far-reaching consequences included the indictment brought against Socrates in 399, when he was charged with atheism and corrupting the youth.

12.1 The Normalization of the Logos

There is a commonplace, as legitimate as it is clichéd, according to which Socrates' death opened a new chapter in the history of ideas. The discipline of philosophy established by Plato, influenced by Ionic and Pythagorean models, adopted the Passion of the sage as its foundational myth. It thus introduced an unprecedented, almost religious seriousness into the quarrels of the learned and of intellectuals. Above all, the story of Socrates' death dramatically widened the gap between the few who were engaged in obtaining real knowledge for themselves or were at least striving for it and the ignorant many. At the same time, Plato delegitimized the poetic expression of the divine, which had thrived in the context of Dionysian festivals, and reclaimed the endeavor to speak truly of God and the divine for the school he founded on the fringes of the city, whose name is supposed to have been taken from an otherwise unknown local hero by the name of Akademos.

This "academization" of the logos was not merely supposed to harm the reputation of poets – whom Plato began to ironically refer to as *theologoi*, implying that they spoke of God without really knowing anything about him. It was also meant to thoroughly delegitimize the eristic discourse that was quite prevalent among Greek men at the time, and indeed to completely delegitimize all forms of the instrumental or strategic use of reason, insofar as the latter involved a claim to public legitimacy. Plato's polemic against the Sophistic movement is supposedly a stable factor in the old European culture of rationality. But there was actually a break here with the older custom of agonal urban speech, and historians can justifiably claim that Platonism, with its odd pathos for the afterlife, its *esprit de sérieux* and its latent Egyptianism, remained a foreign body within Greek culture and only found its proper milieu after the rise of Christianity.

The phenomenon of Plato may well have represented an idealistic exception in its time. However, we are here concerned with the development of a new discursive rule, which stipulates that the conventional techniques for being right in the eristic of opinions, when conversing with others in search of truth and wisdom (with those who will henceforth be called *philosophoi*), have been rendered inoperative. If the Platonic invention of philosophy ended up having far-reaching consequences, this was less because it established a dominant school and more because it introduced a logical practice through which a new type of authority gains ground. The oft-cited Socratic art of dialogue, the dialectic, was not essentially mere eristic, not an art of disputation (lasting more than 2,000 years, until Schopenhauer again evoked this submerged discipline in his short text *The Art of Being Right*),[1] but rather understood itself as a process for disarming the participants in a discussion and leading them out of fruitless strife. The goal of this process was to estrange the holders of an opinion from the ideas they also associated with it, so that they henceforth received their beliefs directly from "truth itself." Thus the Platonic caesura should not merely be interpreted as an alien idealism that has pervasively spread throughout a pragmatically minded environment. Rather, it must be attributed to a much wider development, which could be characterized as the establishment of a new logical norm. This is closely associated with two cultural innovations that led to Greece's special place in the history of rational cultures. On the one hand, we have the emergence of Greek writing, which was connected to the formation of memory capacity for coded knowledge and *eo ipso* connected to an increase of claims to lasting knowledge. On the other hand, we have the discovery of rigorous sciences, particularly in the form of mathematics. It may well be that the Academy, which was nominally devoted to *paideia*, the education of youth, was initially perceived as a foreign body within the framework of the old Athenian institutions – at this time, in the agora, the theater, and the stadium, the city possessed three institutions where citizens could practice stepping out into the light of the public sphere (Hannah Arendt very fittingly called such places, the agora in particular, "spaces of appearance" [*Erscheinungsräume*] for ambitions typical of the polis). Its initial strangeness soon yielded to solid habitualization – this can be seen from the remarkable fact that the Academy pursued its mission uninterrupted for nearly a millennium, and was only shut down in CE 529 due to an imperial order from Byzantium.

The real foreign bodies within the polis-space, however, were novel epistemic disciplines, especially geometry, arithmetic, and philosophical semantics, the emergence of which shook the community's standards of speech and thought. In order to understand this, we must bear in mind that Plato provocatively claimed that he was putting a definitive end to the disoriented and disorienting chatter of the polis, in order to model political argumentation in the agora on the sciences or mathematics – although we do not know how serious he was about this. He was able to make his famous demand for the rule of philosopher-kings only because he had argued for the transition from a rhetorical democracy to an epistemological aristocracy. To see why this idea is excessive, we can refer to Aristotle's objection against Platonic epistemocracy. According to Aristotle, political affairs are subject to the law of the probable, not the law of the true, which entails that rational governance can only be oriented by plausibility, and not by scientific knowledge. The democratic debate of laypersons is sufficient here, while the conversation of the learned remains appropriate for an extra-political realm.

However we care to evaluate the Platonic caesura in the world of Greek discussion, it unquestionably represented a great event in the history of the Western culture of rationality, whose consequences can be traced up to the present day. We could call its *modus operandi* an epistemic domestication of the logos. The word "logos" itself, in its traditional sense, which remains distinct even today, indicates that speech that wishes to be rational in the foundational age of philosophical thought is supposed to undergo a double purification. Its first purgation refers to the doxic origin of true thought – the true logos, initially, at least, takes root in the mire of opinion, as even the philosopher concedes, but must then be uprooted from this mire in order to claim independence from any lower genesis (the reasons for the validity of true utterances are only to be found "above"). The second purgation involves isolating true statements from the passions and particular interests of speakers, since with their inevitable agitation the former disturb the ideal of rest, which from this time on is considered the constitutive feature of *alēthēs logos*. The true judgment's state of rest is the guarantee of impartiality, without which science as a comprehensive practice of neutrality and disinterestedness is inconceivable. It brings about the intellect's free passivity in receiving the final results of logical and empirical investigations.

It is only by means of these two purifications that the improbability known as scientific objectivity can be elevated into a norm and a habitus of the professional and committed pursuit of theory – faced with these stringent demands, we understand why philosophy as a way of life could at first only be made appealing by recommending it to followers as a path to salvation. It formed the core discipline of academic pacifism, without which old European efforts to institutionalize the logos – whether in academies, cathedral schools, universities, archives, or argumentative media – would be unthinkable. To put this emphatically for a moment, we would have to say that the idea of objectively universal truth is inseparable from the supreme tranquility of contemplation that is supposed to occur as soon as evidence and findings have been taken care of. The philosophical path leads from interest to disinterest, from pathos to apathy, from a position to ascendance above positions. With their efforts to come to rest, which alone make philosophically scientific cognition possible, the most resolute adepts of this new discipline imitate nothing less than the being-at-rest of the god of the philosophers. He represents a newcomer in the Greek heavens, distinguished *toto coelo* from the popular gods of Homeric and Hesiodic times by his radicalized cognitive design.

12.2 Divine Cunning, Philosophical Cunning

In contrast, ancient Greek civilization, as depicted in the epic tradition and in the succession of mythic tales, yields a completely different picture of the use of intelligence among gods and human beings. This should not be surprising, since even though Homer's gods already enjoy a privilege of theory (they observe human pursuits from an Olympian distance and make sporting wagers on the outcomes of terrestrial skirmishes), their theoretical attitude initially just means that they are amused as they watch the film of becoming, along with its constantly rotating cast of mortals, but does not yet mean that they possess a comprehensive and unchanging knowledge of the world. Before philosophy, the gods are trapped in pre-epistemic forms of knowledge and the arts, which we see exemplified in the figures of Apollo, Athena, Asclepius, and above all Hermes. For this reason, we readily encounter frequent manifestations of cunning in their behavioral repertoire – the erotic cunning of Zeus, the strategic cunning of Ares, the mercantile cunning of Hermes, indeed even the athletic cunning of the demigod Heracles, who imposes the weight of the firmament upon tired Atlas once more. For rather obvious reasons, a human world full of cunning will flourish beneath a divine sphere pervaded by cunning. The prototype of post-heroic heroism, Odysseus, who not for nothing is endowed in epic poetry with sonorous epithets such as *polytropos* (the man who has wandered far and wide), *polymētis* (full of cunning), and *polymēchanos* (skilled in many arts), is drawn from such divine models.[2] From now on, we are to understand that intelligence, to the extent that it is directed toward practical results, is always also associated with an investment in indirectness, while directness and stupidity are considered to be correlative. The Trojan Horse provides the paradigm of Odyssean cunning, representing a masterful unity of artwork (mimesis of an animal's shape), illusion (the pretense of an offering), and a war machine (a vehicle for invasion). Defined in these various senses, it is considered to be the lasting epitome of profuse cunning, among the Greeks no less than their neighbors in the *imperium romanum* and in modern Europe.

There at least it receives the philosopher's complete attention, and indeed at a very vital point. We are speaking of the critical scene in which the philosopher watches his doppelgänger, the sophist, emerge, that deceptive mimic of the sage, a sham version of the one who truly knows, who from then on is to be unmasked and exposed "by any means necessary." The first, and for a long time only, case in which the philosopher is not merely allowed a cunning of reason, but required to have one, is to be found in the sophistic throwing down of the gauntlet, which, as we now understand, simultaneously

Having made these observations, we can perhaps even plausibly understand why the ancient Western culture of rationality, epistemologically and philosophically re-oriented after Plato, only allows for a limited understanding of pre-philosophical characteristics of human intelligence such as cunning. Because cunning unequivocally represents an expressive form of strategic, instrumental, and positional rationality, it no longer emerges as an object of research in core areas of philosophical concern – at best, it occasionally surfaces in the marginalized peripheries.

There at least it receives the philosopher's complete attention, and indeed at a very vital point. We are speaking of the critical scene in which the philosopher watches his doppelgänger, the sophist, emerge, that deceptive mimic of the sage, a sham version of the one who truly knows, who from then on is to be unmasked and exposed "by any means necessary." The first, and for a long time only, case in which the philosopher is not merely allowed a cunning of reason, but required to have one, is to be found in the sophistic throwing down of the gauntlet, which, as we now understand, simultaneously implied the calling into question of a logos without cunning by a logos that continued to be cunning.

In this context, the phrase "by any means necessary" becomes problematic. To be sure, the philosopher, in fending off the Sophistic movement, must find his own way to convey a pathos, an ardor, an interest, even a will to victory, and must lead an apparatus that reflects this into the field. He is allowed to do this insofar as he is engaged with an implacable foe who never aims at anything but to serve partial interests, to craft deceptive tricks, and to seek out crooked, artful, indirect ways to victory. Nevertheless, the philosopher may not become a sophist himself, if he does not want to lose his superior ontological position. To fight against the Sophistic movement "by any means necessary" thus means precisely to finish off a cunning adversary with the ultimate cunning, the cunning of reason. Yet the cunning of logos is reason's own disciplined activity – the fabrication of conceptuality, insofar as the latter is supposed to enable rule over things that have been illuminated and understood. The sophist is defeated by the cunning of reason the moment that reason provides the true concept of the sophist. In this singular dispute, the labor of the concept and the cunning of reason are one and the same. In the course of the dialogue *Sophist*, after protracted definitions, we finally learn that the philosopher's evil doppelgänger is the deliberate illusionist, the professional deceiver, the all-too-agile and elusive fabricator of cunning paralogisms. This is what Plato triumphantly brings to light at the end of the dialogue, with rather dry logic: the "true sophist" (one should note the irony of the term) is descended from the line of those who are engaged in the following:

> Imitation of the contrary-speech-producing, insincere and unknowing sort, of the appearance-making kind of copy-making, the word-juggling part of production that's marked off as human and not divine.[3]

The philosopher's cunning rival is conceptually articulated in this definition, which contains a number of distinctive features. He is thus petrified, so to speak, and can subsequently be displayed once and for all outside of campus like a statue of eternal falseness. The cunning of the concept is evident in its exposure of the sophist as such, in its capturing of the sophist's essential nature in a definitive portrait. Or to use a different image: the concept is the philosopher's *pharmakon*, as it were – if the sophist accidentally takes it, he will end up permanently paralyzed. In contrast, if those seeking the truth take it, they are forever immunized against the risk of succumbing to sophistic suggestions.

Reference to the banishment of the sophists from the epistemic field does not, of course, merely involve the attempt by academics to get rid of a vexing competitor on the pedagogical market. As we have indicated, it in fact characterizes a restyling of intellectual activity so that the latter is more transpersonally motivated. From this point on, the truth is only supposed to deserve to be called the truth to the extent that the behavior of those inquiring into it is nonstrategic. This requires assuming that contemplation has precedence, in the final analysis – a condition that was relatively easy to meet within the framework of ancient objectivism. If knowledge signifies the reflection of a nature (or a state of affairs) in an intellect, as the tradition teaches, then contemplation *per se* is the recommended path to it – which does not mean that the discursive preparations for contemplation may be bypassed. Inquiring reason is undoubtedly worthwhile in itself – but as soon as it is concerned with results it changes course from activity to passivity. The learned members of medieval Europe understood this fact when they formulated that *intellegere est quoddam pati* [Tr. – "to come to know is to suffer something"] – in this saying, we can still hear echoes of the venerable rhyme cited by the Greeks, *mathein pathein* ("to learn" and "to suffer").

What we referred to above as the disarming of thinkers and their alienation from given opinions in fact aims at the development of an artificial subject that does not spontaneously occur in nature – an inquirer who is qualified to be the authentic bearer of knowledge to the degree that he has become de-pathologized and disinterested by the ascesis of thought. The alienation between knowledge and strategy in the old European culture of rationality is thus ultimately conditioned by the fact that those who think have to undergo a decontextualization and a depersonalization, after which they can no longer simply function as advocates of a particular interest – they no longer receive their mandate from human clients and their interests, nor even from what is called "society," but present themselves as delegates of the objective amidst the bleak confusion of polemical and pathological partisan intellectuals. Whoever treads upon the path of philosophical knowledge has to pay a high price – but a price that is simultaneously supposed to convey the distinction of being able to pay the price. Knowledge requires nothing less than a social death, a radical act of non-solidarity in relation to tribal idols and the transition to a supra-ethnic system of solidarity with those seeking the truth. This is the deeper meaning of the ancient concept of the cosmopolis, as it was popularized from the days of the Stoa on (and which partially survived into the nineteenth century as an important ideal of the European university): it indicates the noble homelessness of the philosopher, who is supposed to know that he is in exile wherever he may be in the empirical world. In antiquity, this negative situation tended to be expressed in positive terms, by emphasizing the sage's capacity to be at home everywhere. The cosmopolitanism of philosophy was not merely based on the intellect's free floating between homelands and above partisan wrangling; it also led to xenophilia, since it ended the age-old privileging of what was familiar in comparison to the foreign: ever since we drank from the river of oblivion true ideas alienate us, although they correspond to our oldest memories, according to Plato, and so we must become estranged from ourselves in order to again make contact with what is really and truly our own. Not for nothing did Plato have a *xenos* (the Stranger) enter the scene at several strategically important points in his dialogues, particularly *Sophist* and *Statesman*.

Reflecting on the alienation of philosophers and scientists from the interests of the communities they originated in may be useful for helping us to understand one of the most conspicuous basic features of the Western culture of reason: the relative strategic blindness of academic pursuits. In fact, there are no "embedded philosophers" in the European tradition, and even where one professes to pursue practical philosophy, as a rule such engagement is just as "quixotic" [*weltfremd*] and impractical as other academic affairs. Only in more recent times, particularly since Heidegger's phenomenological research and a more modern theory of science, have we witnessed attempts to overcome philosophical reflection's notorious lack of position and situation by formulating a theory of situated reflection and the embedding of reason and research within the lifeworld. In this regard, a few names are paramount: Jean-Paul Sartre, Hermann Schmitz, and Bruno Latour.

12.3 The Outwitting of Human Reason

It would be hasty to conclude from what we have just said that these various old European conceptions of reason did not bear any relation at all to the phenomenon of cunning or, to put it more generally, to a method for the indirect realization of goals. On the contrary, over the course of the last two millennia, a variety of figures have emerged who make it possible for us to illustrate in detail how what we ordinarily consider to be reason, primarily theoretical, anti-sophistic, without interests, and above positions, becomes involved with the cunning of superior entities – regardless of whether these entities are addressed as god, nature, idea, or history. Indeed, as we have seen, on its own terms, philosophically and epistemically informed intelligence is not supposed to be in the service of particular interests, pursuing them with partisan cunning and narrow-minded zeal. Yet it can become the object of a superior cunning – particularly when the constraints of the human intellect provoke the intervention of agents operating on a higher level, who pursue superhuman goals by way of human efforts. Conversely, reason can also begin to seem like the subject of a campaign in which we do not have to fight a particular opponent, but have to overcome a superpersonal adversary that is represented by such concepts as nature, lack, necessity, and alienation. In the first case, human reason (or human individuality) has itself been duped, such that there is talk of a cunning of reason, with "of" being used in the sense of an objective genitive. In the second case, human reason reimburses itself for the costs of a generalized other, which is why the subjective genitive is more fitting here.

In what follows, I would like to suggest a few lines of thought that ought to be considered in an intellectual history of duped reason. I will show how talk about the outwitting of human understanding by a higher intelligence is profoundly anchored in the traditions of old European ontology, while talk of outwitting what is without reason through artful human reasoning represents the underlying characteristic feature of rationalism in the modern era. The first kind of outwitting is generally (but not always) associated with mostly forgotten theories of the intellect on the threshold between theology and epistemology, while the second kind is readily apparent in quintessentially modern theories of technology that are articulated on the threshold between the philosophy of nature and the art of engineering. Articulations of the active cunning of reason have been part of Europe's strategic lore since the sixteenth century, and have also played a primary role in aesthetics during this time.

An account of the ways in which an outwitted human reason has manifested itself would inevitably have to begin by recalling Platonic holism. Here we need only refer to the arguments made in Plato's late work *Laws* to bring young men who were inclined to atheism back onto the theistic path. The philosopher draws on a stark ontological ordering principle, according to which a superior creative intelligence arranges the cosmos so that every single thing works together, each in its own place. Order primarily means the seamless integration of parts into the whole. The Athenian Stranger, the main speaker in the dialogue, thus remarks:

These parts, down to the smallest details of their active and passive functions, have each been put under the control of ruling powers that have perfected the minutest constituents of the universe. Now then, you perverse fellow, one such part – a mere speck that nevertheless constantly contributes to the good of the whole – is you, you who have forgotten that nothing is created except to provide the entire universe with a life of prosperity. You forget that creation is not for your benefit: you exist for the sake of the universe.[4]

The goal of argumentation, not without sophistic elements, is quite evidently persuasion – the speaker would like to convince potential and actual dissidents or those who are lawless to give up on the "abduction" of substantive truth based on ignorance and to return to a lawful sphere. The key performative term in the speech can be found in the phrase "you who have forgotten": on the one hand, it points to the doctrine, further elaborated by Plato elsewhere, that no one does wrong willingly (which secures the thesis that everyone is fundamentally educable and also in need of education); on the other hand, it reveals an incisive irony, insofar as the lawless person, who thinks himself more clever than those who are content and integrated, is portrayed as truly ignorant. He allows himself to be duped by the world's empirically conspicuous deficit of rationality, by the appearance of disorder and randomness, and hence misses the logical master plan in which sovereign intellects (all the way up to the *intellectus archetypus*) have ordered the universe – the plan that philosophy is always seeking with receptive admiration as it goes about inquiring and extrapolating.

In our present context, it should be enough to recognize that, with this warning to godless realists, the topos that "the seemingly clever are the foolish ones" is established for future ages. It implies renouncing the popular belief that we learn from our mistakes. In contrast, it aims to demonstrate how we become fools by critically remaining mistaken. This line of thought, which amounts to the repression of regard for the negative, will be most conspicuous where it is considered necessary to have no doubt at all that the world is rationally ordered.

The Stoic doctrine of an all-pervasive providence of cosmic reason is all the evidence we need for this quite broad thesis. In this doctrine, the momentous philosopheme of a foreseeing and foreordaining power of the logos emerges, which is addressed as *Pronoia* (and that recurs after its theological metamorphosis as predestination). From a functional or theoretical-architectonic perspective, it is the task of "providence" [*Vorsehung*] to absorb the future's openness and to incorporate future contingencies into the ordered structure of the universe, as it has been determined from the beginning. Thus only the individual human being, with his inability to understand (which is felt quite strongly in situations of suffering), stands out as an exception – this exceptional status, however, is not supposed to signify foolish behavior, a willful disregard for the good reasons that one must ultimately be able to find for everything. In his lectures on the basic doctrines that typified ancient philosophical schools, with a noticeable emphasis on their agreement, Max Pohlenz notes that:

> In the case of global catastrophes such as earthquakes, we feel compelled to believe that, in view of the whole, providence is imposing a penalty or engaging in a purification, and we do not allow ourselves to run into danger, even if innocents may be affected. We must always think of the whole, of its greatness, purposiveness, and beauty; nagging criticism is then silenced.[5]

According to this logic, the mind that insists on criticism is excluded from insight into the world's purposive structure. It forever remains a loser that allows itself to be duped time after time by a worldwide *Pronoia*.

It would be fascinating to read synoptically the complex history of Platonic, Aristotelian, and Stoic theories of the intellect, along with their extension by Medieval Arabic philosophers and European successors. To pull this off, such a reading would have to be structured broadly enough to allow us to also properly see the methodical pursuit of the humiliation and duping of human intelligence. A sensitive chapter in this history would be devoted to the Augustinian metaphysics of predestination, which very well may be the darkest moment in the European history of ideas. Augustine may have offered one of the most subtle interpretations of human reason when he attempted to show the traces of the trinity within it. Yet, because of his doctrine that human nature is corrupted by original sin, he irrationally obscured the relationship between divine and human intelligence, so that even the most intense religious feeling, the striving for salvation of the soul, was necessarily affected. If our religious obligation requires us to spread the Word, if we must encourage many of our brothers and sisters to strive for salvation, then an inscrutable, even dreadful irony lies concealed in Augustine's admonition: divine omniscience, which acts in unity with divine omnipotence, by virtue of its unfathomable arbitrary mercy has decreed that only chosen individuals may be saved in small numbers – according to criteria that seem unclear to human beings – while the great majority of Christendom, not to mention all non-Christians, are condemned to eternal damnation in advance.

The Augustinian dictum *in experimentis volvimur*, "we are rolled from test to test," perfectly expresses foreordination's macabre duping of human intelligence. On such a view, a wrathful God, wearing the mask of benevolence, seems to use Christendom as bait to lure humanity into recognizing his sovereignty and his right to grant pardon, though he will only opt for the latter in the rarest of cases. As a result, the immense majority of ordinary Christians, despite all of their ascetic practices and confessions, still remain included in the *massa perditionis*, the mass of the corrupted, and will plunge headlong into the depths, however much they would like to delude themselves about the possibility and likelihood of their salvation. The cunning of such arbitrary mercy remains inscrutable. Kurt Flasch has aptly remarked in this regard that ". . . Augustine's God seems like a teacher for whom only a small number of arbitrarily favored students make the grade. He watches as the majority of human beings are unable to do anything with their goodwill."[6]

12.4 Outwitting for the Sake of the Outwitted

We get a completely different impression the moment we consider versions of the figure of outwitted reason in the modern age. As a rule, they exhibit a tendency toward clarification. They offer insight into a series of processes and situations in which we might speak of an outwitting that serves the interests of the outwitted. We must content ourselves here by referring to a few exemplary remarks offered by authors such as Giordano Bruno, Kant, Hegel, and Schopenhauer.

We have the first author on that list to thank for the most impressive version of a fortunate kind of duping. In his work *Degli eroici furori* (*The Heroic Frenzies*), authored in London in 1585, Bruno retold the myth of the hunter Actaeon and gave it a surprising philosophical twist. Actaeon had spied on the goddess Artemis while she bathed in the forest, whereupon the outraged goddess transformed him into a stag (or a buck), which was torn to pieces by her pack of dogs, so that he would not tell others that he had seen her in the nude.[7] Bruno, incidentally, was familiar with hunting metaphors from late-Medieval activist theories of the intellect, through the later work by Nicholas of Cusa, titled *de venatione sapientiae*. Thus for Bruno, Actaeon "signifies the intellect intent on hunting divine wisdom, on grasping divine beauty."[8] Divine subject matter now has to reckon with the guile of objects. They necessarily elude the one seeking them, so long as he or she pursues them merely in terms of their external appearance. They only reveal themselves to the one seeking them when they are conceived in the mode of interiority, that is to say, by their transformation into the seeker's subjectivity.

The thing that has been cognized abandons its position as object and shifts over to become subject, winning those who are cognizing over to its side, so to speak. Bruno summarized this state of affairs with the words of Tansillo, a participant in the dialogue:

> Thus, Acteaon with those thoughts – those dogs – who sought outside himself for goodness, wisdom, beauty – the wild creatures – arrived into the presence of that prey, and was enraptured outside himself by such beauty. He became prey himself, and saw himself converted into what he sought. He realized then that he himself had turned into the longed-for prey of his own dogs, of his own thoughts, because once he had contracted divinity into himself, he no longer needed to seek it outside himself.[9]

The figure of duping for the sake of the duped is prolific in the sixteenth-century history of ideas, with most versions a little more bombastic than the inversion of hunter and prey found in Bruno's myth of epiphany. If, in the Nolan's case, we have what might be called a cunning of the absolute, in Immanuel Kant's case we would have to speak of an episodic cunning of nature. In a series of anthropological writings and works of political theory, which can be considered precursors to the history of philosophy (particularly in the essays *Idea for a Universal History with a Cosmopolitan Purpose* [1784] and *Perpetual Peace* [1795]), Kant hypothetically introduced the figure of a teleology of nature, according to which nature as a whole can be thought of, semi-allegorically, as a kind of provident schoolmistress who uses indirect methods to divert her pupils from their harmful inclinations, to harness them for rational ends. Thus she sees to it that her problem student, the human being, despite a selfish nature that is resistant to reason, is ultimately impelled onto the unlikely path of progress and world peace. Kant is aware that he thereby attributes to nature a role that, in the metaphysical-religious tradition, was given to providence.[10] Yet he does not underestimate how far removed speculations of this sort are from the *terra firma* of solid inquiry – not for nothing does he remark, near the end of his essay from 1784 (under the Eighth Proposition), in an almost confessional tone: "One sees that philosophy, too, can have its chiliastic beliefs . . .," although he immediately continues his digression into the adventurous: ". . . [it] is, for that reason, anything but fanciful."[11] Kant's doctrine of natural intentionality, which wished to be sober despite its exuberance, emphasized the tendency of natural evolution to at some point "develop" all of a creature's natural endowments, completely and expediently.[12] A few sentences later, he formally expresses how the evolutionary cunning of nature is to be understood:

> The means that nature employs in order to bring about the development of all of the predispositions of humans is their antagonism in society, insofar as this antagonism ultimately becomes the cause of a law-governed organization of society. Here I take antagonism to mean the unsociable sociability of human beings, that is, their tendency to enter into society, a tendency connected, however, with a constant resistance that continually threatens to break up this society."[13]

Kant confidently affirms that without the influence of antagonistic forces the endowments of the species would necessarily be condemned to remain undeveloped in a pastoral Arcadian dream world.

> ... thank nature for their quarrelsomeness, for their jealously competitive vanity, and for their insatiable appetite for property and even for power! Without these all of the excellent natural human predispositions would lie in eternal slumber, undeveloped. Humans desire harmony, but nature knows better what is good for their species: it wills discord. Humans wish to live leisurely and enjoy themselves, but nature wills that human beings abandon their sloth and passive contentment and thrust themselves into work and hardship.[14]

Depicted in this manner, Kantian nature assumes the features of a schoolmistress, indeed of a scrupulous factory director, who acts in a strategically clever, but morally questionable manner, to realize her intentions indirectly. At the same time, Kant's argument does not merely provide a philosophical justification of discomfort, it also explicitly sketches a historical pathodicy (a justification of human suffering), including morally objectionable vices, insofar as both dynamically advance the civilizing process by inciting progress.

12.5 Hegel: The Cunning of Reason

After Kant's semi-allegorical talk of natural intentions became an established language game, it fell to his successors to conceptualize still other superhuman entities that harness human beings as a means to various higher purposes. Without doubt, the most famous example of this is the phrase coined by Hegel in the Introduction to his *Lectures on the Philosophy of History* (1822/1831), that of the "cunning of reason." This famous passage is found in the postscript to Hegel's Berlin lectures:

> This may be called the cunning of reason – that it sets the passions to work for itself. . . . The Idea pays the penalty of determinate existence and of corruptibility, not from itself, but from the passions of individuals.[15]

In the light of traditional figures of the duped human intellect, this statement offers nothing new, considered by itself. We once more easily recognize in it the arrangement that usually emerges in the process of the indirect realization of goals by an intelligent being that has been outwitted – the enveloping of local human plans and intentions by a more general plan and a higher-level intention. Hegel's formulation, which not entirely without reason is one of the most well known in his oeuvre, is as popular as it is open to more subtle interpretations – at first glance, we might not view it as much more than an elegant recasting of the proverb according to which man proposes, god disposes [*der Mensch denkt, Gott lenkt*]. On a more subtle interpretation, we would have to work out how the "idea," elevated by Hegel into the guiding principle of history, displays the virtues of a farsighted strategist: the idea sees to it that the chronicle of humanity does not merely remain – to speak with Macbeth – "a tale / Told by an idiot, full of sound and fury,"[16] but can be recounted as a report on the always circuitous process of reason through space and time. It may not be entirely illegitimate to consider whether we do not hear in Hegel's argument an echo of the ideas on political economy offered by Bernard Mandeville and Adam Smith (already present earlier in Kant), according to which the market's regulative power, though based on amoral motives, leads to worthwhile results, a kind of precursor to functionalism and cybernetics.

The real model for Hegel's phrase "cunning of reason" might nevertheless be found in classical philosophy, particularly in Plato's explanations of the trichotomous structure of the human psyche. On Plato's account, the human soul possesses three parts, two emotional motors whose specifications can be roughly character-ized with such terms as lust (*erōs*) and spiritedness (*thymos*), and a piloting function that is free of emotions, the so-called *logistikon*, the site of the capacity of reason. As a psychologist, Plato already possesses a schema of the cunning of reason, insofar as in his model one part of the soul, which does not have any energy of its own, plays the other two parts off of each other in order to obtain its own ends. This generally happens in such a way that the organ of reason mobilizes sensitive spiritedness in matters of honor, in order to stem the potentially offensive inclinations of the lustful part of the soul, while the latter is called upon to offset thymotic surges. In light of this analogy, Hegel's dictum, particularly its second part, becomes a good deal more understandable, since even in the philosophy of history the "idea," as a *logistikon* of higher status, has the empirical, all-too-empirical emotions of historical individuals pay the price for the higher ends of reason. This means that if reason does not wish to remain impotently otherworldly and unreal, but to be historically incarnated in the world, it must work with worldly and historical forces. Such empirical emotions, mainly thymotic or honor-seeking impulses, form the basis for the emergence of great actors in world history. We cannot fail to note that here, too, as in Smith and Kant, an amoralism in the service of morality becomes prominent – in contrast, Hegelian irony (according to which the extraordinary actively serves the ordinary) is unconventional, insofar as all dramatic historical incidents end up fading into a post-historical, undramatic constitutional normalism. As in the Chinese doctrine of cunning, reason as portrayed by Hegel has the appearance of a military commander who always kills with someone else's knife (strategy number three of the thirty-six stratagems on Sun Tzu's list). Cunning reason is a subordinate function of the historical dialectic. Grisly violence – and Hegel's protagonists from Alexander to Napoleon are reckless when it comes to such violence – works toward the salutary goal of establishing a world constitution characterized by the rule of law, with minimal violence.

When considering all of this, we should not overlook the fact that the famous phrase "the cunning of reason," despite its succinctness, remains nothing more than an ad hoc formulation. Hegel himself did not further elaborate it, and indeed for reasons that are to be sought in the logic of his system.

His doctrine is emphatically conceived of as a system of freedom, in which reason's working its way out of the heteronomous conditions it emerged from is on display. Thus it is not in the thinker's interest to push the free subject in service to the idea so far that a new way of being determined by something alien would arise – as would happen if the human mind were completely outwitted by the world mind. To the extent that the agents of history should always be taken seriously as bearers of the historical impulse toward freedom, the interests of the idea, or of reason's superordinate plan, might not be entirely free from the well-understood motivations of human agents, but would have to engage with them in the mode of a semi-transparent kind of cooperation. It must still be said that a "progressive" version of an outwitting in the interests of the outwitted is also encountered in Hegel, in keeping with the prevailing illuminative tendency of the modern Enlightenment culture of reason.

12.6 Schopenhauer: Cunning of the Will

We are faced with a different picture as soon as we turn to post-Hegelian ways of expressing the duping of reason. If darker tendencies surface here, this is due to the naturalistic and functionalistic tendency that shaped thinking about development in the nineteenth and twentieth centuries. From a naturalist and functionalist perspective, human cognition no longer seems to be the earthly projection of a divine intellect, but an organ, or an archetype of programs that have been developed to ensure vital progress on a meta-vital level (or the reflection of the social on the intellectual level). New types of outwitting emerge in this constellation, essentially maintaining the functional alliance between coping with the world and self-deception. Numerous forms of the post-Hegelian critique of reason and ideology target this alliance.

I will content myself with a single example – Schopenhauer's doctrine of *The Metaphysics of Sexual Love*, as we find it in the notorious forty-fourth chapter of the second volume of *The World as Will and Representation* (a passage in which one can recognize the philosophical matrix of Viennese psychoanalysis). First, it must be admitted that Schopenhauer's statements on sexuality are not yet those of a completely developed naturalism, but rather stem from a semi-naturalistic psychological theory, with a conception of nature that is articulated on the basis of a metaphysics of the will. At critical points, the philosopher's argumentative strategy anticipates later figures of cryptic duping. It amounts to ironizing the illusion of freedom in human agents by revealing that we do not handle the most important matters, but rather are handled by them.

Schopenhauer believed that there was no subject that could be more convincingly treated than the love life of human beings, this infiltration of a desire experienced as "our own" by an underlying agent. Even if the love-struck individual obeys an impulse or believes that he or she has obeyed an impulse that arises from deep within, the philosopher still maintains that love is nothing more than the personal guise of a pre-personal force that is directed toward the blind reproduction of the species. The author developed an empathetic interpretation of human love, by taking its heavenliness and its hellishness (in terms of the metaphysics of the will) more seriously than any author before him. He thus remarks:

204   The Other Logos, or the Reason of Cunning

... this longing and this pain of love cannot draw their material
from the needs of an ephemeral individual. On the contrary,
they are the sighs of the spirit of the species, which sees here, to
be won or lost, an irreplaceable means to its ends, and therefore
groans deeply. The species alone has infinite life, and is therefore capable of infinite desire, infinite satisfaction, and infinite
sufferings. But these are here imprisoned in the narrow breast
of a mortal.[17]

Schopenhauer subsequently, somewhat cavalierly, adopts the
Kantian practice of indulging in speculations about the intentions
of nature. In the manner of the best teleology of nature, the philosopher offers a half-psychological, half-metaphysical explanation of
the lover's tendency to highly idealize the object of his or her desire:

Now in this case the sexual impulse, though in itself a subjective
need, knows how to assume very skilfully the mask of an objective admiration, and thus to deceive consciousness; for nature
requires this stratagem in order to attain her ends.[18]

We can easily recognize how Schopenhauer's natural-strategic
derivation of the sublime here anticipates an essential argument of
psychoanalytical naturalism, the reduction of erotic-idealistic phantasms to libidinal urges rooted in the drives. We should bear in mind
that types of cunning reason such as this lose their basis in the theory
of the intellect as they transition into the realm of nature. As philosophical theories about the emotions (or as doctrines of "necessary
false consciousness"), they concern the outwitting of experienced
motives by the more powerful forces of unconscious drives and collective functions. Anyone who would like to learn more about the
development of these and similar theories can consult Heinz Dieter
Kittsteiner's book *Wir werden gelebt*[19] (whose title is taken from a
phrase of Sigmund Freud's) as a guide through the jagged terrain of
the post-Hegelian critiques of consciousness.

12.7 Nature Outwitted: Mechanical Engineering

At this point, I will cease sketching a history of duped subjectivity, or
the passive experience of cunning, and would like to conclude with a
brief allusion to a few motifs of active cunning in modern Europe's
culture of rationality. I would like to cite five fields or disciplines in
which the active use of cunning has tended to manifest itself in the
course of Western civilization since the sixteenth century: in the first

place, we should here think of mechanical engineering, which gave a superpersonal and serial form to European cunning. Next, we should consider the literature of worldly wisdom, as it flourished in the setting of absolutist courts and metropolises, with their worlds of intrigue. A short word will have to suffice for the studies on war and policy in the early modern era, and last but not least,[20] we should refer to the system of arts that crystallized in late-feudal, early bourgeois society, and then freely flourished in the production of entertaining and edifying illusions.

The most influential example of the culture of cunning that is specific to Europe in the modern era is to be found in mechanical engineering, as it was developed in the Old World (associated with ancient models) from the sixteenth century on. To a certain extent, the European art of mechanical engineering freed cunning from its dependence on specific situations and developed into a praxis of cunning in general, of cunning *sans phrase*. A machine is a stratagem whose implementation does not require a strategist. Hence the cunning European operator does not develop an explicit awareness of cunning – to enjoy the benefits of typical operations of machinery, it suffices to fulfil the role of an operator in an appropriate manner. Over the course of centuries, various technologies for power transmission (using gear trains, pulleys, screw presses, and pendulum systems) complemented the discovery of the lever.[21] Around 1500, a historic technological breakthrough (in sociological terms) finally occurred when Peter Henlein invented the pocket watch, his famous Nuremberg eggs. Due to innovations in precision mechanics by the guild of clockmakers, the modern art of mechanical engineering achieved a prestige that indicated a new paradigm in relations between human beings and nature. Thus the mechanical clock was elevated into the universal gadget of the Renaissance and the Baroque. Not only did it offer concrete and descriptive models of the world – particularly with the technical marvel of the *Grande Complication*, which could display the permanent calendar along with the phases of the moon and planetary orbits. Mechanical clockworks and gear trains became metaphors for the world whose predominance only came to an end with the emergence of first-generation thermodynamic machines, the steam engines.[22]

Mechanical engineering in the early modern era can be regarded as a technological translation of the maxim, *natura non nisi parendo vincitur* [Tr. – "nature is only conquered by obedience"], propounded by Francis Bacon in his *Novum Organum*. If ancient mechanics had already been understood by the Greeks to be a pragmatic art of outwitting nature, then Bacon's law that one must obey in order to rule provided a general concept for the principle of this art of outwitting. Because it is depersonalized and decontextualized, technological cunning does not have individual applications. Thus we have a process in which an increasing number of operators become able to handle machines, and hence to participate in the technological power of manipulating nature. The principle of *nisi parendo* is grounded in the turn to experimental methods, which entail a systematic investigation of nature in terms of its regularity. This has traditionally involved an image of nature as only reluctantly willing to unveil itself, yet susceptible to being compelled to betray its secrets by cunning and the coercion of science. Obedience to nature thus signifies the feint of feints, by means of which the universal commander, Western humanity as Baconian progressive collective, exploits a nature that is more outwitted than respected, for the sake of human interests.

12.8 Our Outwitted Fellow Man

The very same Francis Bacon – following the model of Montaigne's essays from 1580 – considered the rules for cleverly accomplishing one's goals in the strategic interactions of courtiers and merchants. The enormous success of this new literary genre indicates the extent to which actors on the early modern social stage were interested in rules offering advice for conducting operations in a realm expanded by trade, seafaring, science, and technology. If we may relate the essay as a literary form to experimental thought in general, we should realize that the variety of new treatments of worldly wisdom opened up a specific kind of access to the field of strategic cunning. In his twenty-second essay, *On Cunning*, Bacon himself compiles a short list of rhetorical and practical advice, which can obviously be read as a rudimentary form of strategic consultancy for courtly and mercantile clientele. In enumerating this list, personal experiences converge with general advice in a seemingly humorous manner.

> I knew one [P. S. – Bacon notes] that, when he wrote a letter, he would put that which was most material in the postscript, as if it had been a bye-matter.
> I knew another that, when he came to have speech, he would pass over that that he intended most; and go forth, and come back again, and speak of it as of a thing that he had almost forgot . . .
> There is a cunning, which we in England call *The turning of the cat in the pan*, which is, when that which a man says to another, he lays it as if another had said to him . . .

It is strange how long some men will lie in wait to speak somewhat they desire to say . . . It is a thing of great patience, but yet of much use.[23]

From the seventeenth century on, the literary market aroused and met an insatiable demand for advisors on existence in a world whose design was increasingly determined by the imperatives of the rivalry between courtiers, bourgeoisie, and the merchant class. The genres of strategic life coaching flourished – collections of maxims, books on etiquette, doctrines of an art of life, textbooks on human anthropology, writings on worldly wisdom – overshadowing anything similar from earlier or later times. What Spanish cultural history called its *Siglo de Oro* signified a golden age of strategic reason for all of Europe – both from the perspective of those who were interested in actively practicing the arts of illusion, as well as from the perspective of those who, since they could see through the illusions of others, wished to be esteemed for their perfection of worldly wisdom. Insofar as the significant authors of the seventeenth century promised their clientele a broad training in resisting deception, we might characterize this era as the incubation period of the Enlightenment – where Enlightenment is to be understood as not merely a time in which the sciences were popularized (paradigmatically exemplified in the project of the French encyclopediasts), but as the melee of urban intelligence with the omnipresent forces of illusion at work in courtly life and the marketplace. One of the key experiences of the epoch is the realization that the human being himself is now able to become the *genius malignus* of the human being – in this regard, it is entirely symptomatic as well as typical of philosophy, when Descartes, in his doubt-experiment, brings the possibility of deception to an acute fever pitch: he hypothetically conceives (*je supposerai*) of "an evil genius, supremely powerful and clever" (*non moins rusé et trompeur que puissant*), who would be able to make it so that all of my perceptions "[are] the bedeviling hoaxes of my dreams, with which he lays snares for my credulity" (*des illusions et trumperies, dont ils se sert pour surprendre ma crédulité*).[24]

Unlike the Cartesian philosopher, the seventeenth-century man of the world does not adhere firmly to the principle of incontrovertible evidence at all, he invests in the virtues of a duelist, such as mobility and presence of mind, and develops a gymnastics of mistrust that allows him to remain sovereign in everyday scuffles with illusions and seductive temptations. No system of true knowledge is established by this man-of-the-world Enlightenment, it is enough to merely ensure our own sobriety by studying the underside of the carpet that, with its thousands of knots, conditions the

world-illusion on top – to use one of Cervantes' images. The general
principle for this worldview can be found in Balthasar Gracián's
advice (in his *The Art of Wordly Wisdom* from 1647) that in matters
of importance, we must look within human beings.[25]

If we had to pick a single example that documents the tone and
tendency of the literature for training modern human beings in the
rigors of moral and strategic fitness, then it would have to be the
masterpiece of the genre, which contained the passage cited above
by the Jesuit-educated Gracián. It can justifiably be claimed that
every single one of the three hundred rules of worldly wisdom
and aphoristic maxims of the portable oracle [*Oráculo manual*][26]
represents an extract from a wealth of strategic situations. Every
single aphorism is a theater of the world in microcosm – each line
seems like it is trying to prove that every human being must now
become a political realist. Where deception is everything, we must
be discreetly clever. We could claim that here the *discreto* – in close
proximity to the figure of the *picaro* – steps onto the stage, the
modern age's first intellectual as member of an artful precariat.
We read in a key aphorism that "Man's life is a warfare against the
malice of men,"[27] and thus a permanent struggle between aggressive cunning and discreet attentiveness. Human knowledge now
means knowledge of the world, and this includes insight into the
strategies that the combatant must master in a continually precarious partisan jockeying for position. In this regard, I would like to
cite rule 26:

> *Find out each Man's Thumbscrew.* 'Tis the art of setting their
> wills in action. It needs more skill than resolution. You must
> know where to get at any one. Every volition has a special
> motive that varies according to taste. All men are idolaters,
> some of fame, others of self-interest, most of pleasure. Skill
> consists in knowing these idols in order to bring them into play.
> Knowing any man's mainspring of motive you have as it were
> the key to his will. Have resort to primary motors, which are
> not always the highest but more often the lowest part of his
> nature: there are more dispositions badly organised than well.
> First guess a man's ruling passion, appeal to it by a word, set it
> in motion by temptation, and you will infallibly give checkmate
> to his freedom of will.[28]

As in many other passages of the manual, Gracián here adopts the
perspective of offering amoral advice on an anthropological basis,
advice that is admittedly general, in order to provide his reader
with insight into the calculations of potential opposing parties.

Sometimes this turns into an outright denunciation of aristocratic cunning – as in Aphorism 149:

> *Know how to put off Ills on Others.* To have a shield against ill-will is a great piece of skill in a ruler. It is not the resort of incapacity, as ill-wishers imagine, but is due to the higher policy of having some one to receive the censure of the disaffected and the punishment of universal detestation. Everything cannot turn out well, nor can every one be satisfied: it is well therefore, even at the cost of our pride, to have such a scapegoat, such a target for unlucky undertakings.[29]

In making this observation, the author calls attention to the risks of jobs involving the future, such as *secretario*, aristocratic advisor, and lawyer. Anyone who runs the risk of getting close to the powerful and their secrets should know that they can lose their life in the bargain. Even Francis Bacon was aware of this when, in his work *De Sapientia Veterum* (*Of the Wisdom of the Ancients* from 1609, though it only appeared in English for the first time in 1619), an anthology of interpretations of ancient myths considered as rationalistic allegories, he translated the story of *Mētis*, who emerged from the union of Sky and Earth, into a contemporary idiom. *Mētis*, a Titan assigned to the planet Mercury, was regarded as the goddess of cunning or wisdom. We read in Bacon's translation that:

> The ancient poets tell us that Jupiter took Metis, whose name plainly signifies Counsel, to wife; that she conceived by him and was with child; which he perceiving did not wait till she brought forth, but ate her up; whereby he became himself with child; but his delivery was of a strange kind; for out of his head or brain he brought forth Pallas armed.
>
> This monstrous and at first sight very foolish fable contains, as I interpret it, a secret of government. It describes the art whereby kings so deal with the councils of state. . . . But when the question grows ripe for a decision (which is the bringing forth), . . . they do not allow the council to deal any further in it, lest their acts should seem to be dependent upon the council's will . . . they take into their own hands whatever has been by the council elaborated . . . so that the decision and execution . . . may seem to emanate from themselves.[30]

In repurposing the myth of *Mētis*, Bacon makes two things clear. On the one hand, he puts his finger on power's increasing dependence on advisement; on the other hand, he indicates that princes, insofar as they have to provide a spectacle of wise governance, must transform themselves into modern-day sophists. The necessary union of ruling and sophistry in the enlightenment of princes has never been more vibrantly imagined than in the legends of the goddess of cunning who was swallowed whole (she is sometimes also portrayed as holding the position of a counselor – which, incidentally, is also a way of handling the theme that a clever woman is always the source of a powerful man's words).[31] This neo-sophistic situation led to the development of a few literary genres that reached their apex with the French moralists. The most significant configuration of a new strategic fostering of reason, Nietzsche's *The Gay Science*, whose subtitle *La gaya scienza* openly suggests its Spanish influences, was crucially indebted to these new genres.

Paradigmatic examples of the literature on the art of war and the science of policy in modern Europe have not been of much philosophical interest – or if they were, it was only insofar as writings of this kind and with this orientation make it possible to document the renaissance of strategic reason. Anyone prepared to note the differentiation of cultures of rationality in the modern Western hemisphere must turn their attention to manifestations of this literature. We limit ourselves here to observing that the more recent library of the strategic sciences, which extends from Carl von Clausewitz through Hans Delbrück all the way to Raymond Aron, John Keegan, and Edward Luttwak, develops an elaborate universe of literature on the theory of war. Similarly, a library of Baroque literature on statecraft, which is concerned with the art of "policey" as a cunning technique for guiding communities,[32] paved the way for the more recent science of politics, which stretches from Montesquieu to John Rawls.

This literature's homage to the genius of indirect reason results from its subject matter. Its strategic tendencies help explain why its basic thrust was no longer understood by the later bourgeois Enlightenment and why it was condemned wholesale: although almost a contemporary, Kant calls the older policey-lore the "twists and turns . . . of an amoral doctrine of prudence,"[33] and condemns it for its incompatibility with the upright disposition of direct goodwill. In the essay *Towards Perpetual Peace*, Kant enumerates three "sophistic maxims" that in his opinion sum up every stratagem of the bad, older statecraft in a nutshell: *fac et excusa* (taking a chance and then making excuses afterward); *si fecisti nega* (deny doing anything and blame someone else); *divide et impera* (sow discord between party leaders and alienate them from the people).[34] In the same work, Kant calls for the condemnation of the Jesuit *reservatio mentalis*, that expedient of a "casuistic false politics,"[35] by virtue of which some Baroque warlords were accustomed to use even the peace treaty as an instrument for the waging of war by other means.[36]

I would like to conclude these reflections by referring to manifestations of the European awareness of cunning, as preserved in literature and works of art. We have recently gained a much better understanding of the literary archive of strategic thought thanks to Peter von Matt's *Die Intrige: Theorie und Praxis der Hinterlist* [*Intrigue: Theory and Practice of Guile*], which has been expanded into a virtual encyclopedia.[37] This work, oriented toward historical motifs, exhaustively treats its subject matter with wonderful comprehensiveness and amazing erudition.

If you would like or are in need of additional material in this vein, then you would have to look into the field of aesthetic theory, insofar as the artwork *per se* represents something that requires cunning-theoretical commentary. In fact, numerous authors in the early modern era spoke of the arts in general and of artworks in particular as examples of the phenomenon of the welcome illusion. To the extent that the domains of art are freed from religious control, in order to affirm themselves as a dimension of autonomous fiction that expresses disinterested truth, a self-conscious demand for messages from the world of beautiful and entertaining semblance begins to take root. The stage is thus set for the centuries-long struggle between the marvelous (*mirabile*) and verisimilitude (*verisimile*). If we wished to update the customary translation of the maxim attributed to Sebastian Brant,[38] *mundus vult decipi* [Tr. – "the world wants to be deceived"],[39] we would have to say: the world wants art – and wants it as a way to appreciate exciting illusions in which the impossible seems plausible and the improbable certain.

The deep alliance between the phenomenon of art and that of cunning – insofar as it is not to be found in the material itself, as is the case in adventure stories, crime stories, and the legends of Reynard the Fox – is based on the fact that artistic production is always also interested in the evocation of "special effects" that play with the audience's perceptual patterns and expectations, aside from its interest in traditional artistic conventions. Arts characteristically strive for the cunning of forms in order to produce effects that could not be achieved by content alone. The novelist Gerhart Schröder has provided a fruitful direction for research into the hitherto little-regarded sphere of aesthetic forms as conveyors of strategic depths in his 1987 book *Logos und List: Zur Entwicklung der Ästhetik in der frühen Neuzeit* [Tr. – Reason and Cunning: The Development of Aesthetics in the Early Modern Era].[40] We should not be surprised to encounter again Balthasar Gracián as one of the key figures in this text.

I will conclude with a personal remark. Harro von Senger, whom I have to thank for suggesting that I entertain these thoughts, has noted in one of his publications on the phenomenon of cunning in the East and West that he would like to toss out a brick to attract jade – which corresponds to a seventeenth-century Chinese stratagem. This has to do with his pointed thesis that Chinese thought is distinguished from European thought by a much more explicit awareness of cunning. In my preceding remarks, I have attempted to indicate just how nuanced this statement can be. In reality, Harro von Senger is too good a strategist not to also attempt a new version of this stratagem. It seems to me that he tossed out jade to prove by means of the brick that he received in return that we Western intellectuals and philosophers, if I may speak with such unseemly inclusiveness, have more to learn from Chinese wisdom and its interpreters, or Sinologists, than we have previously imagined. Harro von Senger, who is very much concerned with the model of duping for the sake of the duped, which we have been discussing here, thus turns out to be an Enlightenment thinker in the best European tradition.

Editorial Note

The following is a list of texts and speeches that have been revised in the making of this book:

"The Anthropocene" is a combination of two essays: the first initially appeared in English under the same title in Ashkan Sepahvand, Christoph Rosol, Bernd M. Scherer (eds.), *Textures of the Anthropocene: Grain Vapor Ray* (Cambridge, MA and London: MIT Press, 2015); the second is drawn from a lecture, "Wie groß ist groß?," given in December 2009 during the United Nations Climate Change Conference in Copenhagen (published in *Das Raumschiff Erde hat keinen Notausgang* [Suhrkamp: Berlin, 2011]).

"From the Domestication of the Human Being to the Civilizing of Cultures" was a lecture delivered on October 11, 2010, in Warsaw under the title *Die Domestikation des Menschen und die Expansion der Solidaritäten.*

"What Happened in the 20th Century?" was the Inaugural Lecture for the Emmanuel Lévinas Chair in Strasburg on March 4, 2005.

"The Thinker in the Haunted Castle" was the opening address for the International Symposium *Derrida's Ghosts* in Naples on October 7, 2009.

"Deep Observation" first appeared in *Geo* 9 (2008), 147ff.

"The Persistent Renaissance" was a lecture delivered in Florence on May 25, 2013.

"Heidegger's Politics: Postponing the End of History" was a lecture given at the Heidegger Conference *le danger et la promesse* in Strasburg on December 5, 2005.

"Odysseus the Sophist" was a lecture given on the occasion of *Ruhrfestspiele* 2009.

"Almost Sacred Text" first appeared in *Das Grundgesetz* (Gütersloh/ Munich: Wissenmedia in der Inmedia-ONE, 2012).

"The Other Logos, or The Reason of Cunning" first appeared in Achim Hecker, Klaus Kammerer, Bernd Schauenberg, Harro von Senger (eds.), *Regel und Abweichung: Strategie und Strategeme. Chinesische Listenlehre im interdisziplinären Dialog* (Berlin: Munster, 2008).

Notes

1 The Anthropocene

1 [Tr. – *Entlastung* and its verbal form, *entlasten*, will generally be translated as "relief" and "to relieve," respectively, but will occasionally be rendered otherwise as context dictates. Here, in a legal framework, it is rendered as "exonerate," and in another, later context as "easing." When used adjectivally, it may be translated as "relaxed." Flexibility is essential for capturing the nuances of Sloterdijk's elusive use of this term.]

2 Stanislaw Lem, *One Human Minute*, trans. Catherine S. Leach (San Diego: Harcourt Brace Jovanovich, 1986), 13.

3 [Tr. – Arthur Schopenhauer, *The World as Will and Representation*, Vol. II, 305–17 ("On Matter").]

4 Jeremy Rifkin, *Beyond Beef: The Rise and Fall of Cattle Culture* (New York: Plume, 1993).

5 Karl Marx and Friedrich Engels, *Collected Works*, Vol. 5 (London: Lawrence & Wishart, 1976), 28n.

6 [Tr. – see Martin Heidegger, *Being and Time*, trans. John Macquarrie & Edward Robinson (New York: Harper & Row, 1962), pp. 304–11.]

7 [Tr. – Robert K. Merton, "The Matthew Effect," in *Science* 159 (1968), no. 3810, 58–63.]

8 [Tr. – New International Version.]

9 [Tr. – Joseph A. Schumpeter, *The Theory of Economic Development*, trans. Redvers Opie (Cambridge, MA: Harvard University Press, 1934), 64.]

10 [Tr. – This German term is similar to the English terms "armchair critic" or "armchair revolutionary," referring to someone who criticizes and condemns political action in the world from the safe distance of their study.]

11 [Tr. – "no-nonsense" is in English in the original.]

12 [Tr. – Hannah Arendt, *The Origins of Totalitarianism* (New York: Schocken, 2004), 376, 379.]

13 Max Weber, *The Protestant Ethic and the Spirit of Capitalism*, trans. Talcott Parsons (London: Routledge, 2001), 123 [Tr. – Translation modified].

14 Werner Sombart, *Der moderne Kapitalismus. Dritter Band: Das Wirtschaftsleben im Zeitalter des Hochkapitalismus* (Munich and Leipzig: Duncker and Humblot, 1927), p. 1010.

15 [Tr. – One of the slogans from the 1968 uprisings in France.]

16 [Tr. – Buckminster Fuller, *Operating Manual for Spaceship Earth* (Mattituck, NY: Aeonian Press, 1976), 53.]

17 Fuller, *Operating Manual for Spaceship Earth*, 45.

18 [Tr. – Friedrich Nietzsche, *The Anti-Christ, Ecce Homo, Twilight of the Idols, and Other Writings* (Cambridge: Cambridge University Press, 2005), pp. 143–4.]

19 [Tr. – Novalis, *Philosophical Writings*, trans. Margaret Mahoney Stoljar (Albany: SUNY Press, 1997), "Miscellaneous Observations," §32, p. 28.]

20 [Tr. – "shareholder" is in English in the original.]

21 [Tr. – Friedrich Nietzsche, *The Birth of Tragedy and Other Writings*, trans. Ronald Speirs (Cambridge: Cambridge University Press, 1999), 75 (§15).]

22 Spinoza, *Ethics* (New York: Everyman's Library, 1910), 87 [Tr. – translation modified].

23 Plato, *Republic*, trans. C. D. C. Reeve (Indianapolis: Hackett, 2004), 51 (372d).

24 Cf. *Note Saved: Essays after Heidegger*, trans. Ian Alexander Moore and Christopher Turner (Cambridge: Polity, 2016), 133–48.

25 Fuller, *Operating Manual for Spaceship Earth*, 50.

26 Ibid., 120.

27 [Tr. – The German here is "*Ständische und Stehende*," which, like every term Sloterdijk is discussing in this passage, is etymologically related to the verb *Stehen* and the noun *Stand* (e.g. *Zustand*), which are in turn etymologically related to the ancient Greek *stēnai* and the Latin *stare* (the latter of which forms the root of "institution"). For this citation, see Karl Marx and Friedrich Engels, *The Manifesto of the Communist Party*, in *Marx/Engels Selected Works*, vol. 1, trans. Samuel Moore (Moscow: Progress Publishers, 1969), 16.]

28 [Tr. – Carl Amery, *Die Botschaft des Jahrtausends: Von Leben, Tod und Würde* (Munich: List, 1994).]

2 From the Domestication of the Human Being to the Civilizing of Cultures

1 [Tr. – Plato, *Statesman*, trans. Robin Waterfield (Cambridge: Cambridge University Press, 1995) 32 (276e).]

2 Friedrich Nietzsche, *Thus Spoke Zarathustra*, trans. Adrian Del Caro (Cambridge: Cambridge University Press, 2006), 135.

3 [Tr. – Heiner Mühlmann, *MSC: The Driving Force of Cultures* (Springer: New York/Vienna, 2005).]

4 [Tr. – "containment" is in English in the original.]

5 [Tr. – In English in the original.]

3 The Ocean Experiment

1 [Tr. – In the present essay, *Vernachlässigung* is being translated as either "disregard" or "negligence" depending on context.]
2 This dialectical conception of the environment is also distinguished from the meta-biological conception of the environment, which was articulated by Jacob von Üexküll, as well as from Niklas Luhmann's systemic conception of the environment.
3 See pp. 11–12 of this volume.
4 [Tr. – "business-as-usual" is in English in the original.]
5 The journal *Science*, June 18, 2010, Vol. 328, p. 1500 began a detailed report on the acidification of the oceans with the thesis that "Humans are caught up in a grand planetary experiment of lowering the ocean's pH, with a potentially devastating toll on marine life." [Tr. – See: http://science.sciencemag.org/content/328/5985 for the full article online.]
6 According to the statements of analysts, the experiment of "industrialized deep-sea fishing" will come to a complete standstill by the 2040s, if the exploitation of the oceans continues at its present pace.
7 An Austrian newspaper, in connection with the leaking of great quantities of petroleum in the deep water of the Gulf of Mexico, recently had the following headline: "Experiment Ölpest" [Tr. – "The Oil-Pollution Experiment"] (*Die Presse*, August 21, 2010).
8 [Tr. – "global governance" is in English in the original.]
9 The inclination toward such dreams is presumably caused by the inception of a credit system, which makes the pressure of interest into the *primum mobile* of entrepreneurial ways of life.
10 See pp. 106–107 of this volume.
11 Apollonius Rhodius, *The Argonautica*, trans. R. C. Seaton (London: Heinemann, 1912), 385.
12 Ibid., 389 [Tr. – translation modified].
13 On the theme of "environment inversion" or "an integral encapsulation of a lifeworld in the enclosing form" cf. my *Spheres III: Foams*, trans. Wieland Hoban (South Pasadena: Semiotext(e), 2016), 315f.

5 What Happened in the 20th Century?

1 [Tr. – Alain Badiou, *The Century*, trans. Alberto Toscano (Cambridge: Polity, 2007), xiv.]
2 It is not entirely implausible that the aphorism also alludes to the title of an article by Maurice Merleau-Ponty from the very first issue of *Les Temps Modernes* in July 1945: "The War Has Taken Place." [Trans. – In: *The Merleau-Ponty Reader*, Ted Toadvine and Leonard Lawlor (eds.) (Evanston: Northwestern University Press, 2007), 41–54.]
3 G. W. F. Hegel, *Phenomenology of Spirit*, trans. A. V. Miller (Oxford: Oxford University Press, 1977), 19.
4 [Tr. – Sophocles, *Four Tragedies: Ajax, Women of Trachis, Electra, Philoctetes* trans. Peter Meineck and Paul Woodruff (Indianopolis: Hackett, 2007), 208 (Line 452).]

5	[Tr. – Emmanuel Levinas, *Otherwise than Being or Beyond Essence*, trans. Alphonso Lingis (Hague: Kluwer, 1981).]
6	[Tr. – François de La Rochefoucauld, *The Maxims of La Rochefoucauld*, trans. Louis Kronenberger (New York: Vintage, 1959), 38 (§26). La Rochefoucauld wrote in the seventeenth century and thus his aphorism was not originally intended as a commentary on the twentieth century, though Sloterdijk here refashions it to that end.]
7	[Tr. – Eric Hobsbawm, *The Age of Extremes: The Short Twentieth Century, 1914–1991* (New York: Vintage, 1994).
8	[Tr. – Karl Jaspers, *Man in the Modern Age* (New York: Routledge, 2010), 173–4.]
9	[Tr. – cf. Jürgen Habermas, "The New Obscurity," in *The New Conservatism: Cultural Criticism and the Historians' Debate*, ed. and trans. Shierry Weber Nicholsen (Cambridge: Polity, 1989), 48–70. It should be noted that *Unübersichtlichkeit* ("obscurity") literally refers to the inability to gain an overview of something, the impossibility of obtaining a comprehensive perspective on a given phenomenon. See Sloterdijk's characterization in the previous paragraph of the twentieth century as "a time devoid of an overview (*ohne Übersicht*)" for an example of what is meant here.]
10	[Tr. – *Weltbürgerkrieg* is an untranslatable term that plays on the fact that the globalized age of cosmopolitanism, *Weltbürgertum*, and of its corresponding world-citizens, *Weltbürger*, is also an era of world wars, *Weltkriege*, between members not of states but rather social systems that span the world – for instance, the worldwide struggle between communist and capitalist factions, both of which seek to impose their socio-economic system on a global scale.]
11	[Tr. – Badiou, *The Century*, 32.]
12	[Tr. – Friedrich Nietzsche, *The Birth of Tragedy and Other Writings*, trans. Ronald Speirs (Cambridge: Cambridge University Press, 1999), 75 (§15).]
13	[Tr. – Georg Wilhelm Friedrich Hegel, *The Philosophy of Right*, trans. S. W. Dyde (Kitchener: Batoche, 2001), 19.]
14	[Tr. – Max Horkheimer and Theodor Adorno, *The Dialectic of Enlightenment*, trans. Edmund Jephcott (Stanford: Stanford University Press, 2002), 92.]
15	[Tr. – See the subtitle of this section.]
16	[Tr. – The title of Section 4 of Nietzsche's *Twilight of the Idols*, in *The Portable Nietzsche*, trans. Walter Kaufmann (New York: Penguin, 1976), 485–6.]
17	[Tr. – Karl Löwith, *From Hegel to Nietzsche: The Revolution in Nineteenth-Century Thought* (New York: Columbia University Press, 1964).]
18	[Tr. – "young realist" on analogy with "young Hegelian." See "Heidegger's Politics" (ch. 9 of this volume) for more context on Sloterdijk's use of this term.]
19	Michael Stausberg's *Zoroaster und die Europaische Religionsgeschichte der Fruhen Neuzeit* (Berlin/New York: Walter de Gruyter, 1998), 2 vols., is quite informative concerning the presence of the figure of Zarathustra in European literature before Nietzsche.

20 [Tr. – Cf., for instance, Karl Marx and Friedrich Engels, *The Holy Family, or Critique of Critical Critique*, trans. R. Dixon (Moscow: Foreign Languages Publishing House, 1956), 29. See also p. 208 of the same text.]

21 [Tr. – Vladimir Ilyich Lenin, "The Three Sources and Three Component Parts of Marxism," in V. I. Lenin, *Collected Works*, trans. George Hanna, Vol. 19 (Moscow: Progress Publishers, 1977), 21–8.]

22 [Tr. – Marquis de Sade, *Justine, Philosophy in the Bedroom, and Other Writings*, trans. Richard Seaver & Austryn Wainhouse (New York: Grove, 1965).]

23 [Tr. – The title of a pamphlet that Chevalier reads in the chapter entitled "Fifth Dialogue" in de Sade's *Philosophy in the Bedroom*.]

24 For an examination of this concept, see *Spheres*, Vol. 3: *Foams*, ch. 3, "The Fiction of the Deficient Being," 651–62. There I show that because of his institutionalistic interests, Gehlen only drew the illiberal line of conclusions from the concept.

25 See Rolf Peter Sieferle, "Gesellschaft im Übergang," in *Archälogie der Arbeit*, ed. Dirk Baecker (Berlin: Kadmos, 2002), 117–54.

26 [Tr. – "hot spot" is in English in the original.]

27 [Tr. – "way of life" is in English in the original.]

28 See Peter Sloterdijk & Hans-Jürgen Heinrichs, *Neither Sun Nor Death*, trans. Steve Corcoran (Los Angeles: Semiotext(e), 2010), 321.

29 See Ulrich Bröckling, "Unternehmer," in *Glossar der Gegenwart*, ed. Ulrich Bröckling, Susanne Krasman, Thomas Lemke (Frankfurt: Suhrkamp, 2004), 275.

30 See Dante Alighieri, *De Monarchia*, book 1, ch. XIV: "every superfluity is displeasing to God and nature, and everything displeasing to God and Nature is evil" (*The De Monarchia of Dante Alighieri*, ed. and trans. Aurelia Henry [Boston & New York: Houghton Mifflin, 1904], p. 50).

31 Smith, *The Wealth of Nations, Books I–IIII*, p. 441.

32 See Sieferle, "Gesellschaft im Übergang," pp. 139f: "The current demand for 'social justice' aims to confiscate property from the productive sector and redirect it 'socially' into the unproductive sector. As those without property (and perhaps even the unproductive or unemployed) could tend toward being in the social majority, we could be faced with a notable change: the democratic state becoming an agency of extra-economic constraint and attempting to tax the productive capitalist economy in order to support the unproductive, parasitic poor."

33 [Tr. – my translation] Sieferle, "Gesellschaft im Übergang," p. 125.

34 The life story of an exemplary agitator on this front is told by Peter Singer, in *Ethics into Action: Henry Spira and the Animal Rights Movement* (Lanham, MD: Rowman & Littlefield, 1998).

35 See Hermann Scheer, *The Solar Economy: Renewable Energy for a Sustainable Global Future*, trans. Andrew Ketley (London: Earthscan, 2002).

36 [TN (Hoban): in Germany, these colors represent the main Conservative Party (CDU) and the Green Party (Bündnis 90/Die Grünen) respectively.]

37 Johannes Fabricius, *Alchemy: The Medieval Alchemists and Their Royal Art* (Copenhagen: Rosenkilde and Bagger, 1976).

6 The Thinker in the Haunted Castle

1 [Tr. – Martin Heidegger, *Being and Time*, trans. John Macquarrie & Edward Robinson (New York: Harper & Row, 1962), 279–311.]
2 "Je suis en guerre contre moimême," *Le Monde*, August 18, 2004. [Tr. – An English version of Derrida's final interview was published in a special issue of the journal *SV* (Studio Visit) in November of 2004 and is the source for the quotations from the interview here.]
3 This colleague was Jürgen Habermas, who provided the quotations cited here in a poignant obituary for Rorty on June 11, 2007.
4 [Tr. – In English in the original.]
5 [Tr. – In English in the original.]
6 [Tr. – In English in the original.]
7 [Tr. – In English in the original.]
8 [Tr. – Karl Marx, "The Eighteenth Brumaire of Louis Bonaparte," in *The Marx-Engels Reader*, ed. by Robert C. Tucker (New York: Norton, 1978), 595.]
9 Dieter Henrich, in particular, has employed this concept to characterize his work on the genetic reconstruction of German idealism. Cf. *Konstellationen. Probleme und Debatten am Ursprung der idealistischen Philosophie* (1789–95) (Stuttgart: Klett-Cotta, 1991).
10 Sigmund Freud, *The Future of an Illusion*, trans. and ed. by James Strachey (New York: W. W. Norton, 1961), 21.
11 Sigmund Freud, *The Future of an Illusion*, 21.
12 Ibid., 43.
13 [Tr. – Sigmund Freud, *The Future of an Illusion*, 49.]
14 Ernst Bloch, *The Spirit of Utopia*, trans. Anthony A. Nassar (Stanford: Stanford University Press, 2000), 34.
15 [Tr. – "Wherever Lenin is, there is the fatherland."]
16 Ernst Bloch, *Logos der Materie. Eine Logik im Werden. Aus dem Nachlaß 1923–1949*, ed. by Gerardo Cunico (Frankfurt am Main: Suhrkamp, 2000). These studies at many points anticipate the late magnum opus, *Experimentum Mundi* (1975).
17 [Tr. – Ernst Bloch, *The Principle of Hope*, Vol. 1, trans. Neville Plaice, Stephen Plaice, and Paul Knight (Cambridge, MA: MIT Press, 1995), 16.]
18 [Tr. – Bloch, *The Spirit of Utopia*, 257.]
19 Bloch, *The Spirit of Utopia*, 257.
20 Ernst Bloch, *Logos der Materie*, 442 [Tr. – my translation].
21 Ersnt Bloch, *Briefe 1903–1975*, 2 vols. (Frankfurt am Main: Suhrkamp, 1985), 66. [Tr. – my translation]
22 On the mediumistic turn in the theory of the subject, cf. my *Weltfremdheit* (Frankfurt am Main: Suhrkamp, 1993), especially beginning on p. 25.
23 Richard Rorty, "Wittgenstein, Heidegger, and the Reification of Language," in *Essays on Heidegger and others. Philosophical Papers Volume 2* (Cambridge: Cambridge University Press, 1991), 80.
24 Jacques Derrida, *Cosmopolitanism and Forgiveness*, trans. Mark Dooley and Michael Hughes (London: Routledge, 2001), 8.
25 Thus his late alliance with the proconsul of Critical Theory, Jürgen Habermas, on questions of European politics dismayed his German

friends, as though he had compromised himself for no apparent reason.

26 [Tr. – the words "deconstruction" and "circumvention" are in English in the original.]

7 Deep Observation

1 [Tr. – "extension of man" is in English in the original.]
2 [Tr. – "symbolic species" is in English in the original.]
3 [Tr. – "life support system" is in English in the original.]

8 The Persistent Renaissance

1 *The Decameron of Giovanni Boccaccio*, trans. John Payne (London: The Villon Society, 1886), 3 ff.
2 [Tr. – "counter culture" is in English in the original.]
3 [Tr. – "the well-being of every mortal."]
4 [Tr. – "side effects" is in English in the original.]
5 [Tr. – Niccolò Machiavelli, *The Prince*, trans. Harvey C. Mansfield (Chicago: University of Chicago Press, 1998), §25, 101.]
6 [Tr. – "good news" and "bad news" are in English in the original.]

9 Heidegger's Politics

1 Cf. Bernd Grün, "Fehlbarkeit auf fremdem Felde. Ein Literaturbericht über Heidegger und die Politik," in *Martin Heidegger, Ein Philosoph und die Politik*, ed. by Gottfried Schramm and Bernd Martin (Rombach: Freiburg, 2001), 13–74.
2 See pp. 59–68 of this volume.
3 Cf. Norbert Bolz, *Auszug aus der entzauberten Welt. Philosophischer Extremismus zwischen den Weltkriegen* (Munich: Wilhelm Fink, 1989).
4 [Tr. – See the very end of G. W. F. Hegel's *Phenomenology of Spirit*, trans. A. V. Miller (Oxford: Oxford University Press, 1977), 493 [§808].]
5 [Tr. – Martin Heidegger, *Being and Time*, trans. John Macquarrie & Edward Robinson (New York: Harper & Row, 1962), 163–8.]
6 [Tr. – Martin Heidegger, *The Fundamental Concepts of Metaphysics: World, Finitude, Solitude*, trans. William McNeill and Nicholas Walker (Bloomington: Indiana University Press, 2001), 78–168.]
7 Heidegger, *The Fundamental Concepts of Metaphysics*, 5. [Tr. – As noted by the translators here, this statement by Novalis can be found in his *Schriften*, ed. by J. Minor (Jena, 1923), Vol. 2, p. 179, Fragment 21.]
8 Heidegger, *The Fundamental Concepts of Metaphysics*, 22.
9 Ibid., 60 [Tr. – translation modified].
10 Ibid., 60.
11 Ibid., 69.
12 [Tr. – Heidegger, *The Fundamental Concepts of Metaphysics*, 75.]
13 Heidegger, *The Fundamental Concepts of Metaphysics*, 80. My italics.

14 Ibid., 79.
15 Fyodor Dostoyevsky, *Notes from Underground*, trans. Richard Pevear and Larissa Volokhonsky (New York: Vintage, 1993), 12.
16 [Tr. – "way of life" is in English in the original.]
17 Dostoyevsky, *Notes from Underground*, 5.
18 [Tr. – "neo-Cynical" in its allusion to a famous anecdote concerning the life of Diogenes of Sinope: "Plato had defined Man as an animal, biped and featherless, and was applauded. Diogenes plucked a fowl and brought it into the lecture-room with the words, 'Here is Plato's man'." See Diogenes Laertius, *Lives of Eminent Philosophers*, trans. R. D. Hicks (Cambridge, MA: Harvard University Press, 1925), VI.40, 47.]
19 [Tr. – This observation can be found in a letter of Nietzsche's to Heinrich Köselitz in March 1886. See Nietzsche's *KGB*, 3.5.814.]
20 Dostoyevsky, *Notes from Underground*, 38.
21 Ibid., 30.
22 [Tr. – Fyodor Dostoyevsky, *Notes from Underground*, 34.]
23 Dostoyevsky, *Notes from Underground*, 22–3.
24 [Tr. – (translation modified) Johann Gottlieb Fichte, *The Characteristics of the Present Age*, trans. William Smith (London: Chapman, 1847), 9.]
25 Martin Heidgger, *Gesamtausgabe IV. Abteilung: Hinweise und Aufzeichnungen*, vol. 96, Überlegungen XII-XV (*Schwarze Hefte 1939–41*), herausgegeben von Peter Trawny (Frankfurt: Klostermann, 2014), 149–57. One finds on p. 149 the para-Fichtean expression "age of complete meaninglessness." [Tr. – English translation forthcoming as *Ponderings XII-XV: Black Notebooks 1939–1941 (Studies in Continental Thought)*, trans. Richard Rojcewicz (Bloomington: Indiana University Press, 2017).]
26 [Tr. – Martin Heidegger, "The Self-Assertion of the German University and The Rectorate 1933/34: Facts and Thoughts," in *Review of Metaphysics*, 38:3 (1985), 480.]
27 [Tr. – "fair play" is in English in the original.]
28 Jean Paul Sartre, *Portraits*, trans. Chris Turner (London: Seagull Books, 2009), 281.
29 [Tr. – Theodor Adorno, *Jargon of Authenticity* (Routledge: London, 2003); Victor Farías, *Heidegger and Nazism* (Philadelphia: Temple University Press, 1991).]
30 [Tr. – "Remarks on the Future of Iraq," in *Selected Speeches of George W. Bush: 2001–2008*, accessed online (April 28, 2017) at: https://georgewbush-whitehouse.archives.gov/infocus/bushrecord/documents/Selected_Speeches_George_W_Bush.pdf, 167.]

10 Odysseus the Sophist

1 This is shown not only in the dramas of the Atridae, but also for the no longer extant Telegony, a sequel to the Odyssey from the sixth century by the poet Eugammon of Cyrene who made use of motifs from the Oedipus mythos: in this mythos, Telegonus ("born far away"),

the illegitimate son of Odysseus with the witch Circe, unknowingly kills his father and marries Penelope, while Odysseus' legitimate son Telemachus is wedded to Circe.

2 [Tr. – Homer, *The Odyssey*, trans. Robert Fitzgerald (New York: Anchor, 1963), 1–2 (I, 1–5, 16–19).]

3 [Tr. – Sloterdijk's original German here is: "The translation cited above, by Anton Weiher from 1955, uses 'the maneuverable man'." Since we obviously could not use Weiher's German translation here, I've opted for Fitzgerald's translation.]

4 [Tr. – In English in the original.]

5 [Tr. – Homer, *The Odyssey*, 175 (X, 329).]

6 [Tr. – Homer, *The Odyssey*, 175 (X, 340).]

7 [Tr. – Homer, *The Odyssey*, 140–1 (VIII, 523/4–531).]

8 [Tr. – Virgil, *The Aeneid*, trans. John Dryden (London: Macmillan, 1885), 15 (I, 465).]

9 [Tr. – Virgil, *The Aeneid*, 15 (I, 662) – translation modified.]

10 [Tr. – Virgil, *The Aeneid*, 24 (II, 3).]

11 Theodor Haecker, *Virgil, Father of the West*, trans. A. W. Wheen (New York: Sheed & Ward, 1934), 24f.

12 Cf. Marcel Detienne and Jean-Pierre Vernant, *Cunning Intelligence in Greek Culture and Society*, trans. Janet Lloyd (Chicago: University of Chicago Press, 1991).

13 [Tr. – Homer, *The Odyssey*, 3.]

14 [Tr. – Homer, *The Odyssey*, 103 (VI, 135f.).]

15 [Tr. – Homer, *The Odyssey*, 103 (VI, 150).]

16 [Tr. – Homer, *The Odyssey*, 103–4 (VI, 149–85).]

17 [Tr. – Homer, *The Odyssey*, 104 (VI, 187).]

18 [Tr. – Erasmus, *Apophthegmata*, III, 70, *Opera*, I–VIII (Basel: 1540), IV, 148.]

19 Cf. *The Older Sophists*, ed. by Rosamond Kent Sprague (Indianapolis: Hackett, 1972), 31.

20 Egon Friedell, *Abschaffung des Genies: Essays bis 1918* (Löcker: Vienna and Munich, 1984), 327.

21 [Tr. – Homer, *The Odyssey*, 166 .]

22 [Tr. – "second thoughts" is in English in the original.]

23 [Tr. – Odysseus is in fact kicked by Melanthius, his disloyal goatherd.]

24 Homer, *The Odyssey*, 317 (XVII, 238).

25 [Tr. – Homer, *The Odyssey*, 1 (I, 3).]

26 [Tr. – Homer, *The Odyssey*, 434.]

27 Homer, *The Odyssey*, 439 (XXIII, 306–9).

28 Particularly in the "Exegesis on the Soul" (Nag Hammadi Codex II.6) [Tr. – see *The Nag Hammadi Library*, ed. by James M. Robinson (New York: HarperCollins, 2008), 127–37.]

29 [Plato, *The Republic*, trans. C. D. C. Reeve (Indianapolis: Hackett, 2004), 325 (620c).]

30 See pp. 187f. of this volume.

31 IX.1.

32 Herodotus, *The History*, trans. G. C. Macaulay (London: Macmillan, 1914), 278 (§111).

11 Almost Sacred Text

1 [Tr. – It should be noted that the German term translated here as "Constitution" is *Grundgesetz*, which literally means "Basic Law."]

12 The Other Logos, or the Reason of Cunning

1 Written around 1830, but only published posthumously in 1864. The essay essentially consists of 38 strategies enabling the participant in a discussion to win an argument, even if he is actually wrong.
2 For more on this, see pp. 187–212 of this volume.
3 [Tr. – Plato, "Sophist," in *The Complete Works*, ed. by John Cooper (Indianapolis: Hackett, 1997), 293 (268c–d).]
4 Plato, "Laws," in *The Complete Works*, 1560 (X, 903b–c).
5 Max Pohlenz, *Die Stoa: Geschichte einer geistigen Bewegung* (Göttingen: Vandenhoeck and Ruprecht, 1978 [first edition 1959], 101.
6 Kurt Flasch, *Augustinus: Einführung in sein Denken* (Stuttgart: Reklam, 1980), 216.
7 Cf. Ovid, *Metamorphoses*, trans. Rolfe Humphries (Bloomington: Indiana University Press, 1955), 61–4 (III, 135–255).
8 [Tr. – Giordano Bruno, *On the Heroic Frenzies*, trans. Ingrid D. Rowland (Toronto: University of Toronto Press, 2013), 107.]
9 Giordano Bruno, *On the Heroic Frenzies*, 109–11. For a synopsis of the literary and philosophical reenactments of the myth of the hunter who becomes prey in early modernity, cf. Wolfgang Cziesla, *Aktaion polypragmon: Variationen eines antiken Themas in der europäischen Renaissance* (Frankfurt: P. Lang, 1989).
10 Thus he explains at one point: "The use of the word *nature* is also, when speaking here merely of theory (not of religion), more appropriate for denoting the limits of human reason (as reason, regarding the relation of effects to their causes, must confine itself within the limits of possible experience) and *more modest* than the expression of a *providence* that is knowable to us. With an expression such as Providence one presumptuously fits oneself with the wings of Icarus, in order to approach the secret of its inscrutable intention." *Towards Perpetual Peace and Other Writings on Politics, Peace, and History*, trans. David L. Colclasure (New Haven: Yale University Press, 2006), 87.
11 Kant, *Towards Perpetual Peace*, 13.
12 [Tr. – Kant, *Towards Perpetual Peace*, 4.]
13 [Tr. – Kant, *Towards Perpetual Peace*, 6.]
14 [Tr. – Kant, *Towards Perpetual Peace*, 7.]
15 [Tr. – Georg Wilhelm Friedrich Hegel, *The Philosophy of History*, trans. J. Sibree (London: Batoche, 2001), 47–8.]
16 [Tr. – William Shakespeare, *The Tragedy of Macbeth*, V.5.]
17 Arthur Schopenhauer, *The World as Will and Representation*, vol. 2, trans. E. F. J. Payne (New York: Dover, 1958), 551.
18 Arthur Schopenhauer, *The World as Will and Representation*, 535.
19 [Heinz Dieter Kittsteiner, *Wir werden gelebt: Formprobleme der Moderne*, (Berlin: Philo, 2005).]

20 [Tr. – "but not least" is in English in the original.]
21 See pp. 171–7 of this volume.
22 [Tr. – "steam engines" is in English in the original.]
23 [Tr. – Francis Bacon, "Of Cunning," in *The Essays of Francis Bacon*, ed. by Mary Augusta Scott (New York: Scribner's, 1908), 102–5.]
24 [Tr. – René Descartes, *Meditations on First Philosophy*, trans. Donald A. Cress (Indianapolis: Hackett, 1993), 16–17.]
25 [Tr. – Balthasar Gracián, *The Art of Worldly Wisdom*, trans. Joseph Jacobs (London: Macmillan, 1904), Aphorism 157: "Do Not Make Mistakes about Character," 94.]
26 [Tr. – The original title of Gracián's book in Spanish is *Oráculo manual*, though its standard title when translated into English is *The Art of Worldly Wisdom*.]
27 [Tr. – Balthasar Gracián, *The Art of Worldly Wisdom*, 7–8.]
28 Balthasar Gracián, *The Art of Worldly Wisdom*, 15–16.
29 Balthasar Gracián, *The Art of Worldly Wisdom*, 88–9.
30 Francis Bacon, *The Works of Francis Bacon*, Vol. XIII (Boston: Houghton Mifflin, 1857–1882), 167–8.
31 *Metis* is also a contemporary German journal in women's studies that is opposed to the reduction of feminine intelligence to a parroting that is in service to masculine domination.
32 [Tr. – "policey," the archaic English spelling of "policy," is in English in the original.]
33 Kant, *Towards Perpetual Peace*, 100.
34 Ibid., 98.
35 Ibid., 108 [Tr. – translation modified].
36 Ibid., 67–8.
37 Peter von Matt, *Die Intrige: Theorie und Praxis der Hinterlist* (Munich: Carl Hanser, 2006).
38 [Tr. – Sebastian Brant, *Ship of Fools*, trans. Edwin H. Zeydel (New York: Columbia University Press, 1944).]
39 Other sources attribute the statement to Caraffa, the papal legate to the later pope Paul IV (who died in 1559).
40 Particularly in the third chapter, "Der Text als List und die Herstellbarkeit des Schönen," in *Logos und List: Zur Entwicklung der Ästhetik in der frühen Neuzeit* (Bodenheim: Athenaeum, 1989), 91–149.